HITLER'S JACKALS

Other Books by the Author

The Black Angels
Battle exploits of the Waffen-SS

The Curse of the Death's Head
An exploration of the SS-Totenkopf Division

Hitler's Young Tigers
The Hitler Youth

Legions of Death
The Nazi occupation and resistance to it in Eastern Europe

Cross of Iron
The Nazi enslavement of Western Europe

Hand of Steel
The wartime campaigns of British and American Commandos and Special Forces

Illustrated History of the Gestapo
An account of Heinrich Himmler's evil empire

HITLER'S JACKALS

by

Rupert Butler

'If you want to join the banquet, you'll
have to help first in the kitchen.'

*Hitler's warning to Admiral Horthy,
Regent of Hungary, 23 August, 1938*

LEO COOPER

First published in Great Britain in 1998
by
Leo Cooper
an imprint of
Pen & Sword Books Ltd,
47 Church Street,
Barnsley, South Yorkshire S70 2AS

A CIP record for this book is available from the British Library

ISBN 0 85052 593 4

Typeset in Sabon by
Phoenix Typesetting, Ilkley, West Yorkshire.

Printed in Great Britain by Redwood Books, Trowbridge, Wilts

CONTENTS

ACKNOWLEDGEMENTS

The preparation of a book of this kind inevitably requires the help and resources of many individuals and organizations. I should like to acknowledge the unstinted and patient help I received in London from the staffs of the Sikorski Institute, Imperial War Museum, the Royal Air Force Museum, the Royal United Services Institute for Defence Studies, the London Library, the Wiener Library and the West Hill, Reference Library, Borough of Wandsworth. Staff at the Hungarian Embassy courteously answered a number of questions and clarified some points. In Munich, I was able to inspect surviving Nazi documents from the archive at the Institut für Zeitgeschichte and here I was fortunate to be helped by Peter Lieb, who, despite being busy on researches of his own, took time to identify and translate crucial documents for me. The most generous and patient help of all was provided by Mark Axworthy who, in addition to allowing me to draw generously on his deeply researched study of Romanian Armed Forces, *Third Axis Fourth Ally*, provided me with additional hitherto unpublished material on Romania. I am grateful to the Editor of *The Spectator* and to Simon Sebag-Montefiore for permission to draw on the latter's interview with King Michael of Romania. I thank Macmillan Publishers Ltd for permission to quote from *The Last Days of Hitler* by H. R. Trevor-Roper and Greenhill Books/ Lionel Leventhal Ltd to quote from Feldmarschall Kesselring's *Memoirs*. Valuable research assistance was also given by Princess Ranier Swidrygiello, Inga Haag, Christine Patel, Dr K.J.W.Leist, C.K.Klinger, Stephen Tyas and James Lucas. A special word of thanks, too, to my good friend Terry Charman who read the manuscript, clarified certain points and made valuable suggestions. I would also thank Brigadier Bryan Watkins for his sensitive editing. As always, I extend my love and admiration to my wife Joyce, who, with patience and humour, has endured my two year preoccupation with Hitler's Jackals.

London   *Rupert Butler*
March, 1998

LIST OF ILLUSTRATIONS

– I –

HOW IT ALL BEGAN

May 22nd 1939. Berlin, the seat of Hitler's Reich was in celebration, its streets dwarfed by vast pylons bearing German and
Italian flags, their Nazi and Fascist emblems writ large. The
stage was set for a joint initiative by Europe's most nakedly aggressive
powers – the signing of the Pact of Steel, by which Germany and Italy
guaranteed to support each other in the event of any future war.

Trapped in a myth of his own creation, Benito Mussolini, Italy's Duce,
on whose behalf his Foreign Minister Count Galeazzo Ciano was present
in Berlin that day, had long proclaimed the military muscle of his debt-
bogged state and, originally, had seen himself as the master of Hitler, his
admiring and willing pupil.

It had not always been like that. Events which had led up to the Pact
of Steel had seen a drastic reversal of roles. The Duce was now, to Adolf
Hitler's lion, the first of what eventually became a clutch of jackals, all
hoping to share in the considerable spoils of war.

It was Hitler who had seized the initiative and done most of the
wooing. Less than two years earlier, on 28 September, 1937, Mussolini's
monstrous vanity had been fed by a lavish state visit to Germany. On that
occasion, too, Berlin had been in the grip of holiday fever. From all over
the Third Reich, flowers and bunting had decked the streets onto
which the crowds debouched from special trains to swell the squares and
pavements.

For the Italians, the reception had been memorable, from the moment
that the Duce had left Rome in his brand new uniform and surrounded
by a phalanx of cohorts. It had not simply been the endless parades of
goose-stepping SS, the army manoeuvres at Mecklenburg or the inspection of the huge Krupp works of Essen. There had been an instance of
pure theatre. The Führer's special train had run at snail's pace directly
opposite Mussolini's, enabling the dictators to talk side-by-side. The

I

correspondent of *Il Popolo d'Italia* had gushed that it was as if the two trains 'signified the parallelism of two revolutions'. Then the *Führersonderzug* had pulled ahead, allowing Hitler to disembark, cross the platform and greet his guest with outstretched hand.

It might well have proved heady stuff for the son of a socialist blacksmith from the village of Dovia, within the anti-clerical cockpit of Italy's bleak Romagna. But, within the very shadow of that birth, the romance of revolutionary politics had been bred into the future *Duce de Fascismo*. The name Benito had been a tribute to the Mexican Benito Juarez, the leader of violent revolt against the Emperor Maximilian. His two other names – Amilcare was after a Romagnal anarchist, while Andrea was a nod to Andrea Costa, a founder member of the Italian Socialist Party.

Mussolini had risen fast in the ranks of left-wing Italian political journalism, becoming editor of the party's newspaper *Avanti!* only to part company with socialist adherents through his support of Italian intervention in the First World War. Robbed of one platform, he created another – the newspaper *Il Popolo d'Italia*, a rabble-rousing tract of extreme nationalism. By March, 1919, after war service and with nationalism burning more fiercely than ever, he had organized the Fasci di Combattimento (Combat Groups), a party with a broad base of appeal among disaffected former soldiers, embittered middle class intellectuals and hungry farmers.

Mussolini's approach to politics mirrored the showy pyrotechnics of the tabloid journalism he knew so well – unabashed populism at the sacrifice of substance. It worked in an Italy laid in economic ruins by war, the country's industrial north paralysed by industrial action, its south seething with the unrest of land-hungry peasants. For the country's industrialists and bourgeoisie, though, here was the stuff of nightmare. Membership figures for the Fascists increased dramatically. Parallels with the rise of Nazism in Germany became all too plain. Rapprochement between the two dictators was surely inevitable.

Everyone who saw Mussolini in Berlin during the 1937 visit, stiff and erect in an open limousine, had admitted he looked the part of a Caesar. According to Paul Schmidt, Hitler's interpreter: 'Firmly erect, swaying from the hips as he talked, his Caesarean head might have been modelled from the old Romans, with its powerful forehead and broad, square chin thrust forward under a wide mouth.'

Mussolini may well have recalled, with some irony, the time, a decade before, when a request had reached his desk in Rome from Major Giuseppe Renzetti, head of the Italian Chamber of Commerce in Berlin. In terms of some besotted fan towards a movie idol, the then largely unknown Adolf Hitler, leader of the Nationalist Socialist Party of some 49,000 members, had expressed fawning admiration for the Duce and sought the honour of a signed photograph. Mussolini had given the memo the barest glance before scrawling across it: 'Request refused.'

The thaw had been slow. In June, 1934, the Führer, in power just eighteen months, had made the first of his trips to meet Mussolini and had placed himself at a severe disadvantage by arriving in Venice in soiled raincoat and battered hat. Faced by a head of government in garb reminiscent, in the words of one observer, of 'a little plumber', the Duce had treated his lank-haired guest with scarcely concealed condescension. Hitler had not even been invited to preside at a military review, but had done most of the talking, causing an irritated Mussolini to explain privately: 'He's mad. He's like a gramophone with only seven tunes to play over and over again.'

For his part, Hitler had scarcely exercised tact, constantly speaking of the superiority of the Nordic races and the decadence of Mediterranean people with Negro blood in their veins. Outwardly, Mussolini had expressed his contempt for the other man: 'a garrulous monk,' a vagabond Austrian who might, however, be impressed by a grand gesture. Mussolini had one in mind.

His onslaught on Ethiopia, to avenge an Ethiopian victory over Italy in 1896, was undertaken the following October. To a delirious crowd of some 400,000, jammed into Rome's Piazza Venezia, the Duce had proclaimed with flamboyant bravado:

> Officers, non-commissioned officers and men. Black Shirts of the Revolution, Italian men and women at home and throughout the world, hearken: a great event has been accomplished. The destiny of Abyssinia has been sealed today in the fourteenth year of the Fascist era. Every knot has been cut by our shining sword, and the Abyssinian victory will remain in the history of our country, complete and pure like the *legionari* who have fallen. Italy has her Empire . . . .

The empire had been gained with twenty-five divisions and 650,000 troops against an enemy of horse-backed tribesmen. Initially popular in Italy, the conquest had been justified, Mussolini declared bombastically, even 'if it meant that the whole of Europe went up in smoke.'

Most of Europe seethed. The adventure was condemned outright by the League of Nations, most forcibly by Britain and France. From then on, Mussolini had fulminated at both countries, condemning them as weak and incapable of striking back under attack. France was not even worth mentioning. The British were cowardly and pacifist and cursed with an effete ruling class. And Germany? Hitler had designs on his native Austria and was pressing for *Anschluss* (union). Clearly, there had been a need for Italy to demonstrate another assertion of authority elsewhere.

Mussolini had fastened his attention on the ferment of Spain and the ascendancy of the nationalist leader, General Francisco Franco. Along with Hitler, the Duce had despatched men and materials. For Italy, here was an opportunity to extend the influence of fascism and toughen the people for war.

One of the first hints that Hitler was making preliminary moves for some measure of serious rapprochement with Mussolini had come after the 1936 Parteitag (Party Day), the annual celebration in the medieval Bavarian city of Nuremberg, where the old streets reverberated to the stridency of bands and the crash of jackboots. To the massed hordes of assembled Brownshirts and SS, Hitler had stormed against the Bolshevik menace. At a lunch for the foreign press following the parade, he had declared: 'People wonder why we are fanatics against Bolshevism. Is it because we – and Italy too – have lived through the same sort of thing which is happening in Spain?'

It was the opening foray in what many interpreted as an impending courtship. Other overtures followed. The Italian-speaking lawyer Hans Frank, head of the legal division of the Nazi Party, had been despatched to Rome, where he delivered his message: Mussolini must come to Germany. Furthermore, he would do so not only as dictator of Italy but as leader of the Fascist revolution.

In the face of a shower of compliments and the repeated insistence that Hitler wanted close co-operation between Italy and Germany, Mussolini retained a frosty exterior. In fact, he was greatly flattered and had made up his mind to accept Hitler's invitation.

The diplomatic niceties inseparable from the planning of any visit outside his own country by a head of state had been entrusted to the Duce's golden boy, the recently appointed Foreign Minister Galeazzo Ciano, Count di Cortelazzo, whose father Costanzo had served with conspicuous gallantry during the First World War in the Italian navy, and had subsequently been one of the architects of the Fascist movement. The son had worked as a journalist on a Rome daily paper, an obvious point of contact with the Duce that could do no harm. But the young Ciano had an infinitely more valuable advantage: he was married to Mussolini's daughter, Edda, who was generally accepted to be the Duce's favourite child.

Ciano's rise had been spectacular: Consul-General in Shanghai within two months of his marriage, then Minister Plenipotentiary in China, eventually Foreign Minister. His idolatry of his father-in-law – even to the extent of copying Mussolini's mannerisms and style of speech – had become a byword.

But many foreign observers remained unimpressed. American Under Secretary of State Sumner Welles, for example, while conceding that

4

Ciano had possessed 'dignity and personal charm', recalled him as a playboy, a man to whom 'morality in public affairs did not exist'. Described by Frank Gervasi, the representative of Hearst Newspapers in Rome, as 'a Fascist from his high hairline to the tips of his well polished boots', Ciano had, as well as visiting Germany to pave the way for the state visit, taken the opportunity to sign a secret protocol with his opposite number, the then Nazi Foreign Minister and Ribbentrop's predecessor, Constantin von Neurath. This created a common foreign policy for the two countries although there was as yet no formal alliance.

Mussolini had lost no time in pressing his suit further. On Sunday 1 November, 1936, in a speech in the Piazza del Duomo in Milan, he had declared:

> One great country has recently gathered a vast amount of sympathy among the masses of the Italian people: I speak of Germany.
> The Berlin conversations have resulted in an understanding between our two countries over certain problems which had been particularly acute ... This Berlin–Rome line is not a diaphragm but rather an axis around which can resolve all those European states with a will to collaboration and peace.

The Germans had taken the speech to be a concrete proposal of alliance. Elsewhere it was sufficient to ring alarm bells. Certainly, in the weeks and months leading up to the Duce's visit to Germany, meetings between Nazi leaders and the Italian hierarchy were stepped up.

The gregarious, flamboyant Herman Göring, Hitler's wily, serpentine plenipotentiary, his front man as the 'socially acceptable' face of Nazism, was entrusted with a number of ongoing missions to Rome. Indeed, Hitler had been keen to establish links with the Fascist regime in Italy.

As well as being probably more privy than anyone to the long-term intentions of his Führer, Göring's gargantuan egotism relished hugely the limelight that the visits to Italy afforded him. The Duce tended at first to dismiss the man as a mere buffoon. It was a view startlingly reinforced for the Duce when, trapped in Goering's sumptuous estate at Karinhall, some 40 miles from Berlin, he had to endure being pawed by his host's pet lioness, as well as being encouraged to enthuse over Göring's elaborate electric train set.

Although nothing could detract from the overall success of the Berlin visit, there had been another irritation for the Duce. What he had planned as his keynote speech, delivered at Berlin's Maifeld, had been all but drowned out by driving rain, the noise of which had rendered Mussolini's halting German even more difficult for the crowd to follow. He bellowed through the downpour: 'When Fascism has a friend, it will march with that friend to the last.'

In a state of exhaustion and soaked to the skin, he had staggered to the shelter of his official car. But by now there could be no going back. He had thrown in his lot with the Germans – 'a great people with proud traditions and a noble future'.

The previous November, the Anti-Comintern Pact, a five-year German–Japanese accord, had been agreed. It had named Communism as the chief enemy of peace in the world and had a secret protocol which provided for the co-ordination of effort directed against the Soviet Union. Italy became the next signatory.

The Axis was poised to grow in strength.

– 2 –

THE PACT OF STEEL

During his various visits to Germany, Mussolini had been deeply impressed by the malign trappings of Nazi dictatorship, the militaristic showmanship and above all, the goose-stepping marching of the SS. His Italy, he had been determined, must have the same. He had decreed that the step should be adopted by his own military. This was too much for some of the army's senior figures. Marshal Emilio de Bono, a hero of the Abyssinian campaign exploded into rich sarcasm: 'The soldier's average height is 5 feet 5 inches . . . you will have a parade of stiff-necked dwarfs.'

More sinister had been the bid to introduce anti-Semitism. Not for the first time, Mussolini somersaulted on previous pronouncements, not least a declaration that 'a specific Jewish problem does not exist in Italy'. This had been backed by an assurance that the Fascist Government had no intention of taking any measures against Jews 'except such as are hostile to the regime'. But now Mussolini himself was talking of 'the acid of Jewish corrosion'.

Measures had included inviting the Nazi's leading racial philosopher, the Balt Alfred Rosenberg, a notorious anti-Semite, to lecture in Italy on the purity of blood. Some leading university professors were also persuaded to declare in the Fascist press that the Italians were in fact Nordic Aryans. While such moves provoked embarrassed amusement, others did not. In September, 1938, a decree had declared that all those whose parents were Jews and who had settled in Italy or the Italian colonies since 1919 (with the exception of Ethiopia) must quit the country. Another measure had been to ban all Jewish teachers from state schools and scientific literary and artistic institutions.

Even so, for all the outward bravado, Mussolini had his anxieties. Threats to the independence of Austria and Czechoslovakia loomed, spectres which had their origins in 1919 when the Treaty of Versailles, following the First World War, had explicitly forbidden Austria's Union or *Anschluss* with Germany, at the same time denying the Bohemian (Sudeten) Germans the right to national determination.

Mussolini's anxieties were not without foundation for in March, 1936, having torn up the Locarno Treaty of 1925, which guaranteed the demilitarization of the Rhineland, Hitler, in defiance of his generals' protests and misgivings, had marched into the Rhineland with a mere three battalions and got clean away with it. His triumph over those who had inflicted the harsh terms of the Versailles Treaty upon Germany was resounding, and not only over them but also over his timid generals. The Army had grown increasingly restive since Hitler had come to power three years earlier and its leaders would have gladly seized any opportunity to overthrow him. However, there could be no prospect of success for such a move unless the weight of public opinion was behind it. The brilliant victory of 7 March marked the beginning of Hitler's dominance over his Service chiefs. The great bulk of the people were now solidly behind this wonderful new leader who was not only restoring the prosperity of their beloved Fatherland but also its standing in the muddled world of European politics. The spirit of *Deutschland über Alles* was reborn and Hitler's lust for power had been given a powerful boost.

By February, 1938, the façade of diplomacy by the Nazis had been ripped aside. The Austrian Chancellor, Dr Kurt Schuschnigg, on a visit to Hitler's mountain retreat at Berchtesgaden in Bavaria, was confronted by the Führer in storm trooper's uniform, flanked by three generals.

In his later account, and subsequently in his affidavit to the Nuremberg tribunal after the war, Schuschnigg described how Hitler, brushing aside all preliminary courtesies, tore into him by fuming: 'You have done everything to avoid a friendly policy. The whole history of Austria is just one uninterrupted act of high treason . . . The German Reich is one of the great powers, and nobody will raise his voice if it settles its border problems.'

Hitler was right. Schuschnigg, aware that there would be no support from Britain or France, was forced to yield to Hitler's bullying demands that an existing ban of Austrian Nazis must be removed, an amnesty declared for those in jail, and the appointment of Dr Arthur Seyss-Inquart, a Viennese lawyer of irreproachable Nazi credentials, to the post of Minister of the Interior. Furthermore, Hitler required closer liaison between the German and Austrian armed forces. Schuschnigg was hustled into signing an agreement that spelt the end of Austrian independence.

For Mussolini the matter of Austria was of more than passing interest. Not so long before, he had made endless references to the inviolability of the country's independence. Italian interests in Central and South-Eastern Europe had to be protected. Now there was the prospect of German troops breathing down the neck of its near neighbour.

The implications were far worse. German dominance in Austria would give Hitler strategic control of the road, rail and river communications of the Middle Danube valley, and hence of the frontiers with, not only Italy, but also Hungary and Yugoslavia. Czechoslovakia would then be surrounded strategically and ripe for conquest.

Schuschnigg went on to put his head further into the lion's mouth by announcing a plebiscite in which those taking part would be able to give their views on the *Anschluss*. Hitler had selected Saturday, 13 March as the day in which he would march into Austria, preceding this with a letter to be delivered in Rome to Mussolini in person. In it, the Führer expressed his determination to restore law and order in his homeland.

With a clear hint that favours done in the past should be matched in full measure by their recipient, Hitler wrote: 'In a critical hour for Italy I proved the steadfastness of my sympathy. Do not doubt that in the future there will be no change in this respect.' The letter was rounded off with a small morsel tossed by the lion to the jackal. The boundary between Italy and Germany, Hitler affirmed, would be the Brenner Pass. This meant that the Führer would not press any claim for the return of the southern Tyrol, which had been taken from Austria and awarded to Italy after the First World War.

Any opposition which Mussolini might have been inclined to offer was, in any case, too late. Hitler's victory in Austria was bloodless. The German soldiers termed it *Der Blumenkrieg*. Pro-German crowds had handed out kisses and posies. Seven million Austrians were added to the Reich, together with the bulk of the country's heavy industry, its national bank and the Austrian Army.

Only a short time earlier, Mussolini had been insisting that Italy had 'never given any pledge, either directly or indirectly, either verbally or in writing, to intervene to save the independence of Austria.' Then, all at once, Hitler was heaping glutinous plaudits on his Axis partner. He charged his special envoy to the Duce, Prince Philip of Hesse:

Please tell Mussolini that I shall never forget him. . . . As soon as the Austrian affair is settled, I shall be ready to go with him, through thick and thin, no matter what happens. . . . If he should ever need any help or be in any danger, he must be assured that I shall stick to him, whatever may happen, even if the whole world were against him.

Hitler's enthusiastic gush had come in such a torrent that the Prince was only able to inject an occasional 'Yes, my Führer'. The Duce's reply was suitably expansive: 'My attitude is determined by the friendship between our two countries, which is consecrated in the Axis.'

Following the *Anschluss*, the rigidly controlled Fascist press and radio had burst forth with unstinted praise for Hitler, who had at last united two countries that had always wanted to be a single entity. Furthermore, Mussolini told the Chamber of Deputies, the *Anschluss* had served to strengthen the Axis.

That Mussolini considered himself an equal partner in that Axis at the very least had been demonstrated by Hitler's state visit to Rome in May, 1938. No longer was the German Führer treated like some greasy suppliant. There had been the horse-drawn royal carriage bearing the German Chancellor with King Victor Emmanuel III to the Quirinal Palace, behind them the jingle of mounted cuirassiers with their gleaming gold and silver helmets and breastplates.

Above all, 30,000 Italian troops had been paraded, along with the ironmongery of tanks, artillery and armoured cars, their might buttressed by poison gas dispensers and flame-throwing units. At the end of the visit, as the two dictators shook hands, the Duce declared: 'Henceforth no force will be able to separate us.'

Back in Berlin, one matter concerned Hitler, the nature of which was made clear to General Franz Halder, appointed that year to be Chief of the German Army General Staff. A decade or so later, he recalled driving with Hitler into Austria at the time of the *Anschluss*. The Führer had remarked thoughtfully: 'This will be very inconvenient to the Czechs.'

The security of the state of Czechoslovakia, stitched together at the end of the First World War out of the former Austrian territories of Bohemia, Moravia, and Austrian Silesia and the former Hungarian territories of Slovakia and Ruthenia, had been plagued by clamorous minorities from its birth. Most vociferous of all were the 3,000,000 Sudeten Germans. For Hitler, they afforded a pretext too good to be missed. They were an aggrieved minority who must be united with the Reich. And there were other considerations, not the least of which were the resources of the Czechs' thriving armaments industry.

Although the so-called Rome–Berlin Axis was not yet a formal alliance, the ongoing belligerence of its two architects was raising temperatures still higher. Another anxiety plagued Mussolini. Stark economics dictated that Italy was too severely stretched to indulge in future armed conflicts. The cost of the Abyssinia war alone had been put at around thirteen billion lire; billions more had been released for strengthening the Italian armed forces. There were still 300,000 Italian troops tied up in occupation duties.

The prospect of Italy being sucked into a major conflict had become insupportable. What were the Führer's intentions in Czechoslovakia?

Were any activities there to be a prelude to all out war? Alarm proved infectious. On the morning of 28 September, 1938, Lord Perth, the British Ambassador, put in an urgent request for an immediate meeting with Ciano. Perth was relaying an urgent request for 'friendly intervention' by the Duce as a last hope for a threatened peace.

For Mussolini, when he received the message, it was a moment of high triumph. He could become the peacemaker of Europe. Hitler had mobilized against the Czechs. If he could be persuaded to postpone his action, however briefly, the heat would be off Italy. Meanwhile, the French and British were exerting their strongest efforts to persuade Hitler that an agreement could be reached on the Sudetenland without recourse to war.

Mussolini suggested that Hitler set up a four-power conference to settle the issue literally within hours. Hitler was conscious that in the short term he could have everything he wanted without firing a shot. Two hours before the ultimatum was due to run out, the Führer turned to Bernard Italico, the Italian Ambassador to Germany: 'Tell the Duce that I accept his proposal.'

The Duce – and his loyal partners at home – were delirious. Adoring crowds gathered in Rome's Gallery Colonna to a chorus of: *'Mussolini ha salivate la pace.'*

The Sudetenland, Hitler stressed in a speech at Berlin's Sportspalast, was 'a territorial demand' – the last that he would be making in Europe. Then came the shaft of steel: 'In 1919, 3,500,000 Germans were torn away from their compatriots by a company of mad statesmen. The Czech state originated in a huge lie . . .'

For the third time during his negotiations with Hitler, the elderly British Prime Minister, Neville Chamberlain, made a visit to Germany, this time to Munich as an increasingly desperate suppliant for world peace.

The conference, held at the *Führerhaus* on the Königsplatz, was attended by, besides Hitler, Mussolini and Chamberlain, Premier Edouard Daladier for France, the respective ambassadors and other senior officials. The Czechs were not invited. According to subsequent accounts by those present, the proceedings were characterized notably by an absence of any agenda or any chairman to control the meeting, but also by serious confusion amongst the interpreters, who found that neither Hitler, Chamberlain nor Daladier, shared a common language.

Not for the first time, Mussolini, who could hold his own in all their tongues, swaggered into the limelight. The besotted Ciano later enthused: 'His great spirit, always ahead of events and men, had already absorbed the idea of agreement and while the others still wasted their breath over more or less formal problems, he had almost ceased to take an interest. He had already passed onto, and was meditating on other things.'

An excitable Hitler dominated the proceedings, declaring that there must be 'a rapid and concrete' solution of the crisis. The agreement signed on 30 September, 1938, split the bulk of the Sudetenland into four zones to be occupied progressively by the German Army. In addition, the Third Reich secured the adjoining fringe of Bohemia that contained the mountain approaches and Czech fortifications. Hitler had indeed won everything for which he had asked; the hour had belonged to the Axis.

From now on, Mussolini gave every appearance of being mesmerized by Hitler. The Duce's fawning and infantile aping of his idol were taken to bizarre and ludicrous lengths. Italians, he declared, must learn to be hard, even 'implacable and hateful'. There must be a mirror image of the Nazi SS with its strong emphasis on harsh athleticism. An example must be set by the most senior of his followers.

Achille Starace, who was not only Secretary General of the Fascist Party but a Lieutenant General in the militia, was detailed to toughen his colleagues for war. Corpulent ministers and senior civil servants were forced to submit to the risible indignity, not only of running in races and taking part in swimming contests, but leaping through flaming hoops and bouncing off trampolines. Army officers were told to eschew anything that might be regarded as soft or self-indulgent. A race of mercurial Latins was to be transformed into one of robotic Teutons. Silk hats were forbidden. Nightclubs were proclaimed out of bounds. Cars were not to be used when it was possible to use a bicycle.

The mood that Mussolini sought to engender in the Italian people was one of perpetual crisis; the Germans orchestrated it. On a visit to Rome, Ribbentrop, now Germany's Foreign Minister, told Mussolini bluntly that war was inevitable, furthermore that the Anti-Comintern Pact, which Germany had originally signed in 1936 with Japan and to which Italy had later put its signature, should be made into a military alliance. Another visitor was the cadaverous peacemaker, Neville Chamberlain, intent on seeking out the Duce – 'Chamberlain and his umbrella are coming', Mussolini sneered. The British were anxious to come to some sort of friendly understanding with Italy so that Mussolini could be weaned away from Hitler.

But in Mussolini's prevailing mood there was no hope of that. Nevertheless, for all his posturing, the Duce was shaken by the news that on 18 March, 1939, Hitler, with no prior consultation with his declared ally, had crossed the Czech frontier. Mussolini considered he would have to show off his own strength elsewhere.

There was a target to hand: Albania, the invasion of which was a pointless piece of muscle-rippling, since the country had been virtually an Italian protectorate since 1926. Hitler was quick to see that this empty bid to assert Italian independence would, as with the invasion of Ethiopia and the intervention in Spain, only draw Italy still closer to the Axis. Whatever his private misgivings, Mussolini put up a good front. Stoutly, he told Ciano: 'We cannot change our policy now. After all, we are not political whores.'

But there were yet more worries, primarily Hitler's designs on Poland where, in 1918, a republic had been hammered out of the Polish-speaking parts of Russia, Austria – and Germany. The Germans constituted a large minority. Hitler's attention was focused on the German-speaking Free City and port of Danzig and the Polish Corridor, that piece of territory between the Baltic Sea and the centre of landlocked Poland, which had been established by the Treaty of Versailles.

Mussolini became seriously alarmed as Hitler appeared to be propelling a roller coaster heading straight for war. There was no way in which Italy could afford to share the same seat, and so a meeting was arranged between Ciano and Ribbentrop in Milan, a city with a strong anti-German feeling.

The two men, both in uniform, were seen to be smiling like old friends. An anxious Duce had briefed Ciano exhaustively. The Germans must be told that in no circumstances could Italy wage any war in under three years. Ribbentrop, for his part, proved reassuring, stating, according to Ciano, 'that Germany too is convinced of the necessity for a period of peace, which should be not less than four or five years.' The Nazi Foreign Minister added that every chance must be taken to improve Axis relations.

An anxious Mussolini, telephoning Ciano for a progress report on the talks, seized on Ribbentrop's remarks with considerable excitement. With characteristic impulsiveness, he instructed his disconcerted son-in-law to announce in a communiqué that Germany and Italy had decided to conclude a military alliance. Hitler acceded to it readily.

From then on, the Duce grew increasingly impatient. The Germans were allowed to draft the treaty; its provisions going unchallenged. Even the proviso of no war for four or five years was conveniently forgotten; Germany, after all, was intent on the rape of Poland. The OKW (*Oberkommando der Wehrmacht*) already had its instructions to prepare for the attack: 'Plans should be made in such a way that the operation can be launched at any time after I.IX.1939.'

Now came the Pact of Steel. Within the pompous grandeur of the Reich Chancellery in Berlin, harsh arc lights accentuated the gaudy splendour of a score of uniforms around the conference table. Present at the signing on 22 May, 1939, in addition to Ribbentrop, Ciano, Hitler and Göring, were the representatives of the German Navy and Army, Grand Admiral Erich Raeder and General Walther von Brauchitsch. After the signing,

Ciano was embraced fondly as 'our good Fascist Italian brother'.

The germ of the Pact was contained in the third of its seven articles:

> If contrary, to the wishes and hopes of the High Contracting Parties,
> [Germany and Italy] it should happen that one of them became involved in
> warlike complications with another Power or Powers, the other High
> Contracting Party would immediately come to its assistance as an ally and
> support it with all its military force on land, at sea and in the air.

To Ciano, who had previously studied the draft of the treaty, this was
'dynamite'. So anxious had Mussolini been to skip at the feet of his
partner that he had not even insisted that the article should include a
clause specifying that it would only be effective in the case of an attack
by an enemy. It was too late for that. Fascist Italy was now locked irrevocably into Nazi Germany.

To an anxious Europe, the Pact of Steel looked like nothing so much
as a bluntly phrased military alliance. Predictably, a blander spin was put
on it by the Italian paper *Messaggero*: 'Rome and Berlin all support one
another vigorously by turn. They will conduct every sort of negotiation
in perfect harmony and avail themselves patiently of all pacific means.'
The sting was in the tail: 'If it proves impossible to negotiate, or if nothing
concrete can be obtained by this means, if too long a time passes without
the opposing party showing signs of yielding to reason, they will make
war.'

The leader writer in *The Times* of London, however, seized on Article
IV of the Pact which stated that the two governments 'will intensify their
collaboration in the military field and the field of war economy. . . . In
other words, they are to prepare jointly and systematically for war, and
are apparently going to organize in common all the resources they possess
for that purpose.'

*　　*　　*

To some of those present at the signing ceremony, Hitler had seemed to
show the strain of the last few weeks and months. Otherwise, he had been
in excellent spirits. And with good reason. Mussolini's Italy had become
irrevocably the jackal of the Third Reich. Others would follow.

- 3 -

HITLER PREPARES FOR WAR : SLOVAKIA UNDER CONTROL

It was Germany's high summer and Adolf Hitler was preparing for war. Any lingering doubt over the Führer's intentions had melted away with the signing of the Pact of Steel. Fourteen senior officers of the armed forces now assembled in the study at the Reich Chancellery to hear Hitler declare bluntly that he would 'attack Poland at the first suitable opportunity'. If such a decision meant conflict with Britain and France, so be it.

Count Ciano, writing in his diary, shared Mussolini's worst misgivings. Both foresaw Italy being dragged into a war she neither wanted nor could afford. On 6 August, 1939, the Italian Foreign Minister wrote: 'Our gold reserves are reduced to almost nothing. . . . We must avoid war.' The entry four days later deepened the pessimism: 'Never has the Duce spoken of the need for peace with so much warmth and without reserve. I agree with him 100 per cent, and this conviction will lead me to redouble my efforts. But I am doubtful as to the results.'

Ciano proposed an urgent meeting with his German opposite number and with Hitler later the same month. The encounter with Ribbentrop was grim:

> The decision to fight is implacable. He rejects any solution which might give satisfaction to Germany and avoid the struggle. I am certain that even if the Germans were given more than they ask for they would attack just the same, because they are possessed by the demon of destruction.

The atmosphere during dinner was arctic. The two Axis foreign ministers did not exchange a word. Ciano later reflected ruefully that it was scarcely necessary. He had enquired of Ribbentrop if Germany was intent on securing either the Polish corridor or Danzig, only to receive the blunt reply: 'Not any more. We want war!' Ribbentrop, and subsequently Hitler, with whom Ciano had two meetings at Obersalzberg, expressed confidence that France and Britain would not take up arms on behalf of Poland.

On such an assumption, Adolf Hitler had laid his plans the previous year, starting in the shadow of the Munich Agreement, with the dismemberment of Czechoslovakia. It was a stage on the way to destroying a country which the Czech President, Eduard Benes, had described as 'a solid, indestructible lighthouse of democracy'.

The division of the spoils of the country, as agreed at Munich, led to an avaricious Poland seizing Teschen, a coveted slice of Czech territory. And there was a prize for those who might serve Hitler's purpose as a future ally. The question was, who had a grievance? Grievances, Hitler felt, existed to be exploited. He sniffed the air and scented Hungary.

At the time of its creation from the old Austro-Hungarian empire, Czechoslovakia had gained Slovakia and Ruthenia (also known as Carpatho-Ukraine) on its eastern tip, while Poland had laid claim to a small area in northern Slovakia. On the other hand, by the Treaty of Trianon of 4 June, 1920, the peace treaty after the First World War, Hungary had lost two thirds of its pre-war lands, a substantial portion of them to Romania, which had been on the side of the victors.

Hungarian anger was a running fuse. The country had been emasculated and made liable for war reparations. Germany now engineered the cession to Hungary of southern Slovakia, and then was to toss it a second morsel: Ruthenia, which formed the eastern tip of Czechoslovakia and a pot pourri of Magyars, Slovakians, Jews and Ukrainians.

For the Nazis, Slovakia had real uses. On 17 October, 1938, a few days after the signing of the Munich Agreement, Ferdinand Durcansky, Deputy Prime Minister of the newly appointed autonomous Slovakia, and Franz Karmasin, leader of the German minority there, were received by Herman Göring who was assured by Durcansky that the Slovaks were anxious for complete independence, with very close political, economic and military ties with Germany. For Göring, this was highly satisfactory. In a secret German Foreign Office memorandum, Göring stated: 'A Czech state minus Slovakia is even more completely at our mercy.' A further highly significant note stated: 'Air base in Slovakia for operation against the East – very important.'

It was fertile territory. Separatist sentiment in Slovakia had bubbled for aeons. Slovaks had long detested the strong influence of their neighbours, the Czechs. Authoritative nationalism, combined with virulent anti-Communism, stalked abroad, embodied in its extreme form in the single Slovak People's Christian Party, which had originally been led by a Catholic priest, Andrei Hlinka, an ardent advocate of Slovak autonomy within the framework of the Czechoslovak state.

For those who were even more radical, this was not good enough. A hitherto respected academic and opponent of the Czech republic, Dr Vojtech Tuka, who had previously been sentenced for political agitation to ten years penal servitude, during which he had lost his sight, was shrill in demands for a totally independent Slovak state.

The time had clearly arrived for the Nazis to stir the cauldron. Language hurled against the Czechs became steadily more inflammatory; there were accusations of Czech 'lawlessness and anarchy'. The Slovaks, thundered the propaganda machine, must be relieved of their 'persecutors'.

It was at this point that the Roman Catholic priest, Monsignor Josef Tiso, took centre stage. The short, rotund gourmandiser had been imprisoned by the Czechs as far back as the early 1920's as an agitator in the Slovak People's Christian Party, to which he would succeed as leader after the death of Andrei Hlinka in August, 1938.

Tiso, a man with a considerable talent for agitation, began to worry the authorities in Prague, who foresaw occupation of Czechoslovakia by the Germans as becoming increasingly likely. At last, President Emil Hacha acted. On 9 March, 1939, the autonomous Slovak government was dismissed in its entirety. Three days earlier, the Ruthenians had suffered the same fate. It was only a beginning. Tiso was placed under house arrest, along with Vojtech Tuka. Durcansky – already a lackey of the Germans, whose travelling expenses to the Reich had been underwritten by the *Sicherheitsdienst* (SD) (the Nazi Party intelligence arm) – was also seized along with members of the Hlinka Guard. Public order was turned over to the Czech armed forces. Karl Sidor, who did not wish to sever all links with the Czechs, was appointed the new Slovak Premier.

Hitler's next move provided a graphic example of Nazi thug tactics. On 11 March, Arthur Seyss-Inquart, the Nazi Governor of Austria, and Josef Burckel, the Nazi Gauleiter of Vienna, encountered Sidor in Bratislava. They carried a blunt message: the independence of Slovakia must be proclaimed forthwith. If it were not, Hitler would have no further interest in the fate of Slovakia.

Then followed the sudden reappearance of Josef Tiso, who had been released from the Jesuit presbytery in Bratislava where the Czechs had confined him, by German officials. He then received a telegram from Burckel inviting him to meet the Führer in Berlin.

It was, of course, a summons rather than an invitation. Refusal would have meant Slovakia being divided forcibly between Germany and Hungary; a process backed by German force of arms. Tiso, accompanied by Durcansky – who had earlier made good his escape to Austria – flew to Berlin to face Hitler at his most truculent and hectoring. It was high time, the Führer declared, that the Slovaks made up their minds. The choice, he informed his visitors, was a simple one. If they stayed with the Czechs, the Germans would wash their hands of them. They would probably be crushed in the embrace of Hungary or Poland. If they wanted guaranteed security from Germany, they must opt for independence. Either way, lightning speed – *Blitzschnell!* – was of the essence. Hitler's powers of assumed anger then went into overdrive: Czech behaviour, he stormed, was intolerable in the face of Germany's supreme self-control. The country should thank its good fortune that it had not been *verstümmelt* (mutilated) earlier. Suspiciously prompt on cue, a grave-faced Ribbentrop then entered with a concocted message to the effect that Hungarian troops were making for the Slovakian border – which was, almost certainly, a bluff.

Tiso kept his nerve but played along with the atmosphere of charade. With the help of the Germans, the priest devised a telegram, which would be sent on his return to Bratislava, proclaiming the independence of Slovakia and urgently requesting Germany's protection of the new state.

On 14 March, 1939, the Slovak Diet (parliament) opted for independence under German protection. Slovakia had become a separate state and a single party, the now re-named *Hlinkovo Slovensko L'udovo Strana* (Slovak People's Party of Hlinka) – more commonly known as the Ludaks – took control. In the new government, Josef Tiso headed the cabinet and was later elected President of the Slovak State. Durcansky became Minister of Foreign Affairs. Ruthenia, as we have already seen, was handed over to Hungary.

One of the new government's first acts was to sign the Treaty of Protection (*Schutzvertrag*) with Ribbentrop. Germany could now interfere in Slovak internal and foreign affairs with virtual impunity.

Anxiety over Slovakia's political complexion had been mounting among British diplomats in Prague as early as the time of Munich. One reported that the Christian Slovak People's Party 'is going ahead on Fascist lines far more openly and obviously than the central government. . . . I fear we must look forward to a period of very crude Slovak nationalism . . .' A few days later, the diplomat added that Tiso and his followers were pursuing an extremist anti-left and anti-Jewish campaign. 'Fascist ideals and practices seem clearly to be the order of the day in the new Slovakia, to which must be added a primitive clericalism.'

Progressively, the new Slovakia took on board many of the trappings of the Axis partners, notably those of Germany. At the time of its avowed 'independence', Slovakia's population was around three million of which some 130,000 were registered as racially German (*Volksdeutsche*). The

German influence proved strong. A busy pro-Nazi movement, the Carpathian German Party (*Karpaten-Deutsche Partei*) sensing the way the tide was flowing, soon simply changed its name to the German Party (*Deutsche Partei*, DP).

As in the Third Reich, a principal aim now became to recruit the eager youth. The Slovak *Deutsche Jugend*, was modelled inevitably on the Hitler Youth which German boys aged between 15 and 18 were, through the official *Hitler Jugend* law, compelled to join. The Slovak model, claimed by the outbreak of the Second World War to have a membership of 12,000 which, by April 1940, was to rise to 17,400. The Slovak bonding with Hitler Youth was so strong that the uniform was virtually identical with that of the German movement, right down to the emblem with its motif of red/white/red with a black swastika at the centre.

For adults, there was the black-uniformed Hlinka Guard, a self-proclaimed élite with pretentions to be compared with Heinrich Himmler's German SS. In addition, the guard had its own young persons' organization, the Hlinka Youth (*Hlinkova Mladez*) which, in its official publication, proclaimed itself 'a voluntary organization for boys and girls of the Roman Catholic faith, of Aryan descent, in sound physical health and without a criminal record.'

For all the aping of Nazi Germany, the emphasis was rigidly national-istic – the pork-pie forage cap, an essential part of the uniform, sported a round badge which featured the Slovak eagle with the double barred cross of St Cyril and St Methodius, the patron saints of the Slavs, on its chest and a *fasces* in its claws.

National pride and pretentions apart, 'independent' Slovakia was, from the start, under the heel of Nazi Germany. The 'Treaty of Protection of the Slovak State by the German Reich' was enshrined by charter from March, 1939. In essence, Slovakia's foreign and military policy was subordinated to Germany, a reality underlined by the presence of German troops. Special orders for troops on Slovakian soil were issued by Generalmajor Alfred Jodl, chief of the operations office of *Oberkommando der Wehrmacht* (OKW), the German High Command. These declared:

Members of the Wehrmacht and its entourage, who are in the Slovakian sovereign area on official business . . . are outside the reach of Slovakian administration and law in principle. The members of the Wehrmacht, the entourage and prisoners of war of the Wehrmacht come under German Wehrmacht courts.

Furthermore, in areas occupied by German troops 'investigations or other official acts can only be carried out by German sections.'

As for the Germany minority, they received certain privileges denied to other Slovaks. More sinister was their right to set up para-military units. Even the independence which President Tiso nominally enjoyed in domestic affairs did not bear close examination. Hitler had declared bombastically that 'Czechoslovakia had ceased to exist'.

The course of events outside Slovakia impacted inevitably on life within the vassal state. Hitler's march into the Sudetenland had been followed on 14 March, 1939, with the ailing, elderly Czech President, Emil Hacha, being ushered into the Führer's presence. Revived from a fainting fit, the trembling Hacha had been forced into signing a communiqué placing 'the fate of the Czech people in the hands of the Führer'.

The bullying of Hacha had been accompanied by draconian demands. Czechoslovakia would be required to quit the League of Nations, reduce the size of its army, surrender a part of its gold reserves to the Reichsbank – and, of course, outlaw Jews. On 15 March, 1939, German troops crossed the frontier. Hitler enjoyed a triumphant entry into Prague.

During the following week, Hungary staked its claim. Troops moved into Ruthenia, the short-lived so-called Republic of Carpatho-Ukraine, following an ultimatum for the withdrawal of Czech forces. This cartographer's blob had compassed a pro-Russian group, those yearning for a greater Ukrainian state that would embrace a three million Ukrainian minority in southern Poland and, eventually, the Soviet Ukraine. Such aspirations were, predictably, fomented by Nazi Germany.

Propaganda initiatives, shrewdly programmed, had included the targeting of Hungarian farmers and country labourers living in adjoining districts who had been taken to the frontier by picked Hungarian pro-Nazis who told them the country on the other side was actually theirs and was to be 'recovered' by them.

The Hungarian leader, Admiral Miklos Horthy, who ruled the country in place of the exiled Hapsburg royal family, had the aid of his fiercely loyal, *Rongyous Garda* (Ragged Guard), guerrilla bands drawn from the ranks of the peasantry and the unemployed who, in addition to Nazi sympathies, afforded Horthy the respect of a spiritual leader. The Guard battled both with the *Sitch* (Carpatho-Ukrainian irregular forces which concentrated on the Romanian frontier) and with Czech troops. Resistance from the *Sitch* was fierce, notably in Chust, the capital. By 18 March, 1939, Hungary was in effective possession of the territory west of a line from Chust to the Polish frontier. The Hungarians and the Poles were not the only ones sniffing around for any territory going; Romanian troops crossed the frontier and occupied the numerous villages in a triangle to the east of Ruthenia.

With Hitler's advance into Prague came the agents of Himmler's SS, buttressed by Gestapo agents, destined to be equally active in Slovakia where life was hardest for the Jewish community. By the summer, *Grenzbote*, the official German minority party organ in Bratislava, was publishing a Slovak government decree dismissing all Jewish members of the Army, in addition to requisitioning 360 former members for slave labour.

There were also wholesale arrests and sequestration of property. In August, 1939, Britain's newspaper, *The Times*, was reporting that 'a large mob, composed chiefly of Germans with a smattering of Slovaks and led by a group of German youth', had stormed through the crowded streets of Bratislava's ancient Jewish quarter, looting and demolishing homes. In the synagogues, rolls of scripture were wantonly destroyed and, in one synagogue, the water hydrants were turned on to flood the entire building. Rioters had the freedom of the streets; although the authorities had been summoned, there was no police presence for four hours.

The Times report left its readers in no doubt that the Slovaks were enthusiastic participants. The paper added that responsibility for the incidents almost certainly rested with Franz Karmasin, leader of the ethnic Germans, who used the pretext that the *Freiwillige Schutzstaffel*, volunteer Slovakian storm troopers, had been attacked and beaten up by Jews in the streets. The powers of both the Hlinka Guard and the *Freiwillige Schutzstaffel* expanded remorselessly. In both groups the right was vested to demand proof of identity from Jews, detain and prosecute them and confiscate their property.

The programme of repression against the Slovaks was also heavily orchestrated from Berlin; Bratislava became almost submerged under an avalanche of 'proposals' from the Reich capital. As well as stepping up the demand that even racial Jews and half Jews who had been born into or converted to Christianity should be considered as Jews, Berlin had eyes for ethnic non-Slovakians, either natives of small villages or former servants of the old Hapsburg empire. Such people, it was reasoned, would make useful recruits for the SS. The government demurred briefly.

Ultimately responsible for the encroachments and prepared to justify them all was the architect of that dark, tangled bureaucracy of terror, which comprised the SS. Heinrich Himmler, *der treue Heinrich*, the Führer's unquestioned and unquestioning acolyte, had enjoyed a steady career progression since 1929 when he had become Reichsführer SS, a pompous rank for a man at that time in command of less than 300 men. By 1935, however, Himmler was the Chief of Reich Political Police and, one year after that, Chief of the entire German police apparatus. This entailed absolute control of the SS, SD and Gestapo. To the job Himmler brought, not simply a beloved filing system, but his own accumulated ideological baggage, into which was stuffed enthusiasms that were to obsess him till his dying day: the efficacy of alternative medicine, hypnosis, herbalism and the unquestioned racial superiority of the Aryan.

Whenever a fresh opportunity to accumulate power presented itself, Himmler was there. Even in the earliest days, when power of even the simplest kind had been only a dream for the Nazis, the movement had recognized the existence of German nationals in other countries, notably in east and south-east Europe. Any future programme of conquest, it was reasoned, would have to take such groupings into account.

One of the earliest organizations dedicated to these German nationals was the *Auslands Organization* (Foreign Organization, AO). Hitler's favourite, Rudolf Hess, was brought in to oversee all matters involving Germans outside the Reich. Inevitably, the appointment came to Himmler's attention. The two men collaborated, fashioning what became known as *Volksdeutsche-Mittelstelle* (Reference Office for Racial Germans, VOMI). Within the SS orbit, VOMI's remit had a broad sweep: to concern itself with all matters relating to Germans living abroad.

Himmler passed day-to-day responsibility for VOMI to Ober-gruppenführer Werner Lorenz, another SS appointee on the make. Lorenz, in his turn, was soon joined by Dr Herman Berends as deputy – an especially significant appointment since Berends happened to be a member of the SD, whose chief was Reinhard Heydrich, unquestion-ably the most sinister figure in the Nazi hierarchy. Increasingly the child of the SD, VOMI's constituents were a network of spy cells, observation posts and informers.

Intent on inflaming the Czechs against their recalcitrant neighbour, a troop of SD agents travelled to Bratislava, amongst other activities, to persuade Tiso to make immediate preparations for Slovakian independence. The SD had no taste for such diplomatic niceties; the intention was to create incidents that would be taken as the work of Slovak nationalists. Such measures included exploding bombs in a Bratislava chocolate factory.

But there was more to do than foment the odd act of terrorism; Germany was on course for full scale war. Priorities switched to the VOMI. Soon it was transforming into a species of press gang, searching out any *Menschenmaterial* (human material) of German extraction.

In addition, came personnel from the *SS-Ergänzungsamt* (Recruitment Office), looking for volunteers for the SS. Press-gang methods were need-less. In Slovakia, as had been seen, there was no shortage of eager young men willing to serve in the *Freiwillige Schutzstaffel*, from whose strength, incidentally, was to be drawn manpower for the future Waffen-SS.

The dismemberment of Czechoslovakia was complete; Horthy's army had, for the moment at least, done all that had been expected of it. The resistance of the *Sitch* guards in Slovakia had been in the vain hope that

1. Mussolini driving through Berlin with Hitler during the State visit to Germany in September, 1937. *(Photo: Topham Picturepoint)*

2. The Pact of Steel is signed in the new Reich Chancellery in Berlin in May, 1939. Seated (from left) Count Ciano, Hitler and Von

3. The young Prince Michael of Romania with his father King Carol, whom he would succeed in September, 1940. *(Photo: Topham Picturepoint)*

4. Admiral Horthy, Regent of Hungary, taking part in a national celebration in Budapest just before making his State visit to Germany in August, 1938. (Photo: Topham Picturepoint)

Hitler would have complied with the request of the Carpatho-Ukraine government and provided some protection against the Hungarians. Tiso's minions marshalled the full resources of their propaganda machine to glorify the country's armed force which now guarded the ridge of the Carpathian mountains.

Hitler's vision was now way beyond the Czechs. Poland was the next country on the agenda; for its conquest, his army began planning for essential co-operation beyond the existing borders of the Reich.

- 4 -

FIRST STRIKE : POLAND

Hitler next turned his attention to Poland, an issue over which the Soviet Union and Nazi Germany were to form a cynical alliance. The Führer's approach to Poland was in many ways predictable; above all, the shrill appeal to nationalist sentiments and condemnation of the hated Versailles Treaty. This was dressed up in lurid language, with talk of the 'bleeding frontiers of the east' – a melodramatic reference to how the Treaty had attempted to re-create the old kingdom of Poland after the First World War.

A major point of contention fastened on by Hitler was Danzig (Gdansk), the ancient seaport on the Baltic at the mouth of the Vistula. Historically it was a Germanic Port, but the architects of Versailles would have none of it; the anomalous position would surely be solved by making Danzig a demilitarized Free City. A strip of land with a coast line was given to Poland to assure access to the sea, the so-called 'Polish Corridor'. Amid shrill propaganda references to sub-human Slavic degenerates, Hitler spelt out his unequivocal demand: Danzig must be returned to Germany.

Significantly, OKW issued its 'Directive for the Uniform Preparation by the Wehrmacht for War in 1939/40', thus making it clear that Poland was one facet of an overall plan for conflict. Part II, which dealt with the invasion of Poland, was designated *Fall Weiss* (Case White) and Part III Danzig.

The blunt preamble was written by Hitler himself. Force was likely to be the only way of solving the Polish problem once and for all. The Wehrmacht would crush the Polish Armed Forces by fast surprise attack. Just when had become clear on 25 August, 1939, with the terse OKH (*Oberkommando des Heeres*, [Army]) order, tagged *Fall Weiss 1. Y-Tag 26.8. Uhrzeit 4.30.* (Attack on the following day with H-hour at 0430 hours.) Seemingly, the die was cast.

Slovakia, firmly in the boa constrictor embrace of Nazi Germany, was assigned a specific role as one of the bases for the forthcoming assault.

Preparations involved concocting a suitable pretext for Bratislava. A German military mission was already in place under the overall direction of General Franz Barckhausen who received his instructions in a Foreign Ministry communication signed in Berlin on 21 August to 'pass on communications or instructions of a military nature to the appropriate Slovak authorities, at the same time informing the German minister at Bratislava.'

The general was further instructed that he should pass to the Slovaks a previously drafted note telling Bratislava:

> The German government are in possession of definite information that the crossing of the Slovak-Polish frontier by Polish units is imminent, and thus a violation of the integrity of its territory.
>
> The advancing troops have received the strictest orders to base their conduct on the fact that the Slovak State is a Power friendly to the German Reich. In order that the German army may carry out its task, it is necessary that the co-operation of the Slovak authorities and of the Slovak people should be secured . . .

The document was forwarded to the German legation in Bratislava to be ready for use at the appropriate time. In a move seeming to sugar the pill, Germany stated that it would guarantee Slovakia's frontiers with Hungary and would help Slovakia to win back the territories it had lost to Poland. Monsignor Tiso, alert to rumours that intransigence could mean Slovakian independence being lost to Hungary, accepted.

Anxiety, meanwhile, gripped the rest of the world. An appeal for peace was broadcast over Vatican Radio by Pope Pius XII. In the United States, President Franklin Roosevelt sent a special plea to Hitler, while in London the House of Commons passed the Emergency Powers Bill.

Optimism rode high among the Wehrmacht generals. It was reasoned that the non-aggression pact with the Soviet Union had taken care of Poland, surely by now a country standing alone and with no stomach to fight. According to Generaloberst (later Generalfeldmarschall) Gerd von Rundstedt, who was in charge of the planning of the German invasion and given command in August of Army Group South, which would attack through Silesia and Slovakia, 'it would be a flower war as in 1938 in the Sudetenland.'

Rundstedt's sphere of responsibility was the planned attack by Germany to the south through Silesia and Slovakia. For the latter, as a Nazi puppet, there was to be a special pre-emptive assignment. One of its chief protagonists, as yet blissfully unaware, was Wehrmacht Leutnant der Reserve Hans Albrecht Herzner, destined to fight, not in the main assault, but in a separate, bizarre shadow war.

Behind Herzner were marshalled the resources of the Abwehr (literally, 'Defence', that branch of the German intelligence machine (*Nachrichtendienst*), answerable to the Wehrmacht). At the head of Abwehr, whose broad function was counter espionage, stood Admiral Wilhelm Canaris, a former First World War naval officer. Since Canaris wielded considerable power; both he and the Abwehr attracted the ongoing jealousy and suspicion of Himmler's SS and its tangled offshoots.

Canaris, from his headquarters at Berlin's Tirpitzufer, activated subordinates within his networks to examine the general complexion of Polish forces, taking in their strengths, dispositions and, where possible, military objectives. To this end, a squadron of high altitude aircraft, an early generation of spy plane, was switched to the Budapest area to survey the Polish–Slovakian–Moravian frontier zone.

At the same time, Dr Theodor von Hippel of Abwehr II, a department originally entrusted with the distribution of propaganda material outside Germany and later broadened to include acts of sabotage in enemy territory, was authorized by the Wehrmacht to lick into shape *Volksdeutsche* (ethnic Germans), dissident Slavs, fascist nationalists, misfit German officers and disgruntled NCOs into what amounted to an army within an army.

Hippel and his staff were accommodated in the Brandenburg barracks of a front line artillery regiment. The new group was originally known innocuously as Deutsche Kompagnie and later as Bau-Lehr-Bataillon z.b.v 800 (800th Special Duties Constructional Training Battalion). Unofficially, though, it was known as *die Brandenburger*, a name derived from its first permanent headquarters. Before long, most people forgot that the Brandenburgers had ever been called anything else.

The Brandenburgers were divided into two parts, K (*Kampf*-Combat) and S (Sabotage). In the initial strike against Poland, one of these K-groups was to conduct its business in the north, while to the south, operating out of north Slovakia territory with a detachment of twenty-four men including a knot of SA (*Sturm Abteilung* – Storm Troopers) and Grenzpolizei (border police).

Another K-group was commanded by the burly, sandy-haired Albrecht Herzner. During the last hours before war broke out, it was tasked with securing the Jablunka Pass through the Beskids mountain range separating Poland from German-protected Slovakia. At this point were two railway tunnels, lying beyond the station at the hamlet of Mosty. Through them passed all traffic between eastern Germany, through south Poland and into the Balkans. The Jablunka Pass was vital to the German invasion plan because the Poles were known to have detonating apparatus there. Herzner's task was to destroy it, occupy the tunnel and remove the explosive charge. This would facilitate the passage of two Panzer divisions in their race for the Polish city of Cracow and the onward drive for Warsaw.

Herzner's K-group hid out in a remote village, waiting for the order to move from Berlin. It came via Abwehr Headquarters where Oberst Lahousen recorded in his diary: 'Notification of the Führer Order. Y Day is 26.8.39.' From Tirpitzufer was flashed the agreed code to all K and S groups. Herzner's crew emerged, some clad in Polish uniform, others in decidedly travel-worn garb, dubbed *Räuberzivil* (robber's civvies). The party crossed into Polish territory where they were supposed to link up with some Hlinka Guard and Slovak volunteers.

At first, luck seemed to be with Herzner. He noted with some satisfaction that the weapon pits and machine-gun emplacements on top of the pass were unmanned. At the station at Mosty there was only token resistance from the staff who were quickly rounded up. Then the Poles opened up from the northern side of the pass, followed by supporting fire in and around the station. Herzner's men held their ground and the Poles were beaten off. The group went ahead, cutting telephone and telegraph lines. Logically, the next step would have been dismantling detonators and explosive charges. But none were found. By now Herzner's early delight had switched to suspicion. It was all far too easy. One Polish guard had been killed but there had been no opposition to speak of. To discover what had happened proved nothing less than a nightmare; the radio had been destroyed and most of the telegraph and telephone lines were down. Eventually, communication was established with the Slovakian railway station at Cadca, near the border.

Here Herzner was ordered by Major Paul Reichelt, 1a (Chief Operations Officer) of 7th Infantry Division: 'The invasion has been cancelled. Retreat at once. Leave behind any prisoners or anything you have taken. Get back over the frontier by the shortest route.'

Meanwhile, enemy resistance had mounted around Mosty station, the bulk of it from police and station guards. There began a steady slog back to the frontier. At 1330 hours on 26 August, Herzner crossed the Slovak border north-north-west of Rakova.

The Brandenburgers had their place in the history books. They had conducted their own little war in what would total six days, four hours and forty-four minutes ahead of their masters in Berlin.

By any standards, the operation had been a shambles. There could be no question of it being repeated – the Poles would see that all fortifications were in place. At the height of fresh developments in Italy, London and Paris, and the resulting postponement of the assault, no one had remembered to cancel the orders which had been given to Special Engineer Battalion 800. As for Slovakia, the incursion across its territory had scarcely amounted to an auspicious beginning for any supporting role it might have played with Germany. But what precisely had happened?

Less than twelve hours before the scheduled attack on Poland, Attolico, the Italian Ambassador, had handed a letter from Mussolini to Hitler in Berlin which, as it turned out, could not have come at a worse time. Hitler had never really considered that the British would go to war over Poland. Now he had been told that Britain had, in fact, just signed a mutual assistance pact with the Poles in the event of German aggression – a significant advance on what had previously been a unilateral guarantee of Polish independence.

That was bad enough. And here was Mussolini writing:

> If Germany attacks Poland and the conflict remains localised, Italy will afford Germany every form of political and economic assistance which is requested of her.
>
> If Germany attacks Poland, and the latter's allies open a counter-attack against Germany, I inform you in advance that it will be inopportune for me to take the initiative in [any] military operations in view of the present state of Italian war preparations. . . .'

This bombshell pole-axed the Führer, who had been constantly expressing his complete confidence in the steadfastness of his Axis partner. Furthermore, Mussolini's letter was accompanied by a request for Germany to deliver substantial military supplies and war materials to Italy before the start of hostilities. If this were done, 'our intervention can . . . take place at once' but not otherwise. The Duce went on to specify a formidable list of requirements which it was obviously impossible for the Germans to satisfy. Hitler ordered his Chief of Staff, General Wilhelm Keitel: 'Stop everything at once. I need time for negotiations.'

Mussolini had left Hitler in the lurch simply because he had no worthwhile military support to offer and, consequently, was hoping vainly that some sort of negotiated settlement would let him off the hook.

In Italy, meanwhile, Fascist window-dressing had continued. The whole mood of the nation was geared to the purifying properties of aggression and self-sacrifice. The process began for the Italian people in childhood; elementary school children were provided with miniature rifles and mock machine guns. As the Duce himself, jaw thrust forward in bellicose pose, rode out on horseback amid adoring spectators in the Borghese Gardens, the Fascist propaganda voice was in full throat.

Almost with one accord, a subservient press thundered that no nation in Europe stood better prepared for war. There was muttered talk of secret weapons, even a death ray that had been perfected from an invention by the late Guglielmo Marconi. Up to the time of the invasion of Poland, Italians were being assured of their country's strength. Precise figures for armament and weaponry were detailed on one day, only to be doubled on the next.

Italy, intoned the national press, could muster eight million men trained to perfection and armed to the teeth. There were a hundred divisions, countless submarines. And, above all, of course, there was the towering genius of the Duce himself.

Mussolini believed his own propaganda, or persuaded himself that he did. The first of the jackals, traditionally sniffing at the lion's prey, still thirsted for action. On the day following his demand for weapons as the price for supporting the invasion of Poland, he informed his military leaders that they must stand ready for war. He received the blunt reply that Italy's capacity for any major engagement was virtually non-existent; at most, ten divisions could be mustered and those would be poorly equipped. As for personnel, the state had, in the words of Robert Farinacci, hitherto one of the regime's most strident supporters, 'a toy army without the least serious training'. No war could be waged with any prospect of success before 1942 at the very earliest.

With the recovery of Hitler's nerve, mobilization continued, but the Führer felt he needed some justification for his attack on Poland. Operation HIMMLER, a raid on the German radio station at Gleiwitz, on the German-Polish border, was concocted. Those responsible for carrying it out were accompanied by concentration camp inmates disguised as Poles in appropriate uniforms and gruesomely dubbed 'canned meat' in the operational order.

After the attack, the 'Poles', who had originally been told that they were taking part in a film, were shot. As an exercise in deception, the operation had been highly successful.

The party newspaper *Völkischer Beobachter* proclaimed 'Polish rebels cross the German frontier.' Hitler himself claimed in his Reichstag speech of 1 September, 1939, that there had been no less than fourteen border incidents of a similar kind; Germany had run out of tolerance. There would be no more negotiations. At 0417 hours on 1 September, 1939, the Germans began firing on the Polish posts in Danzig. At 0445, German armies crossed the frontier, as did bombers and fighters of the Luftwaffe to begin the assault on Polish airfields and aircraft.

Poland had not been mobilized until 1100 hours on 31 August. Throughout the summer leading up to the German attack, the stance of the Poles had been abundantly confident, even arrogant. They had defied Hitler over the Danzig question, standing up to all threats. Their rear, after all, was protected by the Soviets; there had been no reason to expect treachery there.

That dream was blown to pieces. On the opening day of the German attack, the Polish front was held by a mere seventeen divisions, three infantry brigades and six cavalry brigades. By the time hostilities began, thirteen Polish divisions were still on the move to their concentration areas, while another nine were still mustering.

When Rundstedt attacked from the south, it was to face the Polish armies of Poznan, Lodz and Krakow. Generaloberst Fedor von Bock's Army Group North attacked eastward into the Polish Corridor and southward from East Prussia. According to figures later given by Generaloberst Franz Halder, Chief of the German General Staff, the two army groups, consisting of sixty divisions, six of them armoured, numbered 630,000 and 886,000 respectively.

The Slovakian border with Poland was at the disposal of Rundstedt's Army Group South, consisting of VIII, X and XIV Armies. It was included in a huge salient which extended from Suwalki, on the frontier between East Prussia and Lithuania, to the Carpathians south of Przemysl, north-east of Slovakia. This amounted to a front line of some 1,250 miles. Within it, the German army held absolute sway with full freedom to transform the area into a virtual fortress.

Some 115,000 Slovak reservists were called up for service in the 14th Army, which was tasked to pin down the Polish forces around Cracow and Przemysl. The Army consisted of one mountain division, six infantry divisions, one light division, two Panzer divisions and the SS motorized regiment Germania. Slovak forces were made up of three divisions, designated 'Janosik', 'Skultety' and 'Razus'. A group of motorized forces was designated 'Kalincak'.

One division included a so-called *Schnell Gruppe* (Rapid Group) which was to go on to be designated a Division (*Schnell Division*) in its own right for the later invasion of the Soviet Union. A single Slovak air regiment also took part. All forces were expected to withdraw by 8 September.

Under the command of Generalfeldmarschall Wilhelm List, to whom General Ferdinand Catlos, C-in-C of the Slovak force was responsible, one Slovak division managed in a few days to fight through the Dukla Pass, south-west of Lwow province. A specially struck blue, white and red ribboned commemorative badge in the form of an eagle within a wreath of laurel leaves was given for actions against Poland in the Javorina-Orava region, close to the north-west frontier with Slovakia.

There were occasions when progress was a comparatively simple affair. Leutnant Baron von Bogenhardt described the advance of the 6th Motorized Regiment from Slovakia:

There was virtually no resistance. . . . There was a certain amount of sporadic fighting when we got to the river barriers. But the Luftwaffe had already cleared the way for us. Their Stuka dive bombers were deadly accurate, and as there was no opposition they had it all their own way. The roads and fields were swarming with unhappy peasants who had fled in panic from their villages when the bombing began, and we passed hundreds of Polish troops walking dejectedly towards Slovakia . . . there were so many prisoners that no one bothered to guard them. . . .

It was not always like that. On 9 September the Poles were routed at the River Bzura in what had been a large-scale vigorous counter-move. Rundstedt and his Chief of Staff, General Erich von Manstein, held them during the course of a vicious battle on a narrow front. Other units of Army Group South opened the decisive assault on Warsaw. After fourteen days of heroic resistance, the capital surrendered. The Red Army's intervention on 17 September ended any illusions that the Polish High Command might have had of prolonging resistance in a last ditch campaign in eastern Galicia, with their backs to the frontier with Romania. On the morning of 18 September, senior figures in the Polish government fled to Romania and claimed political asylum. The eventual intention was to reach France and continue the war from there.

A Soviet–German Non-Aggression Pact had already been signed at the end of August, which had cleared the way for the German attack on Poland. Now, within days, a fresh settlement to divide the country along the Brest-Litovsk line, was agreed between Moscow and Berlin. The Soviets gained the right to annex eastern Poland.

As for the Slovaks, besides the conventional troops of the Wehrmacht in Army Group South, they too had been in the shadow of the *Einsatzgruppen* (Action Squads of the SS), which, organized jointly by Himmler and Heydrich, had been active in the area of 14th Army, rounding up and shooting Jews in communities caught in the conflict – an activity later extended to clearing the Jews from the land altogether and concentrating them in ghettos. Here was a sharp and sinister portent of what alliance with Nazi Germany could mean. It was to be the first of many.

5

THE JACKAL PACK GROWS : HUNGARY AND ROMANIA

F or months after the fall of Poland, the armies on the Western Front remained in freeze-frame; there were even incidents of German troops waving good naturedly to their enemy across the reaches of the Rhine. This was the so-called Sitzkrieg – the 'Sit-down' or 'Phoney' War.

The only exception had been the four-month sideshow of the Soviet invasion of Finland, a spillover from the Nazi Soviet Pact whose secret protocol had put the Finns within the sphere of the Soviet Union, along with Latvia, Estonia and the eastern province of Bessarabia, which had been stripped from Romania.

Finland had long worried Stalin. The Finnish frontier ran a bare twenty miles north-east of Russia's second largest city, Leningrad. Control of the Gulf of Finland was deemed crucial so as to protect Leningrad and its sea approaches. This could be achieved by the acquisition of a naval base on the port of Hango on the Gulf's north side. On 30 November, 1939, the Soviet leader pressed the button. The Finns, who had been accused of provoking border incidents, were ordered to withdraw their troops from the frontier. A blunt refusal was considered sufficient provocation for war. The Red Army launched the 'Winter War' with a massive air bombardment on Finland's capital, Helsinki, which claimed sixty-one lives.

The Finns held out for three-and-a-half months. For two-and-a-half of these, the fortified Mannerheim Line, covering the Karelian isthmus, deterred the Soviet 7th and 13th Armies attacking through the Isthmus to the north-west of Leningrad. The 9th Army attacked from Soviet Karelia to the north, with 163 and 44 Divisions knifing through to Suomussalmi in the centre but then came up against strong counter-attacks.

Finland is a land of forests and above all snow; the Finns with their white garbed patrols known as 'White Death' defended their woods on skis, harassing flanks and shooting up convoys. Some of the assaults of these patrols caught the Russians off-guard. Many of their over-confident forces had not bothered with winter clothing. In two separate engagements, a couple of Finnish heroes of the Winter War, Paovo Talvela and Hjalmar Siilasvuo, annihilated four Soviet divisions with no more muscle than two regiments. When it came to the official account of the war, the Russians were frank about their shortcomings. The relevant volume of the *History of the Great Patriotic War* of the Soviet Union stated that most of the Soviet troops:

> were simply not prepared for this kind of warfare. They had had no experience of moving on skis through lakes and forest country and had no experience at all of breaking through permanent lines of fortifications, or of storming pillboxes and other reinforced concrete structures.

But, ultimately, Soviet armour proved the turning point. Field Marshal Baron Gustav Mannerheim, the Commander-in-Chief of the Finnish forces, who as a point of irony had once served in the Imperial Russian Army, later stated: 'Their 28 and 45-ton tanks, armed with two guns and four or five machine guns, contributed decisively to the penetration of our lines.'

Stalin, whose Red Army had lost some of its most able commanders in the notorious blood purges and been sorely weakened as a result, was eager to press any and every advantage. The exploitation task was entrusted to General Semyon Timoshenko who, by February, had concentrated twenty-seven divisions against the Mannerheim Line, subjecting it to what has been described as the most powerful barrage since the battle of Verdun in 1916.

Nevertheless, despite their massive superiority in artillery and tanks and in overall strength, the Russians had to pay a high price for victory – estimated by the Finns to have been some 80,000 dead.

Their consolation was to heap draconian demands on Finland, although Stalin stopped short of direct annexation. Even so, the entire Karelian Isthmus, including the town of Viborg and numerous islands, was annexed along with the country north of Lake Ladoga. A thirty-year lease was taken on Hango as a naval base. Stalin had feared that further efforts to subdue the Finns might well have unleashed an all-European coalition to engulf the Soviet Union, possibly with the participation of both Germany and the United States.

The loss of Viborg hurt the Finns particularly and was considered by many to fuel resentment against the Soviet Union, thereby making

Hitler's task of gaining Finnish help that much easier when the time came for the invasion of Russia. The Führer had intimated to Risto Ryti, Finland's future President, that, once Germany had neutralized its enemies, Britain and France, he would turn on Stalin.

Japan, which had signed the Anti-Comintern Pact against Communism with Germany in November, 1936, but had renounced it in August, 1939, now joined the Axis through the signature with Germany and Italy of a ten-year military agreement known as the 'Tripartite Pact'. Its aim was 'to establish and maintain a new order of things calculated to promote the mutual prosperity and welfare of the peoples concerned'. Its unmistakable targets were the United States and the Soviet Union. It was signed in Berlin on 27 September, 1940.

Despite this new development, Mussolini's initial nervousness over being drawn into Hitler's war had by now been matched by that of the smaller countries, potential members of the jackal pack, who had been watching events in Poland with some disquiet.

Notably among them had been Hungary whose Premier, Count Paul Teleki, had in his first of two letters to Hitler, initially shown enthusiasm for making his country's policy conform to that of the Axis. But then he had back-tracked by telling the Führer that, 'on moral grounds', Hungary would not be in a position to take up arms against Poland.

The about-face made Hitler incandescent. In the presence of Count Istvan Csaky, the Foreign Minister, the Führer launched into a ranting reminder that if it had not been for Germany's original generosity, Hungary would not have gained its slice of Czech territory. A suitably cowed Csaky agreed that the two letters should be forgotten, a request he would also make to Mussolini.

Teleki, while his country clung to the apron strings of the Rome–Berlin Axis, privately detested Hitler as an upstart revolutionary intent on undermining the country's political independence for his own designs. At home, various Hungarian neo-Nazi groups fomented social discontent. Elections in Whitsun, 1939, had revealed strong pro-Nazi working class sympathies, orchestrated by shrill anti-Semitism. This had some roots dating from the close of the First World War when, under the leadership of a Hungarian Jew, Bela Kun, Hungary experienced a political whirl-wind. As early as March, 1919, Kun was able to stitch together a short-lived Soviet Republic, which created a deep-rooted fear of Bolshevism among the upper and middle classes.

Even more virulent was hatred for the country's half a million Jews, creating an inevitable breeding ground for Nazism. Prominent among the groups was the extreme right wing Arrow Cross movement of Major Ferenc Szalasi, a former general staff officer who had relinquished a distinguished career to take up a cause which was increasingly compared in ideology with National Socialism.

Four years earlier, Szalasi had gone on a 'study tour' of Nazi Germany, returning to Hungary inspired by the achievement of the Nazis through raucous street corner populism and promises of liberating the working classes from the threat of Marxism. Propaganda for the Arrow Cross, heavily anti-Semitic and anti-Communist, was whipped up by the movement's newspaper *Osszertartas* (Unity) which ran a series of articles on the miserable conditions inflicted on their employees by giant Jewish corporations, financed allegedly from the swollen coffers of Jewish bankers. Alarmed by mounting violence, the authorities clamped down on the activities of the Arrow Cross and similar groups. Szalasi was arrested and flung into gaol. By way of reaction and to counter the threat to the extreme right, adherents of the various factions now banded together as urban terrorists. During early January, 1940, foreign newspapers were reporting serious assaults on anti-Nazis in dark side streets, the drowning of opponents, who were flung from Budapest bridges, and injuries from the elaborate arrangement of traffic 'accidents'.

Neo-Nazi headquarters were raided by police and plans unearthed for overthrowing the existing political and social order, the internment of Liberals and Socialists and the expulsion of Jews. According to other reports in overseas newspapers, Germany reacted in fury to the measures taken against its sympathizers.

Fresh apprehension gripped the Hungarians on 10 May, 1940, when the Germans invaded Holland, Belgium and Luxembourg in easy thrusts with a total of seventy-seven divisions, 3,500 aircraft and three Panzer corps.

Faced with such an example, it had not become difficult to imagine what the consequences might be for Hungary, the most exposed of the Danubian nations, if Hitler were provoked. With its lack of mountains, dense forests and wide rivers, it would be a gift for his Panzer divisions. Furthermore, should he later decide to turn east, he would inevitably look to the Balkan countries for those materials he needed to ensure ultimate victory – bauxite from Hungary and oil from Romania.

Behind the feelings of fear lurked something else: obsession for the return of lost territories, above all for Transylvania, which had been awarded to Romania after the First World War, and Voyvodina, absorbed in north-western Yugoslavia. For Admiral Miklos Horthy, who had been Regent of Hungary since 1920, and Teleki particularly, there was a deep personal interest: both were from Transylvania and both had been dispossessed of their land. Both hated the Romanians.

In the meantime, it was necessary to pay lip service to the Nazis. In an issue of the American *PM* newspaper for Tuesday, 17 September, 1940,

35

Robert Neville, a correspondent in Budapest, wrote: 'When the mayor of Berlin visits Budapest the streets are lined with swastikas. Regent Horthy never fails to send his birthday greetings to Der Führer and her Serene Highness, Magda von Horthy, will willingly break champagne over the bows of Hitler's new warships. A square in Budapest has been obligingly named after Adolf Hitler.'

Horthy's subservience progressed to military muscle, that same September, riding ahead of his troops on a white horse into the area of Nagyvarad and other frontier towns with their Magyar populations who greeted him with enthusiasm.

Contingents from the Nazi *Reichsarbeitsdienst* (RAD, State Labour Service), consisting of labour battalions, were allowed to pass through the country for tasks which included supervising the passage of 90,000 ethnic Germans from Bessarabia, who were being returned to the Reich, and guarding Romanian oil wells against possible disturbances.

German influence went still further. An agreement, involving territory including the whole of south-east Hungary, stretching from the Danube to the Romanian and Slovak borders, was signed between the Hungarian government and a German economic group granting oil-drilling concessions in Hungary.

There was, however, no question of German influence been bought off with the odd concession. Hitler and Ribbentrop were already stepping up pressure on the Hungarian government to make a formal acknowledgement of its subservience to the Axis.

In October, 1938, Germany and Italy had agreed to serve as arbitrators between those central European states where minority problems existed, such as Czechoslovakia, Hungary and Romania. The findings of the Italian and German Arbitration Commission were known as the 'Vienna Awards'. In November of that year, Hungary acquired some 12,000 square miles of Czech territory with a population of 1 million of whom eighty per cent were Magyars. As far as Romania and Hungary were concerned, Hungary was thrown the titbit of Transylvania. Hungarian troops marched in under the eyes of the Germans to acquire a population of 1,370,000 Romanians, 893,000 Hungarians and a total of 235,000 Jews, Germans, Czechs and other nationalities. Predictably, the Romanians seethed with resentment.

On 20 November, Hungary caved in to German blandishments. At Vienna's Belvedere Palace, Count Csaky signed a protocol which bound the country to the Tripartite Pact.

The tone of Ribbentrop's speech before this ceremony had left the Hungarians in little doubt as to their status. Hungary, Ribbentrop proclaimed, was the first Power to 'declare her willingness and her desire to be allowed to join the Three Power Pact'. For their part, the Axis

Powers had condescended to accept Hungary as the first Power to do so.

Hitler looked on while Ribbentrop and Ciano signed for their respective countries, along with Kurusu, the Ambassador in Berlin, for Japan. All equivocation was over for the Hungarians, the country's fate was bound inexorably to the Axis.

As for Romania, it had already proved a thorn in Hitler's side, not least because the Soviet Union had secured the two Romanian provinces of Bessarabia and northern Bukovina, threatening to move still further west. In addition, Hungary had threatened to go to war unless she won Transylvania. Conflict would have meant deprivation from the vital crude oil; worse, the whole of Romania might well be under threat from Russia.

Besides, Hitler had a general distrust of Romania, sharpened by knowledge of events over the preceding sixty years. The country's Hohenzollern king, Carol I, had signed a secret alliance with Imperial Germany and Austria Hungary. But his successor, Ferdinand, had reneged on the agreement and declared war in August, 1916. Although emerging bruised and battered from the conflict, Romania had at least been on the winning side, with consequent territorial gains.

Plainly, Romania had the knack of survival; Hitler had acted to change all that. Force, as he saw it, provided the only answer: five Panzer and three motorized divisions, together with parachute and airborne troops, were to be made ready to seize the oilfields.

Hitler's ultimate motives could be gathered from a single passage of a top-secret directive, destined to be produced at the Nuremberg trials of the Nazi leaders. It proclaimed the need: 'to prepare for deployment from Romanian bases of German and Romanian forces in case a war with Soviet Russia is forced on us.'

The surrender of territory to a clamouring Hungary, Bulgaria and the Soviet Union (the second most powerful power bloc after Germany) had been demanded in return for a guarantee to Romania that what was left would be protected.

After further vacillation on the part of Carol II, surrender had been effected at the Belvedere Palace the previous 30 August. It had all been eerily reminiscent of the way the Czechs had been treated earlier. Romania's wretched Foreign Minister, Mihai Manoilescu, had a map drawn up by the Axis powers thrust under his nose. Dobruja went to Bulgaria and, further to rub salt into the wounds, 16,000 square miles of Transylvania were apportioned to Hungary. Manoilescu's reaction was to slump in a dead faint and physicians had to revive him with camphor.

By mid-October, the initial contingents of the German military mission entered to rebuild the army, followed by droves of economists keen to match the industrial and commercial resources of the country with that of the Third Reich.

As far as at least the outward trappings of Nazism went, the Romania of Carol II had long proved an apt imitator. This was most marked, naturally enough in the areas of *Volksdeutsche*, among them the area of Romanian Banat, with its population to the south-west of Romanian Swabians. Here various pro-Nazi organizations were already in place.

Ever since the occupation of Prague, the Nazis had begun to seek out their own, frequently coming in the guise of tourists to Timisoara, where the hardcore of pro-Nazi activists of the National *Arbeitsbund* were based. From here were established pro-Nazi cells, euphemistically dubbed athletics and music groups and reading circles. In the schools, new faces appeared; teachers who had been to Berlin for 'summer courses' of indoctrination with the tenets of Nazism.

Carol was a firm believer in authoritarian rule and the unquestioned power of the monarchy. A gaggle of Fascist organizations had included the blue-shirted (and misleadingly named) National Christian Party of Octavian Goga. This had adopted the swastika as its emblem and briefly gained power on a frankly anti-Semitic ticket, and the Straji Tarii, Guards of the Fatherland, founded in 1934 by King Carol himself, later renamed Front of National Regeneration.

In a tradition shadowing the Jesuits and the Nazis, the Straji believed in capturing its recruits young. Romanians joined at the age of seven and remained affiliated throughout their teens.

Again, in the manner of the Nazis, they were taught, not simply ideology, but an attitude to life mirroring some of the trappings of Heinrich Himmler's SS with emphasis on the virtues of agronomy farming, the purity of the soil and a lifestyle of rural simplicity. The values of the Hitler Jugend were aped: the boy scout ethos emphasized by the frequent appearances of King Carol decked out in short trousers reminiscent of those worn by British Boy Scouts.

These movements, however, were mere minnows in comparison with the Iron Guard party – originally known as the 'Legion of the Archangel Michael', one of whose earlier leaders had been thirty-eight-year-old Corneliu Codreanu, known as the 'Captain' who operated from a Bucharest headquarters decked out with swastikas and giant pictures of Hitler.

Worshipped by droves of his young followers or Legionnaires, he gained the approval of Hitler who had allegedly proclaimed: 'For me there is only one dictator of Romania and that is Codreanu.'

Policies, apart from proclaiming Christian orthodoxy and worship of the peasantry, took second place to xenophobia, anti-parliamentarianism and virulent anti-Semitism (the Jews were 'moral cancer, a malignant growth'). The League of Nations was opposed bitterly; there would be alliance with Hitler and Mussolini. To the London *Daily Herald*, early in January, 1938, Codreanu declared: 'The Jews are the most urgent and important problem for Romania . . . There are only three solutions – "Assimilation", "Co-operation" and "Elimination". I am for elimination, complete and without reservation.'

By then, the Legion of the Archangel Michael had committed its fair share of atrocities against its opponents. The most notorious of these happened in 1936, when ten Legionaries forced their way into a hospital treating Mikai Stelescu, an Iron Guardist who had defected to another anti-Semitic group. An official account revealed that the intruders pumped 120 shots into Stelescu then 'chopped up the body with an axe, danced around the pieces of flesh, prayed, kissed each other and cried with joy.'

With the situation worsening, Carol took power himself. Codreanu was arrested with thirteen followers on a trumped up charge of high treason. According to some accounts, the prisoners had been bound and gagged, taken out to the forest of Ploiesti, and strangled. Other accounts reported that they were shot 'resisting arrest'.

But, ultimately, all this availed the King nothing. The Romanian delegates, wilting under the hectoring they had received from Ribbentrop, returned to Bucharest in what was wildly perceived as total disgrace. Public resentment at what was seen as their abject surrender boiled over; anger was turned on the King. Anti-royalist demonstrations edged the country to the brink of revolution. By now, King Carol II could not even depend on the loyalty of the police force.

For one man at least there was a twist of fortunes. When Carol assumed his dictatorial powers, he retained the services of Ion Antonescu, a former cavalry officer with an outstanding military record from the First World War. He had also played a major role during the successful war with the Communist regime in Hungary in 1919. Latterly, he had been a military attaché in Paris and London and had become Minister of Defence four years earlier.

He had been twice commandant of the Romanian staff college and the role model for a whole generation of the middle class officer corps. His instincts for diplomacy, however, did not extend to controlling an irascible temper or keeping his relationship with the King in good order. A stern moralist, he had open contempt for Carol's dissolute lifestyle.

As for the stubborn and obstreperous presence of the Iron Guard, Antonescu showed every sign of being tolerant of it. He was an avowed nationalist to whom the surrenders of Bessarabia and Northern Bukovina were the last straw. The King, he intimated, should abdicate as a result.

Carol retaliated by dismissing him from the Army and keeping him in detention.

But Romania's territorial losses spelt the downfall of the King, for they had brought him the contempt of his ministers. He soon came to realize that he had no option but to release Antonescu and hand him supreme power as Prime Minister. Antonescu, sensing that the tide of public feeling was flowing his way, used the power that this gave him to the full. His followers were only too conscious of Germany's threats to step in and occupy the whole country unless the political squabbling ceased. As if those threats were not enough, they were also sharply aware that the Red Army was bunched across the Prut river, which divided Stalin's bailiwick, Bessarabia, from their country.

It had become very clear that the King had become a liability that Romania could ill-afford. Almost as soon as he had assumed power, Antonescu dismissed him, making it clear to Carol that, if he valued his life, he should quit Romania forthwith.

The ex-King and his long-time mistress, the flame-haired Magda Lupescu, crammed as much royal booty as they could lay hands on into a royal train of nine coaches – including it was said three million dollars worth of jewellery and gold coins, together with some Rembrandt portraits and some exotic pets from the royal menagerie. The train sped on its way accompanied by a fusillade of bullets from Iron Guard contingents, a threat which sent Carol diving into a bath tub for protection. The party ultimately reached Lugano, in Switzerland.

Antonescu was affirmed as Prime Minister of a government which included the glum presence of the Iron Guard under its leader, Horia Sima, who believed that he ruled by divine mandate. Carol's son, eighteen-year-old Prince Michael, was proclaimed King but was a mere puppet.

On 7 October, 1940, the Wehrmacht marched into Romania on the twin pretexts of the need to defend the vital Ploiesti oilfields and to help to train the Romanian Army.

The British novelist Olive Manning, whose husband was a British Council lecturer in Bucharest at the time, wrote subsequently:

For the English, life in Bucharest was rapidly coming to an end. . . . Signs of the coming German occupation were everywhere. Officers of the German military mission filled the Athenee Palace, the cafes and the restaurants. Those Romanians who in the past had gained attention by speaking English in the shops, now spoke German. Such friends as remained to us made it clear we should go while the going was good. . . . We flew out of Romania as the German army of occupation marched in from the north.

For Hitler there was now a place man, a new ally, Antonescu, the undisputed dictator, the self-styled 'Conductator'. A month after the German occupation, Romania signed the Tripartite Pact. To pave the way, Antonescu paid a state visit to Italy where he exhibited his notorious scorn of diplomatic niceties by roundly attacking Mussolini over the imposition of the Vienna Award. The Duce was well aware that he was beholden to Romania for oil supplies and was obliged to guard his tongue; understandably, there were to be no further meetings between the two dictators. Hitler's relations with Antonescu were more positive, not least because of their shared views on Slavs, Hungarians and Jews. And, for Germany also there was the enticement of the Romanian oilfields.

– 6 –

AND NOW BULGARIA
AND YUGOSLAVIA

The memorandum on the desk of the Abwehr chief, Admiral Canaris, carried the signature of General Wilhelm Keitel, now promoted to Generalfeldmarschall and Chief of the High Command of the German Armed Forces. It declared that, as the highest priority, measures should be undertaken to safeguard supplies of Romanian oil destined for Germany.

In May, 1940, Germany commanded more than 500,000 tons of shipping on the Danube. Domination of the waterway, and especially of its Iron Gates, a narrow channel at the point where it became the boundary between Yugoslavia and Romania, was crucial; loss of control would mean a sudden halt to the chief supply of oil, necessary to fuelling the war and particularly for pursuing any conflict further east. Hungary, Germany's nearest neighbour on the Danube, was confronted with blunt demands that Nazi gunboats should be admitted to its territorial waters to guard the Reich's oil and food traffic. The Danube, Hitler and Keitel insisted, must be policed thoroughly. To be successful, there was need for the clandestine approach; in such matters the Abwehr of Admiral Canaris was in the ascendant.

Canaris despatched Edrich Ferdinand Pruck, a former Wehrmacht officer turned Abwehr agent, to contact Eugen Christescu, Chief of the Siguranza, the Romanian intelligence services. A joint programme evolved, centring on carefully selected oil firms in which Germany had major control.

Hauptmann Doctor Paul Leverkuehn, a lawyer turned Abwehr officer, who worked closely with Canaris, later wrote of setting up:

An intelligence organisation which was spread over the whole of the oilfields and which was concerned with the detection of any sort of planning which might conceivably be aimed at sabotage. The Bulgarian and Hungarian Intelligence Services . . . not only condoned the activities of the German Abwehr in their own sovereign territory, but also supported it and shielded it when necessary.

The task of surveillance went to the men of the Brandenburgers, straining at the leash after being confined to barracks following the farcical events preceding the invasion of Poland. Soldiers of the regiment donned civilian clothes and were posted as security guards. They were made responsible for searching goods trains on their way through Hungary and every oil-tanker on the Danube. None gave any trouble.

For Hitler, the next hurdle was Bulgaria. One serious miscalculation continued to haunt King Boris III, the short, swarthy monarch of this Slavic state in the eastern Balkans, which had long been dominated by Turkey. It had thrown in its lot with Germany in the First World War and the reward had been the total defeat of its armed forces, followed by French occupation. Above all, national pride had been deflated by the loss of the Dobrudja area, a rich strip of land between the Black Sea and the Danube to Romania and its Macedonian possessions to Greece.

Anglo-French sentiment had been in no mood for forgiveness. By September, 1939, Bulgaria had been the only power defeated in 1918 not to receive at least some territorial redress. However, a degree of compensation came, at a price, a year later with the gift of part of Dobrudja.

Hitler and Ribbentrop had operated with characteristic high-handedness. The Bulgarian and Romanian foreign ministers had been summoned to Salzburg to determine the future of Dobrudja. As far as Romania was concerned, the Germans, with their overwhelming military might, held all the cards. There was talk of 'discussion' of the Dobrudja question but, in fact, Bucharest had been given its orders. Bulgaria received southern Dobrudja, but the north remained with Romania.

A mood of euphoria gripped the Bulgarians. On 21 September, 1940, units of the Third Bulgarian Army moved in to reclaim the country's former territory. Its path was strewn with flowers; there was wistful talk of nation unification. King Boris was magnanimous: political prisoners were pardoned. For the King, of course, there was the requirement of commitment to Germany. When he finally made it, Hitler was ready for him.

In the meantime, there was plenty of groundwork to be done and the Abwehr was chosen for it. Canaris had grasped eagerly at the chance of setting up KO (*Krieg Organization*) Bulgaria in an area so near to Russia and the Dardanelles. It was an agreeable expansion of his power; Major

Otto Wagner of Abwehr III was despatched to Sofia by way of Romania.

Wagner was not slow to discover that Fascist factions within Bulgaria had been, for the most part, ill-organized, ineffective and short-lived. Prominent among them had been the Bulgarian National Socialist Workers' Party (NSBAP), founded in 1932 by Christo Kuntscheff, a medical student working in Berlin.

Something of a mirror image of the German National Socialist Party (NSDAP), the design of its badge nicely symbolized the chaos of Balkan politics: it featured the lion of Bulgaria holding aloft the hammer and sickle – with the background of a swastika. It was, however, a fractured affair that within two years of its foundation had split into two squabbling factions, each half claiming to be the sole NSBAP. The government of the time however was not ready for such blatant pro-Nazi sentiment and banned both halves, along with the pro-Nazi Union of the Young National Legion and the Italian-orientated NZF (National Union of Fascists).

A bid to be taken far more seriously, however, was that of the brown-uniformed Brannik ('Defender') Youth Organisation which, formed just three months before Germany marched into Bulgaria, had extended its tentacles into German universities where young Bulgarians were studying. A watch on potentially useful Neo-Nazi and Neo-Fascist movements was useful; for the Abwehr's Wagner though, there was far more serious work.

The first three months of 1941 were characterized by the discreet arrival of various military staffs into Bulgaria. All were given elaborately non-committal labels. But all had one overall function: to make all preparations necessary for the progress of the Wehrmacht. The springboard for the planned onslaught on Greece and Yugoslavia would be Romania. Then would come the advance through Bulgaria.

Hitler's plans had already been thrown out of gear by the actions of his senior Axis partner. In July, 1940, Hitler had felt content enough to take a small break at his mountain retreat at Berchtesgaden and dream of a brand new opera house proposed for Linz. Within three months, that cosy reverie was shattered.

The Führer's occupation of Romania had enraged Benito Mussolini. To Ciano, whom he had summoned to the Palazzo Venezia on 12 October, the Duce complained volubly that Hitler had stolen his thunder, that the occupation had made a bad impression on the Italian public. Fascist Italy must have a triumph of its own. He stormed:

> Hitler always faces me with a *fait accompli*. This time I am going to pay him back in his own coin. He will find out from the papers that I have occupied Greece. In this way the equilibrium will be re-established.

Ciano asked the Duce if he had consulted his chief-of-staff, Marshal Badoglio, only to receive the astounding reply: 'Not yet, but I shall send in my resignation as an Italian if anyone objects to our fighting the Greeks.' The Italian service chiefs were appalled. Only three weeks before, Mussolini had ordered mass demobilization. Now he proposed to attack Greece within twelve days – at dawn on 28 October. Hitler had tried to talk Mussolini out of so potentially disastrous an adventure which involved attacking Greek mountain troops at a time of year when the weather was likely to be frozen and many roads impassable. But late in the day of the invasion, the Führer was alighting from his special train in Florence to be greeted by a triumphant Mussolini announcing in German: 'Führer! We are on the march! Victorious Italian troops crossed the Greco-Albanian frontier at dawn today.'

Intent on a cheap conquest, the Duce had been deaf to all advice, asserting that his troops could walk through Greece and that the campaign had been planned down to the smallest detail. In fact, the troops to whom he referred had been some 100,000 hastily mustered raw recruits. The Greeks mobilized quickly and had at their disposal fifteen infantry divisions, four infantry brigades and a cavalry division. They had the edge, fighting against invaders soaked by rain, bogged down by mud and frozen by temperatures plummeting to 20 degrees below zero.

In Rome, the newspapers, with their customary sense of self-preservation, either remained silent or spoke of the welcome the troops were receiving. What was more, busts of the Duce were being handed out as gifts to the delirious Greeks. The reality was rather different: there was scarcely a section of Greek opinion that did not loathe Mussolini.

The diminutive Greek dictator General Ioannis Metaxas, thinning and bespectacled, was known to have pro-Axis leanings, to the extent of aping the Third Reich with his grandiose conception of the 'Third Hellenic Civilisation' – respectively, ancient Greece, medieval Byzantium and an individualistic pot-pourri of both. But, although no liberal, Metaxas also happened to be a fierce Greek patriot with no intention of caving in to Mussolini's ultimatum, which had torn him out of a deep sleep on the early morning of the invasion. Attired only in dressing gown and slippers, he had snapped at Count Emmanuele Grazzi, Mussolini's envoy, a contemptuous refusal.

The terms of the ultimatum were that, since the Greeks had collaborated with the British by allowing them to use Greek ports and airfields for refuelling ships and aircraft, the Italians would now demand access to 'strategic points' within Greece. Metaxas had been given precisely three hours to concur. He had told Grazzi: 'I could not make a decision to sell my own house on a few hours notice. How do you expect me to sell my own country?'

The Italian army had mustered motorized Bersaglieri in Albania – élite riflemen with the traditional insignia of black cockerel feathers sweeping from their helmets – who poured into Greece. Within a matter of days, the Greek 9th Division counter-attacked from the Macedonian mountains. Greek General Papagos's forces of around 150,000 men and weak in armour, swept down. An Evone force, made up of crack infantrymen who also served as the royal guard, trapped the Italian 'Julia' Alpine Division within the Pindus mountains and cut off an Italian column.

By as early as 3 November, the Greeks were firmly on the offensive. Their troops counter-attacked at points near Klissura, Yanina and further north at Koritsa and Kastoria; the enemy was forced back into Albania.

In the churning, chomping seas, matters were scarcely better. An intended amphibious operation against Corfu was scrapped. The weather set at naught any effective air support. By mid-January, the Greeks were masters of a quarter of Albania. A final counter-attack in early March availed the Italians nothing.

*   *   *

By this time, Hitler was in the grip of one of his longest lasting obsessions – the strategic importance of the oil wells at Ploiesti that German troops had been sent into Romania to protect. The wells were now threatened by the presence of British forces in Crete and Lemnos. Orders were forwarded to the Army to prepare plans immediately to invade Greece through Bulgaria; initially, ten divisions would be sent to Romania via Hungary.

Anxieties plagued the Bulgarian monarch; he cast worrried glances at a near neighbour. He knew that talks between Ribbentrop and Molotov had already discussed the possibility of including Bulgaria in the Soviet sphere of influence. Propelled by circumstances rather than fuelled by ideology, Boris had been edging towards the Nazi camp from the previous summer. When it came to requests from Germany to sign the Tripartite Pact, to which Hungary, Romania and Slovakia were already signatories, Boris temporised. Such a move, he hinted, might be possible some time in the future.

Compromises, though, were made. In pre-war Bulgaria, the Jews, who had formed some one per cent of the population, had enjoyed a long period of freedom and tolerance. German influence gradually eroded all that; on 24 September, 1940, a Defence of the Nation Act was passed by the *Sobranije* (parliament); all sexual relations between Jews and non-Jews, whether married or not were forbidden, although there was some exemption for those who denied their Judaism. Progressively, Jews were banned from the key professions and from senior posts in industry.

Pressure by Germany on Bulgaria to abandon neutrality had not yet worked, although Boris walked a dangerous tightrope. In a special King's Speech from the throne, delivered early in November, he was careful to express gratitude to Germany and Italy for their part in restoring the southern part of Dobrudja. Civilities out of the way, he went on to make it clear how much he valued his country's independence by stressing the importance of Bulgaria's treaties of non-aggression and friendship with Turkey and Yugoslavia. There had been encouraging progress in political and economic relations with the Soviet Union.

But Hitler's patience had only months to run. In the closing days of February, 1941, giant swastika flags were serving as funeral banners at the burial of yet another independent state. It was a quiet Saturday afternoon and the occupation had begun with the advent of troops in field grey. Fleets of fighter aircraft and Junkers troop carriers swept over Sofia. There were instances of cordial reception for German troops; advance elements of 12th Army were received with the traditional bread and salt; the impression was that, since Germany and Russia were allies, they would march together and that there was now nothing to fear from any of Stalin's demands.

Away in Vienna, at the Belvedere Palace, with its imposing salon draped in Gobelin tapestries, the obsequies were being conducted. The usual summons had been served: Bogdan Filov, the Bulgarian Prime Minister, signed the Tripartite Pact, joining the Axis powers; not just because of their help in obtaining southern Dobrudja, but because the Pact would 'secure for the nation the possibility of developing in peace, strengthen its welfare, and safeguard a just and permanent peace'. Friendly relations with the Soviet Union and Turkey, he declared, would not be affected.

Ribbentrop, later to be the recipient of the highest Bulgarian distinction, the Order of Saints Cyrill and Methodius, with its Maltese cross and sash badge of blue enamel, was flanked by Filov and Ciano and declared:

> We are gathered together again to greet a new country which is joining the Pact. I am particularly glad that it is Bulgaria. In spirit, Bulgaria was always with us. Now they have taken the decision to join us formally.

On cue, Nazi radio parroted: 'In agreement with the Bulgarian government, German troops crossed the Bulgarian frontier today in order to counteract intentions of spreading the war in the Balkans and in order to protect Bulgarian interests.' The *Sobranije* was told by Filov: 'Bulgaria adhered to the Three-Power Pact owing to the pressure of events, which produced a new situation around us.'

Bulgaria was now cast as the next jackal of the Third Reich. For Britain, the alarm bells jangled. The British, deeply concerned over the extent of the danger which now faced the Thracian frontier of Greece, and at the time engaged in talks with the Greek military and political leaders, were promptly cast by the Germans in the role of aggressors.

On the streets of Sofia, German repression was turned on Britain. Radio Berlin announced that some fifty people in the employ of British intelligence had been arrested, including British and American journalists. Britain riposted by officially breaking off relations with Bulgaria within days of the signing of the Tripartite Pact. Hitler's overall plans had been outlined as early as 8 and 9 January, when Mussolini had been suffering defeat in North Africa. He saw it as imperative to come to the Duce's aid. During a war council at the Berghof, the Führer announced Operation MARITA, the attack on Greece. This would involve a significant role for his Tripartite Pact partners.

Hitler knew that Bulgaria, in particular, had no love for the Greeks. Under the Neuilly Treaty of November, 1919, following defeat in the First World War, Bulgaria had lost Western Thrace to Greece, which had meant being cut off from the Aegean. Recovery of lost territory had become something of a political mantra between the wars.

Directive No 20, issued on 13 December, 1940, by the Supreme Commander of the Armed Forces from Führer Headquarters reflected Hitler's continuing anxiety over the Ploiesti oilfields. The opening clause stated:

> The outcome of the battles in Albania is still uncertain. In the light of the threatening situation in Albania it is doubly important to frustrate English efforts to establish, behind the protection of a Balkan front, an air base which would threaten Italy in the first place and, incidentally, the Romanian oilfields.

Hitler then went on to state his intention:

> **a.** To establish in the coming months a constantly increasing force in Southern Romania.
> **b.** On the arrival of favourable weather – probably in March – to move this force across Bulgaria to occupy the north coast of the Aegean and, should this be necessary, the entire mainland of Greece (Operation MARITA).

He declared: 'We can rely on Bulgarian support.'

Once again, the Bulgarians had displayed their uncanny knack of picking the wrong side, believing firmly that Germany had indisputedly won the war so far. There was no reason to suppose that the pattern of hitherto easy victories would not be repeated. Glittering prizes were dangled: the prospect of securing Greek territory to the south, with consequent access to the Aegean.

In return, participation in MARITA was required in the shape of allowing passage to German troops which had been assembled in Romania. Minutes have survived of a German–Bulgarian conference held on 8 February, 1941, at which Generalfeldmarschall List was the Wehrmacht delegate, together with representatives of the Royal Bulgarian General Staff. The substance of the conference was that:

> . . . at least six Bulgarian divisions [would be deployed] on the Bulgarian Turkish border; sufficient forces for the protection of the border, on the Greek border; reinforced border protection on the Yugoslav border. Later on, the Bulgarian Army is also responsible for adequate protection along these fronts where German forces will not become offensive.

It was made clear that the German and Bulgarian General Staffs would work in full cahoots and would 'take all measures in order to camouflage the preparation of the operations and to assure in this way the most favourable conditions for the execution of German operations as planned.'

The minutes continued:

> From the beginning, a sufficient quantity of German forces – mainly armoured and motorized divisions – will be moved in the shortest time behind the Bulgarian border protection troops. . . . The other forces provided for the operations, that means more infantry and armoured divisions, will follow behind, depending on weather, road and bridge situation.

In addition, the Germans required the Bulgarian railway network and accompanying rolling stock to be placed at their disposal; transportation of German forces was to be provided by the Bulgarian general staff.

The fruits of that agreement fell thick and fast. Pontoon bridges were slung across the Danube at three points from which German forces arrowed towards the Greek frontier, one arm of them to make for a mountain pass where the Struma river flowed into Greece.

The able and ruthless Generalfeldmarschall List, an assiduous apostle of *Blitzkrieg*, arrived from Romania to 'direct operations'. By the end of February, he and his staff had requisitioned some fifty mountain villas and pensions at Tschankouria, a ski-resort some 70 miles from the Greek frontier. All visits to the area, which was placed under special guard, were forbidden. From Belgrade, reports came of the closure to traffic of the Danube for 60 miles. The Germans had thrown the pontoon bridges across the river from Romania to the Bulgarian bank.

The German General Staff in Romania had moved westward from Bucharest to Craiova, 40 miles from the Danube. Predictably, Hitler was thinking ahead. He wanted Yugoslavia as the next signatory to the Tripartite Pact but the Yugoslavs were proving intractable. On 4-5 March, the Regent, Prince Paul, was summoned to the Berghof and, like so many before him subjected to Hitler's bullying, with the proffered consolation of the morsel of Salonika after Greece had been successfully overwhelmed.

Three weeks later, a knot of police guarded a suburban wayside station. Two men boarded a special train which pulled out of an obscure suburban station on the way to Vienna. The men were Yugoslav Premier, Dragisha Cvetkovic and Foreign Minister Aleksander Cincar-Markovic.

Their arrival was greeted with drums and flags. The Yellow Hall of the Belvedere Palace was ablaze with lights and thick with microphones and newsreel cameras. In the presence of Ribbentrop, Count Ciano and the Japanese Ambassador in Berlin, General Oshima, Yugoslavia was signed up to the Tripartite Pact on 25 March.

The protocol scarcely differed from those already signed by Slovakia, Hungary, Romania and Bulgaria. The sole concessions made by Germany were embodied in two letters from Ribbentrop declaring that the sovereignty and territorial integrity of Yugoslavia would be respected, and that no demands would be made during the war for the passage of troops.

In a comment far wiser than he knew, the Diplomatic Correspondent of *The Times* newspaper in London wrote:

> Germany's record shows the value of such promises . . . If the Germans wished their troops to go into Yugoslavia . . . they would simply send them over the frontier either by trickery or by force. No promise on their own part would stop them, but only the continued resolution and watchfulness of the Yugoslav people.

As for Hitler, he had every reason to be pleased with his widened Axis. An anxiety that there would be a strong rapprochement between Turkey and Yugoslavia in the face of a common threat had been removed. And, as the Führer told Ciano, a compliant Yugoslavia would make the assault on the northern frontier of Greece that much easier.

For once, however, the German warlord was taking rather too much for granted.

- 7 -

GREECE OVERWHELMED

The composition of Yugoslavia in the early days of the Second World War set a pattern which was to become sadly familiar – a clutch of squabbling nations whose only area of agreement was deep mutual hatred.

A vain attempt at reconciliation between widely disparate groups had been made on 1 December, 1918, with the creation of the Kingdom of the 'Serbs, Croats and Slovenes', bundling together the former Austro-Hungarian provinces of Slovenia, Croatia-Slavonia, Dalmatia, Bosnia and Herzegovina. Included were the kingdoms of Serbia, Macedonia, Vopjvodina, Kosovo and Montenegro. Many had misty dreams of individual sovereignty. The Serbian King had assumed the crown. Nine years later, the kingdom was renamed Yugoslavia.

Heavy-handed control was vested in the Serbs who lorded it over not only the Croats, Slovenians and Macedonians, but also a heterogeneous sprawl of Albanians, Hungarians, Germans, Montenegrins, Czechs, Slovaks, Romanians, Jews and Gypsies. The process of government was paralysed by inefficiency and corruption; the Croatians were sullen in the face of coercion by the Serbs. King Alexander, who had led the Serbian armies during the First World War, set up as dictator, a move which he saw as the only practical alternative to civil war.

Croat nationalists struck in October, 1934. Whilst on a state visit to France, Alexander was shot dead in an open limousine in Marseilles, an easy target for the terrorist agents of Dr Ante Pavelic, head of the Ustachi, the fanatically nationalist movement of Croatia, which was still, technically, a kingdom under the absentee King Tomislav II.

In a state that was anti-Serb, anti-Semitic and pro-Axis, Pavelic could depend on the protection both of Nazi Germany and Fascist Italy, who, looking for allies, had seized every opportunity of fomenting discontent among the Yugoslavs. Belgrade sent an indictment to the League of

Nations, alleging that one of the terrorists involved in Alexander's murder had received his passport in Hungary, while two others had found shelter in Italy. The weapons used in the killing were, it was further alleged, supplied by Germany.

The successor to Alexander was nine year old King Peter II but power passed to the English-educated Regent, Prince Paul, who had reluctantly committed Yugoslavia to the Tripartite Pact. Hitler had seen no reason to be unduly worried, assuming that the government of Prime Minister Dragisha Cvetkovic would dutifully abide by it.

The Nazi approach would be courtship rather than seduction. Once the country had been wooed, then Germany would have a free passage across it by rail. A potentially hostile Yugoslavia could not be considered. This time the Führer was firmly set on his course to invade the Soviet Union.

If Hitler was reasonably sanguine, the British secret service was not. The signing of the Tripartite Pact by Yugoslavia scarcely came as a surprise to Winston Churchill. On 14 January, 1941, the British Prime Minister, minuting Foreign Secretary Anthony Eden, described Prince Paul's attitude as looking like that 'of an unfortunate man in a cage with a tiger, hoping not to provoke him when dinner time approaches.'

At Churchill's urging, British agents began overtures to dissident groups in Serbia who congregated at the Reserve Officers Club in Belgrade. The British air attaché fastened on General Bora Mirkovic, the deputy commander of the Yugoslav Air Force. Mirkovic was known as a loyal Serb patriot, sentiments which the air attaché set out to exploit.

Mirkovic was persuaded that nothing less than the overthrow of the Regency would do for his country. A plan was concocted among a small number of officers who were deemed to be absolutely trustworthy. Once the decision had been taken, a network of conspirators, led by General Dustan Simonvic, was built up in the country's main garrisons. On 26 March came the signal – seize the key points in Belgrade, seal off the royal residence and secure the safety of the young King Peter II by the following day.

Tanks and artillery rumbled through the streets. The Ministry of War was occupied; Cvetkovic was induced to resign and, by dawn, a wireless proclamation had announced the overthrow of the Regency. In Zagreb, an unsuspecting Prince Paul, was euphemistically 'requested' to return to Belgrade. After signing the instrument of abdication, he decamped for Greece.

Acutely aware of the way things were going, the young King Peter had escaped the Regent's clutches by shinning down a drainpipe in the place where he was held. On 28 March, amid an enthusiastic welcome, he attended divine service in Belgrade Cathedral. It was reckoned that a successful challenge had been mounted against disaster. In the words of Winston Churchill:

> The Yugoslav nation found its soul . . . A people paralysed in action, hitherto ill-governed and ill-led, long haunted by the sense of being ensnared, flung their reckless heroic defiance at the tyrant and conqueror in the moment of his greatest power.

It was also possibly the moment of Hitler's greatest anger. The coup had put paid to his wish for a solidly pro-Axis group of Balkan states. Incandescent with rage, he summoned the senior members of his High Command. His plans, he proclaimed, had been seriously disrupted; the dubious consolation was that the action had been taken before the intended launch of the invasion of the Soviet Union.

In all their unambiguous harshness, Hitler's deliberations to Göring, Keitel, Jodl and Ribbentrop survived as evidence at the Nuremberg Trial:

> The Führer is determined, without waiting for possible declarations of loyalty from the new government, to make all preparations in order to destroy Yugoslavia militarily and as a national unit. . . . Politically it is especially important that the blow against Yugoslavia is carried out with *merciless harshness* and that the military destruction is done in a lightning-like undertaking. In this way, Turkey would become sufficiently frightened and the campaign against Greece later on would be influenced in a favourable way.

Sarcastically, Hitler added, Italy, Hungary and Bulgaria, united in collective greed, would doubtless be happy. In now familiar fashion, thieves' gold would be parcelled out to the jackals: Italy would get the Adriatic coast, Hungary the Serbian Banat and Bulgaria would be tossed Macedonia.

Keitel, responsible for the practical details, spent the entire night with his generals planning invasion logistics. At Nuremberg he stated in evidence:

> The decision to attack Yugoslavia meant completely upsetting all military movements and arrangements made up to that time. MARITA had to be completely readjusted. New forces had to be brought through Hungary from the north. All had to be improvised. Operation STRAFE (Punishment) was to coincide with MARITA. Furthermore, the invasion of Russia would have to be postponed.

Alongside the military preparations, there was the pressing need to prepare Hungary, most immediately affected by the invasion of Yugoslavia; all lines would be through Hungarian territory which would be a transit zone. For Hungary this was the point of no return. Horthy was only too well aware that opposition to Hitler's demands would mean occupation of his country. But there would be gains: among them territories of her southern frontiers which had previously been lost to Yugoslavia.

On 30 March, the details of the joint offensive were prepared during a visit to Budapest by General Friedrich Paulus; Hungary agreed to co-operate with Germany. Operation STRAFE was also to involve Romania and Bulgaria.

The Hungarian Prime Minister, Count Paul Teleki, could not stomach the fact that the agreement with Germany came within months of a treaty of 'eternal' friendship with the Yugoslavs.

Depressed and ill, he retired to his apartment in the Sandor Palace and, at dawn, put a bullet through his head. At first, a badly rattled government attempted to conceal the death altogether. When it became obvious that such a stance could not be maintained, an official statement took refuge in a lie. The Prime Minister, it was said, had been found dead in bed by his valet following a heart attack. The evasion did no good. Teleki had sent an emotionally charged letter to Horthy: 'We betrayed our words – out of cowardice – the words of our treaty of eternal peace. . . . We will become the despoilers of corpses.'

Hungary, he had argued, was no longer proof against German domination. He felt that he had failed and that his foreign policy had brought the country into entanglements from which there was no escape.

Teleki's gesture was empty. Hungary's behaviour and, above all, that of Germany changed not one iota. The formalities were obeyed. As was customary, the Hungarian government resigned at the death of the Premier and his likely successor was discussed. The choice fell eventually on the pro-Axis Lazlo Bardossy. Within nine hours of Teleki's suicide, German armour rumbled through Budapest.

By way of justification for its contribution to the invasion of Yugoslavia – 4th, 5th and Mobile Corps (eight brigades) – Hungary cited a General Staff report, never confirmed, that Yugoslav aircraft had violated Hungarian air space and dropped bombs. Across to the east, Bulgaria, as far as possible, was keeping its head down. King Boris, a shrewd operator, at first, had no wish to be drawn into any adventure in Yugoslavia or Greece. He claimed that all divisions likely to be of any use in battle were in 3rd Army guarding the German flank against any possible move by Turkey. However, because of the agreement reached by Generalfeldmarschall Wilhelm List, the German

5. King Boris of Bulgaria with the German Commander-in-Chief in the Balkans, Generalfeldmarshall Wilhelm List, in April, 1941, discussing troop deployments before the entry into Yugoslavia. *(Photo: Topham Picturepoint)*

6. Hitler meeting Marshal Antonescu of Romania in Munich just before the launch of Operation BARBAROSSA in June, 1941.

7. Monsignor Josef Tiso, President of Slovakia from 1939-44. *(Photo: Topham Picturepoint)*

8. Dr Pavelić, the Croatian Head of State, with Von Ribbentrop, Hitler and Göring, June 1941. *(Photo: Imperial War Museum)*

9. German troops under heavy Russian fire in the suburbs of Leningrad, November, 1941. *(Photo: Associated Press/Topham Picturepoint)*

12th Army was already committed to using Bulgaria as the springboard.

The Germans wasted no time. Luftwaffe bases were established on Bulgarian soil, while German anti-aircraft gun emplacements sprang up on the Bulgarian–Yugoslav frontier. Romania also played its part. A bridge was slung over the Danube at Bechet, crossed by German supply columns.

The vanguard of List's main attack towards Skopje was formed by IX Panzer Division and the Leibstandarte Adolf Hitler of the Waffen-SS, the object being to cut off the Yugoslavs from Greece. The advance of the Leibstandarte was through Skopje. Within three days it had captured the stronghold of Monastir near the border. The attack was through mountainous territory from within Bulgaria, the major route being along the Nishava valley and a network of roads, one spearhead making for the Vardar River, south of Kosovo, while another arrowed south to Salonika.

Two days later, General von Kleist's XIV Corps struck north from the Bulgarian–Yugoslav frontier, making for Belgrade. By 19 April, Bulgaria's 5th Army had occupied Macedonia and some districts of Eastern Serbia which, with Western Thrace and Eastern Greek Macedonia (the Aegean Province), Bulgarian forces were to annex.

The Nazi party newspaper, the *Völkischer Beobachter*, screamed its headlines: 'The German soldier answers the traitors'. Under Hitler's Operation CASTIGO, for two days from 6 April, Palm Sunday, bombs had fallen on Belgrade, reducing the city to a mass of burning rubble. More than 17,000 people had been killed.

The Yugoslavs had been taken totally by surprise, having assumed that if war came at all, it would be preceded by an ultimatum. An almost surrealist instance of the unpreparedness was provided by the spectacle of the air force Commander-in-Chief, General Simovic, in top hat and tails for his daughter's wedding, threading his way gingerly in his official car past deep bomb craters and back to the war ministry.

Hitler's satellites had played their part. Eighty miles to the north of the capital, an observation post had reported the progress of fifty German aircraft flying in tight formation from Hungary.

As for the Yugoslav Army, it suffered from weakness of resources, internal feuds and tactical miscalculation. It could mobilize twenty-eight infantry and three cavalry divisions at the most. The onward march of the German Army rendered the Yugoslavs tired and dispirited and many were only too glad to surrender. When Zagreb fell on 10 April, 15,000 men went into captivity.

Propaganda bids to stir up the *Volksdeutsche* had paid off by 9 April, at Maribor, just north of the Drava river between the German and Hungarian borders. Smuggled weapons had enabled public buildings to be seized by armed force for the harassing of Yugoslav troops. Over the next three days, the Hungarian forces followed the Germans across the Yugoslav border. The collapse of Yugoslavia made further advances needless.

Horthy's reaction was a pious disclaimer. Hungary had begun defensive measures 'only when the Yugoslavs made a series of air attacks upon Hungary and made armed raids on Hungarian territories.' The national radio broadcast a statement from Bucharest in the Regent's name (widely thought to have been dictated by the Germans) that he had hoped to win back Hungary's territories bloodlessly, but the Yugoslav *coup d'état* – 'caused by the same powers that brought so many tears, so much blood and suffering to Europe in 1914' – had caused differences between Yugoslavia and the Axis powers.

By 12 April, when reports of the broadcast were carried by the world press, Hungarian troops had begun occupying the north-east regions of the Banat, with its mixed population of Germans, Hungarians, Croats, Slovenians and Serbs.

Justification for this was Hitler's speedy tearing apart of Yugoslavia. A separate Croatian state came into being on 10 April when General Slavko Kvaternik, the underground Croat leader, proclaimed on the radio 'the Independent State of Croatia.' His peroration was accompanied, appropriately enough, by the playing of *Deutschland über Alles*. Six days later, Dr Ante Pavelic returned from exile in Turin to become *poglavnik* (leader) of the new state. He named a cabinet and, shunning German-Italian approval, appointed a series of *zupani* (district leaders) from among his loyal cronies. Already Dr Andrijö Artukovitch, described by the German radio announcer as an 'outstanding member of the insurgent movement', had urged the Croat people to turn their weapons against 'our accursed enemy the Serbs.'

The doling out of the spoils then followed. By way of agreement with the Germans, the Ustachi accepted Italy's annexation of central Dalmatia and a titular Italian king for Croatia in exchange for the chance to take power. The Independent State of Croatia swallowed all of Pavelic's native Bosnia-Hercegovina and the Srem region of Slavonia, the area to the north-east abutting Hungary, from Vukovar on the Danube to Zemun, across the Danube from Belgrade. The Germans and Italians lost no time in moving in to establish a permanent presence. Hungary received the triangle of territory between the Danube and the Tisza into which her forces had moved. This embodied the area of the Böcksa and of Voivodina with its Serbian population, which had originally been Hungarian territory before the First World War.

Macedonia (known to the Yugoslavs as 'South Serbia'), was the gift parcel handed to Bulgaria. For Mussolini, who had done little beyond fulminating that Yugoslavia was the invention of the Treaty of Versailles and had no right to exist in a Europe designed for Fascism, there was southern Slovenia, the Dalmatian coast from Split southwards, Montenegro and the Kosovo region of Macedonia. It was sweet revenge for the humiliation of the earlier failed invasion.

For the Germans, preparations were made for the setting up of a puppet Serbian government in Belgrade; in the meantime, for the Third Reich came northern Slovenia and the remnants of the former Yugoslav kingdom.

Hitler had become accustomed to conquests coming cheap and Yugoslavia was no exception. Operation STRAFE had lasted a mere twelve days at a cost of 151 killed, 15 missing and 392 wounded. Some 300,000 men, however, evaded capture. They made for the mountains; it was good terrain for an already flowering movement of resistance.

*   *   *

The simultaneous invasion of Greece was like a thunderbolt. The Wehrmacht, which had contended with bad weather and poor roads, had started its crossing of the country's mountainous frontier from Bulgaria through Macedonia and Thrace. List's 12th Army, headed by XL Panzer Corps, knifed through Skopje in Yugoslavia in a fevered race for the Monastir Gap, strategically set at the juncture of the Albanian, Yugoslav and Greek borders. Orchestrators of the attack were Stukas of VIII Fliegerkorps but they had to reckon with a heavy anti-aircraft barrage from the stoutly defended Metaxas Line, straddling Macedonia. On the left of XL Panzer's advance, had come XVIII (Mountain) and XXX Corps which, along with Bulgarian forces, had captured Salonika within three days. Thrace and Eastern Macedonia were cut off from the rest of Greece. The cause of the region was hopeless; the next day, all Greeks there surrendered.

The collapse of the Yugoslavian resistance had made it inevitable that the Germans would be able to outflank the Aliakmon Line in the north-west, where General Maitland Wilson's British and Commonwealth W Force was fighting gallantly with their Greek allies. A withdrawal first to the area of Mount Olympus and then to the historic battlefield of Thermopylae, though delaying the Germans and inflicting heavy casualties, could do no more than that and the final Greek collapse followed swiftly, the bulk of the W Force being evacuated to Crete and Egypt. That only 8,000 men had to be abandoned in such a situation speaks volumes for the conduct of Wilson's withdrawal and the heroism of the Royal Navy. This salutary defeat of the British, when added to the triumph of the elimination of Greek resistance, must have given

Hitler no small satisfaction. His control over the Balkans was now absolute.

As for the Bulgarian Army, it had taken no part in the fighting. In fact, the armed forces had been poorly and inadequately equipped; the Royal Bulgarian Air Force, with its hopelessly outdated Italian, Czech and Polish aircraft, would have proved a severe embarrassment if they had been put to the test. The end of the Greek campaign was signalled by the rumble of German trucks entering Athens. On 27 April, 1941, the swastika was hoisted on the Acropolis.

Meanwhile, the Bulgarians were not slow in proclaiming the 'reunion of the liberated Aegean provinces'; a purely Bulgarian administration was set up. In reality, the seven divisions the country possessed were assigned to what amounted to police duties: defending vital lines of communication between southern Yugoslavia and Greece. In addition, the hospitals in Bulgaria served as reception areas for the Greek wounded and private houses were commandeered for the same purpose.

The Germans retained direct control of Salonica and a large part of Western Macedonia, of some areas and islands near Athens, and the port area of Piraeus. For the two-and-a-half years remaining to his regime, Mussolini had the rest of Greece under his control, with the annexation of the Ionian islands and part of north-west Greece given to the Albanians.

Such territory as was assigned to the Italians came at Hitler's behest, with the Duce being given little say in the matter. Despite everything, Hitler still retained some loyalty to his senior Axis partner, stating smoothly that the German intervention in Yugoslavia and Greece was a 'precautionary measure against the British attempt to enrich themselves in the Balkans.' In reality, the credibility of Mussolini, dented by the early fiasco in Greece, was in tatters.

As for Bulgaria, it incurred the contempt and hatred of the Greeks. For their part, the Bulgarians countered with consummate viciousness. Greek inhabitants were driven from eastern Macedonia and western Thrace and replaced by Bulgarian settlers. The result was eventually to force westward over 100,000 refugees from Greek soil. Bulgar schools were established throughout the region; attendance was compulsory for Greek children.

By December, 1941, British newspapers, reporting from the safety of Istanbul in neutral Turkey, referred to the recruitment of Greek and Yugoslav subjects for work in military labour camps in the areas that Hitler had awarded to Bulgaria. The Bulgarian fiscal system was also foisted on Macedonia.

In addition, details emerged of Bulgarian and German outrages in both Thrace, with its Jewish communities of sephardic origin, and in

Macedonia. A figure was given of 3,500 Greeks slaughtered in the occupied areas, particularly in villages where entire populations of women and children under sixteen were reported to have been executed.

Prime sufferers among the Slavic population of Vardar Macedonia (the area around Skopje) were the Serbian clergy, many of whom were taken from their villages and executed. For the more fortunate, the mildest fate was humiliation; they were ousted from office and replaced by Bulgarians.

On the morning of 12 September, revolt coursed like a running fuse around Greek Macedonia. The Bulgarian police were the object of particular hatred and a crowd stormed the city hall at Drama where they murdered four policemen. In other towns and villages, there were scenes of even more prodigious slaughter. The outcome was inevitable. By the month's end, Bulgarian troops had moved into the centres of revolt, seizing all men between the ages of eighteen and forty-five. Execution squads were running riot. Comfortably ensconced in *Sonderzug Amerika*, his special train, Hitler had watched the progress of the campaign in the Balkans from the little southern Austrian village of Monichkirchen, receiving there Admiral Horthy, who went out of his way to proclaim his allegiance, declaring: 'If Russia's inexhaustible riches are once in German hands, you can hold out for all eternity.'

The vast reaches of Russia had indeed become Hitler's main preoccupation. The plan was for the invasion, Operation BARBAROSSA, to be launched on 22 June, 1941. By then, at the inevitable ceremony at the Doge's Palace in Vienna, Croatia became yet another adherent to the Axis Pact. The protocol was signed by Ante Pavelic in the presence, among others, of Ribbentrop and Count Ciano. The Italian Foreign Minister declared that Italy, Germany and Japan were already organizing an enduring peace which would follow the overthrow of England.

But for now all sights were on Russia. Of the Nazi's chieftains, Heinrich Himmler was the most transported. His greatest ambition was within his grasp – the chance, closely nurtured since the outbreak of war, to expand, beyond any previous imaginings, the boundaries of his own closely nurtured, jealously guarded empire. Those who had thrown in their luck with the Axis were to prove willing servants.

– 8 –

HITLER'S FATAL MISTAKE : OPERATION BARBAROSSA

The telephone rang in the private apartments of the Pelesh Palace in Bucharest at 1.30 am on Sunday, 22 June, 1941. Conscious that all lines were tapped and conversations recorded, the caller to King Michael of Romania was terse: 'The Germans have been at war with the Soviet Union since midnight.' Then the line went dead. That message had only one meaning for the King. His country too was committed to that war.

Hitherto, declaration of war had been the prerogative of the Crown but Ion Antonescu had chosen to ignore that convention. Efforts to find out more proved fruitless. The King and Helen, the Queen Mother, quit Bucharest and headed for the mountains, halting on a lonely road to tune the car radio to the BBC frequency in London.

From the early spring, when Antonescu had begun meetings both with Hitler and with German officers in Bucharest, Romanian forces had been committed to the first phase of BARBAROSSA, predominantly for the purpose of liberating Bessarabia and Northern Bukovina. Hitler, however, wanted no risk of the Soviet Union being forewarned and Antonescu had been asked to delay his full contribution until after the launch date.

Five days later, Hungary declared war on the Soviet Union. Hitler had also made an agreement with Finland to place troops in the North.

The overall purpose of Directive No 21 for BARBAROSSA declared:

The bulk of the Russian Army stationed in Western Russia will be destroyed by daring operations led by deeply penetrating armoured spearheads. Russian forces still capable of giving battle will be prevented from withdrawing into the depths of Russia.

The enemy will then be energetically pursued and a line will be reached from which the Russian Air Force can no longer attack German territory. The final objective of the operation is to erect a barrier against Asiatic Russia on the general line Volga-Archangel. The last surviving industrial area of Russia in the Urals can then, if necessary, be eliminated by the Air Force.

At this stage, the Germans had preserved a stance of arrogant optimism over the Russian campaign. The tone had been set by Hitler himself. The Führer had lectured his generals on the Soviet military machine, which he had seen as a creaking inefficient structure bled dry by the Stalin purges of the 1930s as well as being riddled with insecurity and constipated with ideology. It was, Hitler declared, utterly incapable of fighting effectively: 'You have only to kick in the door and the whole rotten structure will come crashing down.'

Initially, this had been hard to dispute. In the early hours of 22 June, to the sole accompaniment of croaking frogs along the River Bug, German soldiers had wrapped rifles, gas masks and bayonets in blankets to deaden the sound. The hands of synchronized watches reached 3.15 am and it was as if the world had exploded. Russian frontier guards stared in horror at a dawn sky suddenly fractured with the brilliance of 6,000 flashes from the German guns. Punch drunk with sleep and fumbling for their tunic buttons, the guards stumbled from their barracks, gasping and choking through the acrid smoke. To the sound and sight of the guns had been added the squeal and the clatter and the thud of tanks. As others sought feverishly to detonate demolition charges, assault parties dashed across bridges while elsewhere Heinkel 111 bombers bombed Soviet airfields and dropped mines in the Black Sea and Baltic.

Three Army Groups had been tasked to deliver the gargantuan thrusts. The Baltic and, above all, Leningrad, would be secured by Army Group North while the drive on Moscow would be the responsibility of Army Group Centre. Generalfeldmarschall Rundstedt, commander of Army Group South, intent on thrusting deep into the Ukraine, was the ultimate authority for the Romanian forces involved and ultimately for the Hungarian ones also. Rundstedt's force had a total of forty-one German divisions, five were Panzer and three motorized. The equivalent of fourteen Romanian divisions were under his control.

The satellite forces immediately created problems for Rundstedt who, as well as commanding an army group, had been obliged to call on additional skills as a diplomat. With memories of the Vienna Awards still smarting, neither Romania nor Hungary, who incidentally shared a meagre armoury of obsolete French weapons, poorly trained commanders and peasant conscripts, were prepared to be docile comrades in arms. They had to be kept apart.

The fact that Hitler deeply distrusted the Hungarians scarcely helped either. Rundstedt also had an Italian corps and a Slovakian mountain division wished upon him. As for the Slovakians, some 57,000 had been drafted early in 1941 and total Slovak combatants amounted to just over 90,000 – only 60 per cent of the army's size at the time of the Polish offensive.

Neither the civilian population of Slovakia nor the Army were able to work up much enthusiasm about the attack on the Soviet Union. An SD report, issued from Gestapo headquarters at Prinz Albrecht Strasse in Berlin on 17 July, 1941, noted sourly: 'Wide circles are of the opinion that the fight against Bolshevism by Slovaks against their own brethren has to be condemned.' Things were seen to be little better in the Army where there was widespread feeling that the Soviet Union was the home of Russians, Ukrainians and White Russians with whom they had no quarrel.

Hitler knew full well that if he was to get the full support from Romania that he was counting on, account would have to be taken of Antonescu's stubborn nationalist pride. With characteristic cunning, he appointed him to the command of Army Group Antonescu, a force consisting of the fourteen divisions of the 3rd and 4th Romanian Armies and Generaloberst Ritter von Schobert's 11th German Army of seven divisions, some of which were armoured and some motorized. The Army Group would remain in being for as long as the coming campaign in Northern Bukovina and Bessarabia lasted.

Swollen with pride and nationalistic fervour, Antonescu refused resolutely to place his Romanians under overall German command, insisting that rather they would operate under Rundstedt's strategic direction.

General von Schobert's mission was to bolster the Romanian advance to the rivers Prut and Dniester and push ahead into Bessarabia and the Ukraine. The liberation of Northern Bukovina was to be entrusted to the Romanian Army. That an attack was going to be made on Soviet territory from Romania gave new life to the long-standing spectre in Hitler's mind of a savage Russian riposte against the vital Ploiesti oilfields and he now ordered the switch of Schobert's Panzer divisions from 11th Army to reinforce 1st Panzer Army in southern Poland.

At 0100 hours on 22 June, 1941, Army Group South reported their readiness for operations by passing the codeword WOTAN to OKW. Two hours later, the entire German invasion force swept forward on a front of 500 miles, from the Baltic to the Hungarian border – Operation BARBAROSSA was launched.

Rundstedt's opponents were the four armies of the Kiev Special Military District, commanded by a veteran of the Russo-Finnish War, Lieutenant General Mikail Kirponos. Generaloberst Ewald von Kleist's Panzergruppe was to spearhead the advance towards Kiev and soon found that they had a tougher fight on their hands than they had bargained for. The stubborn resistance they encountered as they advanced towards the Dnieper imposed a delay on Rundstedt's plans and it was not until 2 July that 11th Army was able to lead the way over the Prut for Army Group Antonescu. With fine bombast, Antonescu proclaimed on the national radio 'Romania has gone into action by the side of her German ally. I, the Conductator, now give the Army the order *"Treceti Prutu!"* (Cross the Prut!).'

Despite the loss of his Panzer divisions, Schobert was across the Prut on that same day and followed this by a rapid thrust towards Mogilev on the Dniester, having brushed aside all attempts by three mechanized corps to stop him. By 8 July, he had a bridgehead over that river. Meanwhile, the 3rd Romanian Army had found that the province of Northern Bukovina was only lightly defended and its liberation was completed by the 9th.

Further south, however, the Romanian 4th Army had to contend first with flooding on the Prut and then with Russian counter-attacks. Toughest of these was at Cornesti Massif, directly in line with the Prut. German LIV Corps, spearheaded by the 1st Panzer Division, sped from the north, unhinging the Russian defences, at the cost of four destroyed and five damaged tanks. Army Group Antonescu was reckoned to have achieved its aims and was dissolved.

For the 4th Army, which had strained at the leash for the major assault on the Soviet Union, the cost had been daunting. The total of wounded, dead and missing was put at more than 21,000. And that was only the beginning. Nevertheless, army morale remained high; Antonescu made no attempt to lessen his allegiance to Hitler, his vanity duly flattered with the award of the *Ritterkreuz*. On 3 August, 4th Army began crossing the Dniester. The mission, to be accomplished while 11th Army pressed on to the Crimea, was to cut off the key naval base of Odessa, from the main retreating Soviet front.

The Russians, who had been encircled at Uman and Kiev, threw in everything they had in Odessa's defence. Throughout the siege, the city, which fell after two-and-a-half months of bitter fighting, was able to maintain communications with both the Crimea and the Caucasus; the Black Sea Navy and marines were in the forefront of defence. Furthermore, the Russians moved a substantial amount of military hardware from Odessa to Sebastopol and the Caucasus, although much of the equipment had ultimately to be abandoned.

Romanian forces were not long alone in Odessa; Himmler's SS had seen to that. Special mobile formations charged with carrying out liquidations in Eastern countries were a component of Amt (Office) IV of the RSHA under Reinhard Heydrich. These were the *Einsatzgruppen* (SS Special Action groups or extermination squads) which, through the individual detachment, designated *Einsatzkommando*, operated throughout the Eastern Theatre with SD and Gestapo operatives as components.

For their work in the Soviet Union, four *Einsatzgruppen*, each with a strength of between 1,000 and 1,200 were created. Group D worked within the Ukraine, and was under the command of Oberführer Dr Otto Ohlendorff with headquarters at Nikolayev, near Odessa.

On 12 November, 1945, Lieutenant Colonel Traian Borcescu testified before the post-war People's Court in Bucharest that *Einsatzkommando II B* from *Einsatzgruppen D* contained an entire operational company from Romanian intelligence. This service had been established by Antonescu shortly before the outbreak of war with the purpose of protecting the rear of the Romanian Army against espionage, sabotage and terror. The speciality of the *Einsatzkommando IIB* was to press victims into warehouses or huts which had been drilled with holes into which machine-gun muzzles were inserted. The warehouses were then set on fire to ensure that there was no escape for those who had survived the fire power. For work in the Soviet Union, there were four *Einsatzgruppen*. Their function was referred to in SD directives in characteristically euphemistic language. The *Einsatzgruppen* would ensure 'the security of political life' and would conduct all 'enterprises necessary to the national economy and so, also, to the war economy'. In fact, 'security of political life' involved mass murder.

Assessments of the Romanians as battlefield fighters varied. The contemporary Russian born historian Alexander Werth revealed: 'The Russians were very surprised by the toughness of the Romanian troops, since Romania's military record, particularly in the First World War, had not been exactly glorious.' Rundstedt, though, considered that they had made heavy weather of Odessa. The average Romanian infantry division had been revealed as having little offensive potential; training and leadership had been inadequate. According to Soviet figures, overall losses at Odessa, the majority of which were Romanian, stood at 110,000, of which more than 4,500 were officers.

Above all, there had been a harsh role for the aircraft of *Fortele Aeriene Regaleale Romaniei* (the Royal Romanian Air Force, FARR). The cost at Odessa was high, inevitably, since FARR was an outdated, mongrel affair made up of Italian, French, British and Polish aircraft purchased before the war. Spares came mostly from Germany and were scarcely enough to cope with a high wastage rate. The bomber force had remained at eight squadrons, but the numbers of observation, fighter and reconnaissance squadrons had been severely reduced in combat.

The Luftwaffe had pushed on into the Soviet Union, so the bulk of the air sorties fell to the FARR who were at the mercy of heavy Soviet anti-aircraft defences. At the siege of Odessa, women pilots flew with the *Escadrilla Aviatie Sanitare*, a casualty evacuation squadron whose aircraft sported the internationally recognized Red Cross. Although popularly known as the Escadrilla Alb (White Squadron), at the outbreak of BARBAROSSA, the women's white aircraft were over-painted with camouflage colours; few had confidence in Soviet respect for the Geneva Convention, although the Red Cross was retained.

Three pilots, Nadia Russo, Mariana Dragescu and Virginia Thomas, later to receive official Red Cross medals, scooped up wounded from the forward airstrips, flying at low altitudes to avoid enemy fighters. By the time the siege of Odessa was over, some 700 seriously wounded had been evacuated. The Squadron worked round the clock and there were no rest periods. The women slept on stretchers aboard the aircraft.

Throughout, Romania's 4th Army was pushed to its limits and beyond. There had been no armoured assistance from Germany in support of the offensive in Odessa. The achievement there was considered a cause for celebration – triumphs were marked in part by the creation of 'Transnistra', an area which was incorporated into Greater Romania and comprised territory between the Dniester and the Bug in the southernmost corner of the Ukraine.

The main celebration, however, was reserved for a grandiose victory parade on 8 November in Bucharest when those who had fought at Odessa paraded through the Arc de Triomphe, which had been restored by King Carol in commemoration of the outcome of the First World War.

Generalfeldmarschall Keitel, who attended as Hitler's representative and as head of OKW, showed due deference to Antonescu, a courtesy which did not prevent him from commenting later on the poor standard of the troops' drill. King Michael, who presented decorations to officers and men, had remained in blind ignorance of the progress of the war until he received a wire from Hitler congratulating him on the capture of Odessa.

Relations between King and dictator remained arctic. Michael had already witnessed something of the harsh realities of war. From divisional headquarters, on a hill overlooking Bessarabia, he had watched an attack by Romanian troops and the riposte of Russian shells cutting down men whose columns had continued to advance. He had seen too Antonescu's harsh treatment of his men. The King noted at Cernauti, in

Bukovina, the absence of even the simplest medical facilities for the wounded.

Not everyone shared Antonescu's elation. There were politicians who argued that Romania had done enough, that there was no reason for troops to advance beyond the Dniester. Their voices had been drowned by belligerent cries at the victory parade of '*Vrem Ardealul!*' (We want Transylvania!) and there was general dismay when, a month later, Britain declared war on Romania. On 12 December, prompted by Hitler and Mussolini, Antonescu, declared war on the United States. There was now no going back.

If Antonescu was unashamedly elated over the prospect of war, Miklos Horthy and Hungary had mixed feelings, not least because the country's armed forces were woefully ill-equipped. A basic distrust of Hungary had led Hitler to be cautious about his intentions, although hints had been dropped for some time in what the Führer considered to be the safest quarters. According to a Hungarian witness at the Nuremberg trials, Colonel Istvön Ujszöszy, a letter in November, 1940, from General Franz Halder to General Henrik Werth, the Hungarian Chief of the General Staff, had informed Werth that Hungary would have to participate in a preventative war 'if only in her own interests.' The phrasing was significant when the letter came to outlining objectives: 'possibly against Yugoslavia but definitely against the Soviet Union.' The tempting prospect of further territory was also dangled before the Hungarians: they might well find themselves in possession of land at the foot of the Carpathian mountains, up to the Dniester.

At any event, the official reasons for the final decision came four days after the German declaration of war against Russia. Military aircraft, carrying Soviet markings, appeared over the north-eastern city of Kassa, causing casualties and damage. Casualties were given as twenty dead and forty-one wounded, with direct hits on a number of buildings, including military ones.

A communiqué from the Hungarian General Staff read:

In retaliation for the Russian air raids on Hungary, strong units of the Hungarian air arm this morning carried out successful raids on Soviet military objectives. Fires were caused and considerable damage was done. At several points along the front, Soviet batteries began an artillery duel and their fire was returned.

Then, to dispel all doubts, Bardossy, the Prime Minister, declared a state of war between Hungary and the Soviet Union.

The truth about these raids has never been established but there was no shortage of theories and general perplexity as to why, Russia, at that time in the throes of withstanding German invasion, should gratuitously bomb Hungary. There was even a suggestion that the raid was either an error by Russians bombing off target from the eastern front or the work of disguised German aircraft seeking to provide Hungary with a pretext for declaring war. It made no difference; by now, the country had scented blood.

Resources were few. The regular army was made up of nine army corps which comprised twenty-seven brigades or light divisions with a total infantry strength of 216,000, to which could be added two cavalry brigades and two motorized brigades.

The figures, however, told only half the story since fighting men had to rely on sub-standard equipment. Rifles frequently jammed and there was a shortage of anti-tank guns. As for the tanks themselves, these consisted at first of Ansaldo light armoured vehicles with fixed turrets. Home-grown Toldi and Turón tanks could not be produced fast enough and, for the start of BARBAROSSA, only 190 were in service.

At first sight it was remarkable that Hungary's so called Mobile Corps, under the ethnic German General Ferenc Szombathelyi and in reality only partly mobilized, did so well in its role of accompanying General Karl Heinrich von Stülpnagel's German 17th Army and later First Armoured Group, of Army Group South, on its advance to the Dniester and the Donets rivers. Casualties overall were put at a modest 977, sustained under the fire of a Red Army in retreat.

The fact that their forces had carried their tasks both with credit and light casualties seemed sufficient reason to many Hungarians for the Mobile Corps to be withdrawn for a period of rest and recovery, sufficient resources being left in place to resist partisans. For once, the suggestion caught Hitler in a benevolent mood. He concurred.

There was still a whiff of euphoria from those early victories; the winter, after all, seemed far off. Besides, it could scarcely be denied that the triumphs had been considerable. By the end of June, two tank forces – Panzer Groups 2 and 3 of Bock's Army Group Centre – had cut through the grass and wheat landscapes of Belorussia towards Minsk, east of the German-Soviet border through occupied Poland. Three Russian armies, the Third, Fourth and Tenth had been ripped apart as if by giant claws.

In charge of Panzer Group 2, was General Heinz Guderian, already a living legend within the German Army – reckoned, not without good reason, to be the architect of the concept of fast moving Panzer forces on *Blitzkrieg*. His men were less reverential: they dubbed him '*Der Schnelle Heinz*' (Hurrying Heinz) or 'Hard arse Guderian.'

Minsk fell on 9 July, yielding some 324,000 prisoners. Ahead lay the ancient fortress of Smolensk, which was quickly to succumb to the German *Blitzkrieg*. Such victories as these were responsible for Halder writing in his diary: 'It is probably no exaggeration when I contend that the campaign in Russia had been won in fourteen days.'

Smolensk was regarded as the key to victory and not just by the senior commanders. German troops, borne on a high tide of optimism, erected hand-painted signs. They read 'To Moscow.'

- 9 -

THE THRUSTS FOR LENINGRAD AND MOSCOW

From the start of BARBAROSSA, Adolf Hitler, cocooned in his *Führerhauptquartier* set deep in the sweating pine forests of Rastenburg in East Prussia, had been mesmerized by both the rich economic resources of the Ukraine and the Romanian oilfields which would be at threat unless the Russian air arm was deprived of its bases in the Crimea.

The Führer's preoccupations were to shatter the schemes of Heinz Guderian who had envisaged a quick burst through the Smolensk line, followed by a ruthless, knockout blow at Moscow itself: quintessential 'Hurrying Heinz.' Guderian had outlined his reasons to Hitler in terms later outlined in his memoirs: 'Moscow was the great Russian road, rail and communications centre: it was the political solar plexus; it was an important industrial area; and its capture would not only have an enormous psychological effect on the Russian people but on the whole of the rest of the world as well.' Besides, his troops had become conditioned for nothing less.

Hitler had not been willing to change his mind. It was true that Smolensk had fallen but the Russians had re-grouped in strength some 25 miles to the east and that position had to be annihilated. There was also a need to smash Kiev, the capital of the Ukraine. That achieved, there would be time enough then to think of Moscow.

Orders were issued to Panzergruppe Hoth and Panzergruppe Guderian to diverge, with Hoth wheeling northwards, serving as a pincer for the drive on Leningrad by Generalfeldmarschall Ritter von Leeb's Army Group North, while Guderian would link up with Rundstedt's

Army Group South, only to revert to the Central Front with the fall of Kiev.

*　　*　　*

Why Leningrad? To Russians, Leningrad, was the former St Petersburg where Czar Peter the Great had first sunk massive piles into the morass of the Neva estuary, at the cost of tens of thousands of lives, to build first the fortress of Peter and Paul, then the Kronstadt naval base on one of the hundreds of islands of the Neva delta, and finally palaces, boulevards and grandiose squares. The result had been a city of slender bridges, lowering skies and the endless cold and snow of winter. Here Mussorgsky had written dark, tempestuous musical whirlpools, Pavlova had danced and the Imperial Ballet had spawned Diaghilev, Fokine and Nijinsky.

To Hitler, Leningrad was the hated cradle of Bolshevism to be 'wiped off the face of the earth. . . . The further existence of this large city is of no interest once Soviet Russia is overthrown.' Capitulation was 'not to be accepted, even if offered.' Leeb started with a race through the Baltic states, then crossed four major rivers, tearing open a gap between Lakes Peipus, Pskov and Ilmen. It appeared effortless. Army Group North, after all, had the patent advantage of 16th and 18th Armies and General Erich Hoepner's Panzer Group 4.

The two Russian armies, commanded by General Fyodor Kuznetsov, were woefully understrength. Far from being puny, though, was Soviet armour – 43-tonne KV-1 and 52-tonne KV-2 tanks with their three inch armoured plating. German shells fired against them as were puny as peas.

The only way to tackle the clumsy leviathans was by explosive charges and the demolition of the tank tracks. This was achieved but it meant delay for Generalleutnant George-Hans Reinhardt's XLI Panzer Corps, fretting to drive on to the broad Dvina river, reached early in July. By the middle of the month Reinhardt had reached the Luga river, the last major obstacle before Leningrad.

In his bid to unlock the northern front, Hitler had needed help. He remembered the Finns. Their territorial losses after the war with Russia in November, 1939, had been harsh and fears of a wholesale Soviet takeover widespread. Forever cynical, Hitler recognised that the return of territory to Finland would, with victory, cost him nothing.

Generaloberst Nicolaus von Falkenhorst, had two Finnish divisions in the far north as well as responsibility for troops in Norway. Their adversaries were the Soviet 14th and 17th Armies. In the south, the Finnish Karelian Army, under General Erik Heinrichs, would, with the addition of a German division, drive south from the Finnish border on both sides of Lake Ladoga.

Meanwhile, predictably, the acolytes of Heinrich Himmler were hard at work. Most notable of these was former gymnast instructor SS Brigadeführer Gottlob Berger, a sawmiller's son who, in April, 1941, had created the Waffen-SS Recruiting Office, even though the title of 'Waffen-SS' had not then been official. Berger's power had burgeoned since. Diligent enquiries in pro-German Finnish circles, revealed that there were at least enough men in Finland available to form a Waffen-SS battalion. Subterfuge was necessary. Some 1,000 Finns found their way to the Reich, ostensibly as 'workers for the German war industry'.

Within OKW, there was uneasiness. If the Finns were to co-operate, tactful treatment would be necessary. 'Guidelines for the behaviour of troops in Finland' was prepared. The document proclaimed: 'The Finn is a member of a cultured people, feeling strong associations to the other Scandinavian peoples, proud of his achievements and with a distinct sense of national pride. The freedom and independence of his country are valued above all. His friendliness towards Germans is genuine. For this reason anything that could hurt his national pride has to be avoided and his military achievement in particular has to be acknowledged.' Indeed, the Finns were far from being as biddable as Himmler would have liked; the government made the stipulation that they were only to fight Russians. The standard Waffen-SS oath was not acceptable and the Finns made it clear that they wished to be under the command of their own officers.

Some 400 men who had fought in the Winter War were seconded to 5th SS Wiking Division, going in at the start of BARBAROSSA. Fiercely independent, they insisted on their own volunteer battalion name, *Finnisches Freiwilligen Bataillon der Waffen SS*. The battalion had its own banner in the form of the blue cross flag of Finland incorporating, among other motifs, the national emblem of a gold lion and swords and the commemorative cross of the 27 Jägerbataillon of the First World War.

The Germans needed the Finns to stiffen their formations, and the Finns knew it. An offer to the Finnish Commander-in-Chief, Field Marshal Carl Gustav von Mannerheim, of overall command of all German troops in Finland was turned down. Mannerheim was very much his own man and had no intention of tying his country directly to Hitler's ambitions beyond seeking recovery of the territory they had lost in the Winter War.

Mannerheim delayed his offensive for a week after the launch of BARBAROSSA. Then a Finnish division besieged Hango on the south coast, while two corps advanced, one north of Lake Onega and one south, in a bid to trap Soviet troops against the water's edge before the frozen lakes would provide an escape route. But the Finns had no intention of wasting their forces, of whose weaknesses they were well aware.

Of their disposable divisions only seven were at full strength. The greatest weakness was in armour; every model of tank was inferior to the Soviet T-34.

By then, Germany's Army Group North, amid heavy driving rain on 8 August, had burst from bridgeheads over the Luga, which was forming the outermost line of the defences of Leningrad. The city itself was protected from the rear by the vast waters of Lake Ladoga. The group secured Schlusselburg (later Petrokrepost) at the lake's southern tip; Finns and Germans were separated by a mere forty miles. All the territory that had been lost to Finland in the Winter War had been rolled up; Vyborg occupied on 29 August, Terijoki, on the old Soviet Finnish frontier on 31 August. A further push into the northern suburbs of Leningrad would have been possible. But Mannerheim called a halt to any further territorial ambitions.

Generalfeldmarschall Ritter von Leeb had called on some extra muscle. The Spanish dictator, General Francisco Franco, had felt under an obligation to Hitler who, from July, 1936, onwards, had supplied the forces of the Condor Legion to help secure Franco's victory against the Republicans in the Civil War.

The Spanish 250th Infantry Division, drawn principally from the Army and the Fascist party, *Falange Espanola*, had been formed and, due to the colour of the *Falange* shirts, became better known as the Blue Division. There was no shortage of volunteers besieging the Infantry Academy at Saragossa. In September, 1941, the Division was on the northern front where Leeb had begun his encirclement.

The first of the Spanish battalions became a component of XXXVIIIth Corps of the 18th Army of Army Group North, responsible for a front of 50 kilometres, from Lubkovo on the west bank of the river Volkov in the north, to Kurisko on the west shore of Lake Ilmen in the south. The Spanish headquarters were sited north-west of Novgorod, the ancient city to the north of the lake.

Former combatant Nationalists, under the command of the Civil War veteran and former corps commander General Augustin Munoz Grandes, swelled the ranks of the 2nd Battalion of the 269th Regiment. On the night of 12 October, a Soviet battalion inched across the Volkov, trusting that it would be unobserved under the cloak of darkness. An hour of firepower erupted from the Spaniards; after that the Russians withdrew, the blood of fifty of their dead staining the snow. Further skirmishes were punctuated by desperate Russian bids to block reinforcements reaching the 269th but the Spanish units on the eastern side held on. Soon came new orders: the Blue Division was to seize the villages of Otenski, Possad and Posselok, taking the heat off the holding German 18th Division. The Spanish swiftly learnt what manner of fighting men were these: the Russians were fanatics, seemingly equally careless of the appalling cold or whether they lived or died. They stormed the trenches and bunkers of Possad and Posselok, eventually torching Posselok which within hours was serving as a funeral pyre for the corpses of both sides.

Blue Division survivors, whipped by the Russians, were driven north without quarter. When they reached Possad they were treated to a rerun of Posselok: an inferno of shells and burning houses. There was no luxury of retreat. The Spaniards pitched into the waves of Soviet assault troops with their old Civil War battle-cry: *Arriba Espana!* But by now there was another enemy, as equally ruthless as any battlefield combatants. The icy fingers of winter were there to freeze the oil on bolts of weapons or render bread so rock hard that it had to be cleaved with an axe.

As for the casualties, by early December, the volunteers of the 269th Regiment had lost 120 dead, 440 wounded and 20 missing. Death was not always through straight combat; the Soviet troops were merciless to those they captured. There was the instance of the platoon under the command of Alfred (Ensign) Mosques manning a fortified position between the villages of Udarnik and Lubkovo. The Russian battalion penetrating Udarnik, seized Mosques and his men and stripped off their uniforms. Pick axes were then driven into chests and the corpses nailed to the ground with their owners' own bayonets.

Leningrad by now had fire in its belly. The formidable peasant bulk of Marshal Georgi Zhukov, the one-time Czarist conscript turned cavalry-man, who had given the Japanese a bloody nose along the Mongolian border in the Far East in 1939, had arrived in the city in mid-September. Stalin, who had previously dismissed Zhukov, his Chief-of-Staff, for daring to suggest the abandonment of Kiev to prevent encirclement, was now all forgiveness. Zhukov had been sent to stiffen the Leningrad Front defences entrusted to another wily survivor, Kliment Voroshilov, who not only had emerged intact from the notorious purges but also from his role in the initially disastrous earlier war with Finland.

Zhukov prepared the city for siege with the erection of a massive network of anti-tank ditches, barbed wire entaglements, pillboxes and earthworks. Factories, bridges and public buildings were mined, ready to blow up at the entry of the Germans. Some 300,000 members of the Young Communist League were mustered by the Leningrad Command and, where necessary, under threat from the NKVD.

Leningrad stood firm. Civilian casualties were certainly high and a number of fires had been started, but an exasperated Leeb reported to Hitler the frustration of the Panzer thrusts, stymied on the lines of trenches and concrete erected by the men and women of the city.

But by now the Führer's eyes were elsewhere. Given time, he declared, the city would 'fall like a leaf'. He was now persuaded that with Kiev all but reduced to a blackened shell and 665,000 prisoners claimed – one third of the total Red Army strength at the opening of BARBAROSSA – the assault on Moscow, to be designated Operation TAIFUN (Typhoon), could go ahead.

As for Leningrad, it was to hold out for close on 900 days in a state of siege; victim to disease and near starvation, a situation which was slightly eased as the waters of Lake Ladoga froze over and supplies could be carried across the ice from the east.

In the south, Hitler had pushed his increasingly fatigued troops ever further east and Rundstedt's men cursed at the driving autumn rains, which had become routine on their marches of over 20 miles a day. Schobert of 11th Army had been killed when his aircraft had landed in a minefield and his place had been taken by General (later General-feldmarschall) Erich von Manstein, who had commanded LVI Panzer Corps in the advance on Leningrad and whose objective now was the Crimea.

The link between the 11th and the 17th Army of General von Stülpnagel, also by now across the Dnieper, was provided by the Romanian Third Army which had also helped to clear the Uman pocket, south of Kiev, where the Russians had delayed their withdrawal at the cost of their 6th and 12th Armies. The Germans claimed to have taken 103,000 prisoners, including the two army commanders, seven corps headquarters, 300 tanks and 800 guns. The Romanians pressed on to Krivoi Rog, north-east of Odessa.

These figures, impressive though they were, were only made possible through the hideous demands made on the physical resources of the Germans and their allies. Men had been reduced to little more than stumbling zombies, robbed of sleep and even of any sense of time. If they had become divorced from reality, so in a different way had OKW; Franz Halder had expressed the optimistic view that the whole of the Russian south-west front was cracking. But this was far from being the experience of those who had to contend with the merciless Soviet resistance.

Manstein, meanwhile, had been watching his back. Two corps and six German infantry divisions were far from being sufficient for the job of occupying the Crimea decisively. Once he had broken into the peninsula, there had been a need for coastal protection. An approach was made to Antonescu for reinforcements.

It was not the first such request. In mid-August, the Conductator's troops had acted as Hitler's fire brigade by speeding to plug a dangerous gap that had yawned between the Bug and the Dnieper. The Third Romanian Army, north of Berislav on the Dnieper, fended off forays by the Soviet 18th Army, which was seeking to divert German reserves, thus frustrating the bid by 11th Army to cross the river.

Manstein was again proffering his begging bowl. Antonescu gave him his Mountain Corps for protection and it followed 11th Army on its final breakthrough to the interior of the Crimea on 28 October. By then the 11th had pushed the Russians into the fortress city of Sevastopol.

For all his dependence on the help of the Romanians, Manstein had been fully aware of their faults. In his memoirs, he wrote:

Although the Romanian soldier – who was usually of peasant origin – was modest in his wants and usually a capable, brave fighter, the possibilities of training him as an individual fighting man who could think for himself in action, let alone a non-commissioned officer, were to a great extent limited by the low standard of general education in Romania.

He added sarcastically that such outmoded practices as flogging were unlikely to improve the quality of the rank and file.

The Romanian leaders thought in terms of the First World War and their weapons and equipment were partly obsolete and inadequate. More fundamental, Manstein considered, was the cold fact that their heart was not in the conflict. There had been enthusiasm for the recovery of Bessarabia, little interest in the territory between the Dniester and the Bug known as 'Transnistra' and absolutely none at all for pushing even further into Russia with which, Manstein believed, the Romanian people felt some Slavic affinity.

Hitherto the situation maps at OKW had given their almost monotonous message of advance. But what they could not signify to Hitler and Halder was the deteriorating weather. Such sun as there was proved worse than useless; it was too weak to dry out roads made into glutinous slime under the autumn rains.

The securing of Rostov at the mouth of the Caucasus proved of dubious benefit; the Soviets counter-attacked and threw out the Germans in eight days. Blunted too was Generalfeldmarschall Walter von Reichenau's achievement in taking Kharkov on 24 October. Stalin ordered the city to be abandoned; there were but meagre pickings for the Germans, in terms of weapons and prisoners. As for the Donets basin, the Russians had stripped it of its industrial equipment, which was now stored beyond the Urals.

Any further advance was frustrated because the retreating Russians had blown the railway bridges across the Dnieper. This meant a severe reduction of motor transport and essential supplies for the troops, who were forced to forage. Rundstedt ordered Generalfeldmarschall Kleist's 1st Panzer Army, which was under pressure from Soviet forces and in imminent danger of being cut off at Rostov, to withdraw to the south of the river Mius, some 40 miles west.

To the Führer any talk of withdrawal, reasonable or otherwise, was a lighted fuse. Withdrawal was unnecessary, he declared. Once the frost arrived, the roads would harden and the advance could go ahead. Hitler's full fury was turned on Walther Brauchitsch, the Army's Commander-in-Chief, who had no stomach for argument and was easy prey to his Führer's tirades. Why, Hitler demanded, had Rundstedt's order not been countermanded? A new order was issued via the compliant Brauchitsch; Kleist was to remain east of the Mius. It drew the riposte from Rundstedt: 'Should confidence in my leadership no longer exist, I beg to request someone be substituted who enjoys the necessary confidence of the Supreme Command.' He got his wish and was relieved of his post.

On the assault on Moscow, Hitler had boasted on 6 September, 1941: 'Today begins the last – the great battle of this year. . . . At last we have created the prerequisites for the final, tremendous blow which, before the onset of winter, will lead to the enemy's destruction.'

However, the danger signs were there, literally, on the Führer's doorstep. On 7 October, the first snowflakes fell at Rastenburg. But Hitler was either blind or indifferent to the weather. He had obsessive confidence in the sapping of the morale of the Russian forces. While it was true that fifteen Russian armies – 800,000 men – were in the front line blocking any approach to the city, all the signs were that they were in a state of near exhaustion and severely short of armour. They could muster a mere 770 tanks and 364 aircraft.

But Hitler had reckoned without another steadfast ally for Mother Russia, the weather. It was not simply the snow that threatened the German advance. There were the severe night frosts which the ill-clothed men of the Wehrmacht could not withstand. Man-management of the fighting force now scarcely existed. Fortifications into which the Army might retire from the effects of the winter were sparse. Hitler required his armies to keep on the move, not to hold themselves back. All doubts were thrust aside.

There had been jubilation for the first ten days of the operation as the German Army had driven forward on the long road to Moscow. The Russians were driven back by Bock's Army Group Centre to Vyazma and Bryansk, 220 miles south-west of the city. Both were ultimately abandoned. They were also forced out of Dnepropetrovsk to the south. Edward Wagner, the Army's Quartermaster General, wrote: 'Tonight the Kremlin is packing its bags.' Eight Russian armies had been annihilated and around 650,000 men entered the prisoner-of-war cages.

One of the biggest prizes had already gone to Guderian's newly designated Second Panzer Army, which had doubled back from the Ukraine and taken Orel, 75 miles behind the Russian front line. The final German drive, aimed to encircle Moscow and cut it off from supplies, reached Klin in the northwest and Tula in the south with its armaments plants.

By then, Stalin had prised Zhukov out of Leningrad, which was experiencing the first pangs of starvation, to take command of a newly formed Western Front. As well as the determined people of Moscow, he had the supreme ally of that dreadful weather. By October, the bright sunshine had been superseded by flooded rivers, roads knee-deep in mud and fields churned into quagmire. Then came the cold. On 12 November, the temperature on the Moscow front plunged to minus 12 degrees Celsius.

In vain, the tank crews lit fires in pits under their vehicles in a bid to thaw out the engines. The goal had been tantalisingly near. Troops reached the tram terminus of a line running near the Kremlin, which was by no means the same as Red Square where there were fresh regiments of Siberian riflemen, who knew that, if they were going to be allowed to live, there was but a single order: 'Drive back the Fascist invaders!'

As in Leningrad – and with the same dire penalties for disobedience – there was the citizen army, battalions of workmen, hastily mustered and with the minimum of arms, stood among the tanks and guns of the Red Army. As if in deliberate mockery, there was some sunshine in the brief December days when all that most German troops were ever to see of their Army Group objective were the domes of the Kremlin.

The capital of the Soviet Union lay a mere 50 miles from the German front. But for ill-clothed troops, plagued by dysentery and frostbite, it had been 50 miles too far. On Friday, 5 December, when the temperature had plunged to minus 25 degrees to 30 degrees Celsius, Stalin's counter-offensive sent Army Group Centre hurtling into retreat.

Three days later, Hitler agreed to call off the offensive. Moscow remained in Russian hands. But the Führer made it abundantly clear that there could be no question of further withdrawal.

Those who did so question were bundled out of office. The wretched Feldmarschall Brauchitsch, the overall Commander-in-Chief, who had already suffered a severe heart attack and been constantly humiliated by Hitler, brushing him aside and issuing instructions direct to army commanders, was dismissed and declared to be 'a vain cowardly wretch and a nincompoop'. The commanders of Army Group South and North, Leeb and Bock also went (the latter was relieved of his command through ill health).

By then, Britain and the Commonwealth had declared war on the three subordinate partners involved in the war on Russia – Finland, Hungary and Romania.

On the Eastern Front, the hammer was all set to become the anvil. But the Wehrmacht was not the only arm of the Third Reich at work in the lands Hitler sought to conquer. Within these lands, Heinrich Himmler, the insatiable power seeker, had unquestioned control of the bureaucracy of terror. Regardless of the fortunes of the battlefield, he would continue to exercise it until the end.

– 10 –

HIMMLER'S EMPIRE

The elephantine structure of which Heinrich Himmler, former chicken farmer and herbalist had become the ultimate head, had gone through several metamorphoses in its creation.

By the end of September, 1939, it had become the *Reichssicherheitshauptamt* (RSHA: Reich Central Security Office). Under its umbrella was both the Gestapo (*Geheime Staats Polizei*, Secret State Police) and the *Sicherheitsdienst* (SD – The Security Service) – the latter being the jealously guarded territory of Reinhard Heydrich, Himmler's icy subordinate, whom nervous colleagues had long dubbed 'Germany's most dangerous man.'

The prissy, bespectacled Reichsführer, the arch-pedant who spent most of a twelve hour working day blinking through incriminating files and dossiers, was soon looking beyond the confines of Germany to those anxious to cling to the coat tails of the Reich. Such spare time as Himmler permitted himself was spent dipping into the pages of the superman philosopher Friedrich Nietzsche, with his glorification of brutalism, the breathless worship of 'the strong men, the masters – monsters filled with joy.'

In the black uniform of his SS, Himmler detected shadows of an earlier Germany of forests and hunters, of supermen who lived by the dagger, of the religiously fanatical 12th century Teutonic knights. Where in the first quarter of the 20th century would it be possible to recreate such men?

*   *   *

Adolf Hitler had emerged on 29 July, 1921, as leader of the still minuscule *Nationalsozialistische Deutsche Arbeiterpartei* (National Socialist German Workers' Party: Nazis). Acts of political violence, the threat of rival groups and the need to build on what meagre power he already possessed, had led Hitler to write:

> I told myself that I needed a bodyguard, even a restricted one, but made up of men who would be enlisted unconditionally, ready even to march against their own brothers, only twenty men to a city . . . rather than a dubious mass.

The beginnings of that bodyguard formed in April, 1925, the nucleus being the *Stabswache* or Headquarters Guard. It was shortly renamed the *Schutzstaffel* (Protection Guard), whose new recruit, number 168, was Heinrich Himmler, with his dream of becoming a special warrior in an elite force – and this from a man whose own military service had been as a mere officer cadet in the 11th Bavarian Infantry Regiment.

On 1 January, 1929, that dream began to burgeon when he was given command of the SS, still a body of only about 200 men. In the following year, he was elected to the Reichstag as the Nazi deputy for Weser-Ems and his meteoric rise to power had taken off. By 1933, the SS had reached a strength of no less than 52,000.

Hitler's agenda, of course, was wider and infinitely more sinister. In a speech on 16 March, 1935, to his assembled robots in the Reichstag, he announced that Germany would reintroduce military conscription, with the eventual aim of securing an army with a strength of thirty-six divisions. Moreover, a handful of SS men whom Himmler had jealously guarded for security and ceremonial use, would serve as the nucleus of a future SS division under the name of SS *Verfügungstruppe* (SS-VT, Order Troops).

Expansion was cautious; there were the susceptibilities of the established army, survivors of the old imperial order, to be considered. In stages, the SS-VT went on to incorporate the *Leibstandarte SS Adolf Hitler*, the Führer's elite personal bodyguard, along with members of the SS-*Totenkopfverbande* (SS-VT, Death's Head formations of concentration camp guard units). By 1936, the SS-VT was boasting two regiments, four within two years. Hitler still moved delicately; no SS formation was designated a division until after war had broken out.

In laying down the conditions for entry, Himmler was able to indulge his racial preoccupations to the full. The amassing of the beloved files delighted the Reichsführer: they bulged with minutiae indicating the possible racial traits of putative recruits. From the end of 1935, all SS men were required to produce a record of ancestry, for officers back to 1750, for other ranks from 1800.

No one knew when Himmler would pounce on a suspected transgressor. A trace of Jewish blood, however remote, entailed instant dismissal. In January, 1937, Himmler declared:

> I insist on a height of 1.70 metres. I personally select a hundred or two a year and insist on photographs which reveal if there are any Slav or Mongolian characteristics. I personally want to avoid such types as the members of the 'Soldiers Councils' of 1918–19, people who look somewhat comic in our German eyes and often give the impression of being foreigners . . .'

To those less patient with Himmler's hobby-horses, such as Sepp Dietrich, the former Bavarian baker's errand boy, who emerged as the iron-hard commander of the Leibstandarte, such limitations were a decidedly mixed blessing. Dietrich was known to have grumbled: 'Some forty good specimens at least are kept from joining the Leibstandarte every year due to doubts concerning racial ancestry.' Nonetheless, as far as training and preparation for war were concerned, and despite the sneers of the Wehrmacht, who did what they could to obstruct the new forces, the SS-VT (designated the *Waffen-SS* on 1 December, 1939) emerged as a formidable fighting machine.

Training exercises were often so realistic as to be indistinguishable from the real thing. With the use of live ammunition and artillery fire there were the inevitable casualties and even fatalities. The Army, to whom the SS troopers were officially subordinate, protested vigorously, only to be told by the sententious Himmler: 'Every drop of blood in peacetime saves streams of blood in battle.' By the close of 1937, the military academies were producing around 400 officers a year from original volunteers: men who had become hardened by aggressive training and made ready for action. To achieve this, Himmler depended on two men, united in total lack of interest in the racial ramblings of their Reichsführer.

The first of these was Felix Steiner, a former Reichswehr officer from East Prussia, now carrying the rank of SS-Sturmbannführer, who had witnessed at first hand the severe limitations of trench warfare in the First World War, where thousands of troops had literally been pinned down for wasteful mass slaughter. He declared that what was needed were mobile formations of elite troops of the highest class, a force which 'by blows of lightning rapidity would split the enemy in fragments and then destroy the dislocated remnants.'

Meanwhile, Himmler's personal ambitions for expansion were soaring way ahead of acquiring mere native Germans. For his armed SS, volunteers could – and would – be enlisted from Slovaks, Hungarians, Romanians, Bulgarians. They would be drawn from the ranks of the

Volksdeutsche, the German-speaking communities within those countries, and also foreign nationals.

Officers of the Leibstandarte were left in no doubt of Himmler's intentions when in September, 1940, he declared: 'We must attract all the Nordic blood in the world to us, depriving our enemies of it, so that never again will Nordic or German blood fight against us.' Racial trappings of the Reichsführer aside, there was an admirably practical reason why volunteers from outside Germany should be welcomed: they were free from what was regarded as Wehrmacht interference.

The task of bringing all this about had fallen to the second trusty, Gottlob Berger, whose Waffen-SS recruiting stations, in parallel to those of the Wehrmacht, mushroomed across the Reich.

From the beginning, Berger subjected Himmler to a blizzard of memoranda. On 7 September, 1940, he told the Reichsführer-SS that a pool of 600,000 reserves for the Waffen-SS could be found in southern Romania and Yugoslavia and that Hungary could supply 500,000 ethnic Germans. Berger declared: 'It can be assumed that once peace has been made, recruitment for the Waffen-SS in these countries will be possible. We can expect an annual yield of about 1,000 to 1,500 men under most stringent selection.' As it turned out, volunteers among Hitler's partners were not slow in coming forward.

In quest of *Volksdeutsche*, Himmler and Berger looked favourably on Romania whose Germanic links had always been taken seriously. As it turned out, the choice of Romania was particularly convenient. Berger worked through twenty-eight-year-old Andreas Schmidt, who was not only the political leader of the German community in Transylvania – many of Swabian origin – but also Berger's son-in-law. Nazi influence there stretched back to 1933 with the forming of the National Self-Help Movement of the Germans in Romania. Himmler, however, was cautious about the extent of German infiltration and the likely repercussions; Berger was told to avoid any possible diplomatic embarrassment.

On 27 November, 1940, the Reichsführer-SS wrote to Berger from Berlin:

> I am sure Andreas Schmidt believes that he has achieved a great victory by constituting a National Socialist Party in Romania and by getting the Romanian government to agree that the swastika flag be displayed. Of course this represents a success to a degree. Politically, however, it could be damaging; there is a danger that other Balkan states will become anxious about losing some of their independence. . . . This could be very dangerous with regard to Russia which is very suspicious of anything to do with Romania.

To lull any fears, Himmler went on to order that the swastika should be displayed as little as possible and that the National Socialist Party should be advertised as representing German ethnic groups.

Romanian and Hungarian service chiefs were particularly anxious that none of their men liable for military service should defect to a foreign army. In an earlier report to Himmler, dated 5 January, 1940, and labelled Top Secret, Berger explained that racial Germans who attempted to cross the frontiers were seized in both Hungary and Yugoslavia, sent back, and treated as deserters.

Berger was soon grumbling to Himmler about the 'duplicitous' conduct of the Romanian government in seeking to prevent 1,200 would-be recruits leaving the country on the grounds that they might be 'educated in the wrong spirit and might prove disobedient in the future.'

Any future worries of the Romanian government were scarcely Berger's concern; he needed some 3,000 men immediately. To get round the susceptibilities of the Romanians, he suggested to Himmler that 'agricultural and industrial workers' should be demanded by the Reich Foreign Ministry and that they should be transferred in that guise to Germany in mass transports. He reported: 'In Transylvania and Bessarabia 1,000 young men have already been enlisted and are immediately available as soon as the frontiers are in any way passable. They can also cross the frontier illegally if Hungary does not return them to Romania.' The Romanians gave in; the volunteers reached the Reich in this guise. The progress of what was at first clandestine recruitment was reported to Himmler by Berger in a string of reports.

Bolstered by Schmidt's successes, Berger became even more ambitious, dashing off a Top Secret memo to Himmler, entitled 'Population movement.' This suggested that the Balkans would provide the most fruitful area for recruitment. In Hungary and Yugoslavia there were estimated to be a total of a million-and-a-half ethnic Germans.

Not long after the fall of Yugoslavia, a modest recruiting initiative in Serbia yielded a clutch of ethnic German volunteers to be absorbed into SS Division Das Reich. On 16 April, Berger was reporting a similar success in Slovakia.

As the need for manpower steadily increased under the demands of war, particularly following the invasion of Russia, means of securing foreign recruits for the SS had to be widened. The methods used were by no means secured with universal approval.

In Croatia, SS Gruppenführer und General der Polizei Werner Lorenz, of VOMI, ordered SS Obersturmführer Hermann, the recruitment officer for the Waffen-SS, to draft all men from the *Arbeitsdienst* – compulsory labour camps – into the ranks of the Waffen-SS. An emissary of the Foreign Office grumbled to Berlin, who sent a sharp telegram to Lorenz:

'We have undertaken to form a Croat Labour Service as an instrument of education. If we now dissolve these units only after a few weeks by carrying out such recruitments, we not only hinder the continuation of practical work but also lose the trust of the Croatian side. . . .' The telegram went on to grumble that 556 men from the Arbeitsdienst had been examined and 327 chosen. In the end, Lorenz had to be content with seven leaders and 100 men poached from the Croat Labour Service.

But instances like these ultimately proved little more than pinpricks. When it came to gaining recruits, florid propaganda worked wonders. When it failed, there was no shortage of strong-arm squads to make good the deficiency. Berger was sharp and to the point: 'Those who do not volunteer will have their houses broken up.' As it turned out, there was no shortage of racial Germans willing to serve. Their devotion was not confined to being fighting men; on matters of racial persecution they proved equally willing to ape the Germans, particularly when it came to the Jews.

Alongside the encroachment of *Volksdeutsche* and nationals into the Waffen-SS, preparations for anti-Jewish measures of varying degrees of harshness went ahead in all the countries that were Hitler's allies.

In Bulgaria, King Boris refused to join in the invasion of Russia; nevertheless, with the appointment in February, 1940, of Bogdan Filov as premier, the country's stance had become progressively pro-German. Jews were forbidden to serve in the armed forces but were mustered for labour battalions in the Army. The repressive role of the SS lay in the future. Meantime, there were minor irritations with the introduction of a special tax on Jewish-held property. Jews had to obey a curfew and suffer the confiscation of telephones and radios.

In Romania, on King Carol's abdication in 1940, there followed closely the founding of a National Legionary State commanded jointly by Marshal Antonescu and Horia Sima, the head of the Iron Guard. For countless Jews it seemed to signify the inevitability of sustained persecution; there was a massive exodus from Romanian ports for Palestine, where the British refused to permit the entry of Jews from an enemy country.

Then, at the turn of the year, events highlighted Himmler's malign role in events in Romania. Eternally in conflict with Ribbentrop's foreign ministry and keen to consolidate his own power, the Reichsführer-SS turned to the SD to force the pace. The Iron Guard, keen to topple Antonescu, launched a short-lived bid for power. Ribbentrop, Himmler knew, had always been in favour of Antonescu as leader, whereas he and Reinhard Heydrich supported Horia Sima, not least because the Iron Guard was anti-Semitic. Antonescu had retained Hitler's support because the Führer was anxious for a stable routine on the eve of BARBAROSSA.

The Iron Guard's hold on power lasted from September, 1940, to January, 1941; Sima and his supporters were bundled into Germany and held as useful fallback hostages should Antonescu ever be considered dubious in his Axis loyalties. In retaliation, Antonescu successfully demanded the withdrawal of Hitler's SD – but it did not last long.

When it came to terrorizing the Jews, the Iron Guard had made the most of its brief tenure of power. Synagogues in Bucharest were torched, business premises and private apartments ripped apart. Butchered naked bodies littered the streets. Leaders of the Jewish community who survived, identified 630 of the dead and recorded 400 missing.

Under torture, Isidore Goldstein, the secretary of the Jewish community, surrendered the complete list of all Jewish leaders in Bucharest before being shot. Jews were rounded up, stuffed into military trucks seized from the Army, decanted on roadsides and then mown down. The German military attaché, collating casualty reports, wrote: 'In the Bucharest morgue, one can see hundreds of corpses, but they are mostly Jews.'

By the time of BARBAROSSA in June, 1941, German participation was evident in the first deportations of Jews, from the province of Bessarabia. They were driven from their towns and villages, crammed into trains and deported eastwards, frequently assaulted both by Romanian and German troops.

A particularly cruel fate was reserved for the inhabitants of Jassy, north-east of Romania's regional capital, which had been the centre for Jewish life and culture since the 16th century. Jassy was singled out for conspicuously vicious persecution: there were arbitrary arrests, extortion, confiscation of property and seizure of businesses, accompanied by a series of show trials of Jews alleged to be 'pro-Communist'.

By malign fate, Jassy became an assembly point for Romanian and German Army units destined for the Russian front. Tension was fanned between Jews and non-Jews. The Romanian Special Intelligence Service, functioning as a liaison office for all military units, charged the Jews with having sent signals to Soviet aircraft. Mass arrests followed dragnets by Romanian and German Army patrols.

Events during the worst of the pogroms, between 23 and 30 June, 1941, were recalled after the war by survivors interrogated by the Romanian public prosecutor. A war crimes trial in June, 1948, indicted some of those responsible. Joint German–Romanian responsibility emerged – the German Commandant at Jassy, Jerman von Stransky, was revealed as being one of those responsible for pillaging and acts of violence. Also involved were Germans serving in the Todt Organization, consisting of a pool of men and women providing labour in industrial and munitions factories throughout the Reich and its satellites.

Repression spread far beyond Romania. One month before the invasion of Russia, *The Times* of London, citing 'very reliable sources', carried a report on the extent of repression in Yugoslavia where racial tensions and hatreds were still kept on the boil. Croatia, Montenegro and Serbia had been divided into three states – the residue after the Axis powers and signatories had dismembered as much as they could. The victims were the hated Serbs: Hungarians and Bulgarians competed with one another and with the Germans in the extent of their persecution. Villages and towns were subjected to a dragnet of slaughter with the routine arrest of the local priests and politically active students; Gestapo agents drew up lists of known opponents of Yugoslavia's signature to the Tripartite Pact.

Serbian Macedonia was subjected to particular savagery by the Bulgarians. Filed from Istanbul on 19 May, 1941, a despatch from *The Times* revealed: 'The Patriarch Gavril, who had been arrested in Montenegro, was brought to Belgrade and, after the removal of his clerical robes, confined in his underclothes on the ground floor of a building where passers-by could see him.' As in Greece, wholesale 'Bulgarisation' was attempted in some cases. The Germans viewed this as a display of excessive zeal and took over the administration of some districts themselves.

The Hungarians also emerged as apt pupils of the Germans, particularly when it came to deportation and killings. By October, 1941, letters smuggled out of Budapest had reached the United States, describing how some 18,000 Jews, mostly refugees from Germany or Poland, or naturalized Hungarian citizens, had been deported from Hungary to eastern Galicia. The letters, many of them from Hungarian officers who had witnessed the deportations, focused particularly on the region of Kamenec-Podolsk, which had been invaded by German and Hungarian armies at the start of the war with Russia.

In a single incident, SS-Gruppenführer Franz Jackeln took on responsibility for some 23,000 Jews whom the Hungarians had deported and who had been wished on the Germans. The Jews were stripped of their clothes and then cut down by machine gun fire. The bodies were then tumbled into bomb craters.

Ante Pavelic and his Croatian Fascists had also lost no time in proving themselves adept pupils of the Nazis. Besides the predictable banning of political parties, trade unions and a free press, there was the ongoing persecution of Serbs and Jews. Within days, decree XXV-33Z became law, proscribing the use of Cyrillic (Serbian) letters, both in official and private correspondence. From there it was but a step to forcing Serbs to wear a blue armband with the P, the initial for Orthodox (Pravoslavac). Jews were required to wear the Star of David on their sleeves and even across their backs.

10. Operation BARBAROSSA. The fight against 'General Winter'. German horse-drawn transport snowed in at Stalingrad. *(Photo: Associated Press/Topham Picturepoint)*

11. Stalingrad. February, 1943. German prisoners on their way to captivity. *(Photo: Topham Picturepoint)*

12. The Victor of Stalingrad. Marshal Fyodor Tolbukhin *(Photo: Topham Picturepoint)*

13 & 14. Hitler's worst fears fulfilled. 178 B-24s of the 9th US Air Force attack Ploiesti on 1 August, 1943. *(Photo: Topham Picturepoint)*

15. Heinrich Himmler, Reichsführer-SS. *(Photo: Associated Press/Topham Picturepoint)*

Neither Serbs nor Jews were allowed on the pavements. There was also the proliferation of posters, proclaiming 'No Serbs, Jews, Nomads or dogs allowed.' One published decree was concerned with 'The protection of Aryan blood and the honour of the Croatian people.'

By as early as 1940, 280 miles of new second-class roads leading east and north-east had been built by German firms; the Slovaks had been expected to pick up the bills. A railway line from Oderburg in East Germany running south-east to Kosice in Slovakia, with access to Halmi in northern Romania, came under German control, as well as the main Hungarian railway lines leading from the Danube Valley to Romania.

There were those in Slovakia quite prepared to gear up for war. Lorenz had been proud of his work there. On the eve of BARBAROSSA, he told Himmler:

> Until November, 1940, the Hlinka Guard had a poor public image due to bad behaviour in public, frequent changes in leadership and higher ranks being filled exclusively with men who were close to President Tiso . . . Today, we can report that the HG is well organised, sound, National Socialist and pro-German in all respects.

Seventy leadership and teaching courses were being held with the strong involvement of leaders of the Waffen and General SS.

By October of the following year, Himmler was reporting to Berger that over the teacups he had met Tiso and Alexander Mach, head of the Hlinka Guard. Here the chance to net even greater power proved irresistible to the Reichsführer SS. He told Berger:

> I have agreed that we will take over the administration of the Hlinka Guard. I suggested myself . . . that particularly good young Slovaks from the Hlinka Guards could volunteer to join the Waffen-SS. Mach agreed enthusiastically.

Even with his new triumph, Himmler was unable to jettison his racial preoccupations. Berger was told sternly:

> Not very many must be accepted. Those who are taken in must have a minimum height of 1.74 metres and follow the most stringent Germanic standards racially. It must never be possible to distinguish a Slovakian Waffen-SS volunteer in uniform from a German or Germanic volunteer.

Furthermore, each year some thirty of the volunteers would be required to visit the Junker training school to be groomed as leaders.

The new responsibilities of the Hlinka Guard inevitably involved its adherents in repressive measures against Jews. The task was entrusted to SS-Hauptsturmführer Dieter Wisliceny of Section IV B 4 of the RHSA, whose territory also included Hungary and Greece.

It was small wonder that Himmler, sitting on the top of his pyramid of files, was in the seventh heaven, his precious Waffen-SS legions truly an unassailable elite. The primeval forests, steppes, tundras and wide rivers of Soviet Russia were to prove otherwise. But that, at the time of the expansion of his empire into Slovakia, had been four years away.

– II –

STALINGRAD

Stalingrad, focus of Hitler's fresh obsession, sprawled along the western banks of the Volga, consisting of vast armament factories, industrial sites of glum concrete, wooden buildings, broad boulevards and homes for half a million. It was earmarked for destruction as part of the Führer's summer campaign for 1942.

Operation BLAU, released as Führer Directive No 41 on 5 April, paid tribute by way of preamble to the soldiers on the Eastern Front and then proclaimed: 'We must seize the initiative again and through the superiority of German leadership and the German soldier force our will upon the enemy.'

On 8 May, at the start of BLAU, Manstein and his 11th Army punched their way through the Kersh peninsula. The city of Kharkov fell at the cost of some 70,000 Russian lives and the loss of 200,000 prisoners. Hitler reckoned he was now free to launch his next major offensives south and east towards Stalingrad and into the Caucasus, some 350 miles away from the city. The distance alone pointed to the monumental risks of such a two-point gamble. The Wehrmacht would cross the Volga in the area of Stalingrad, cutting Russia's main north-south line of communications. At the same time, the fruits of the rich oil-fields of the Caucasus, which were vital if Germany was to stay in the war, could be secured. All this must be achieved before the next terrible winter visitation.

Stalingrad itself was to be shelled and bombed under the direction of Army Group B, commanded by General Maximilian von Weichs, which was intent on preventing a build up of Russian forces. The plan was to take the city with two armies in three stages. General Friedrich Paulus's 6th Army would penetrate the north, followed by General Hermann Hoth's 4th Panzer Army pushing up from the south. The final task of the mass of Paulus's army was to sweep up any further Russian opposition and annihilate it on the Volga.

Hitler scheduled the start of his assault on Stalingrad for 23 August. The dawn of that day belonged to the men and tanks of 16th Panzer Division, spearhead of 6th Army, which was safely across the Don and on course for the city, an enticing 35 miles to the east. Junkers and Stukas stormed above the advancing troops.

For this adventure, Hitler had use for his jackal allies, who had become progressively more suspicious of each other and of their allegiance to the Vienna Accord. The creation and occupation of Transnistra by Romania had led to declarations of war, first by Britain then, in retaliation, by Romania itself on the United States, as a sign of solidarity with Germany and Japan, developments which many Romanians had viewed with alarm.

As for Antonescu, when he had been received by Hitler in February to discuss the Romanian contribution to the German summer campaign in Russia, he had been preoccupied with his country's hurt pride over Hungary's continuing occupation of Northern Transylvania. Hitler pressed that Romania and Hungary should sink their differences. He had wanted to see an increased contribution by Romanian forces for the war in Russia. Furthermore he had made it clear that the Vienna Awards were not negotiable; a figure of half a million men was agreed on.

As for Hungary's forces, their strength was pathetic. Figures available in 1941 had shown that the country could produce between 300 and 360 aircraft of questionable combat readiness. As for armour, by the time that the country entered the war, only 190 Italian-made light machines had been commissioned and most of those were out of date.

The air force had launched a dummy run against the Russian towns at the end of June, 1941, ahead of the launch of BARBAROSSA. A short foray across the Hungarian–Soviet border had ended in farce. Of the twenty aircraft involved – nineteen bombers and one fighter – none had reached their targets, two had been shot down and four either damaged on take-off or obliged to make forced landings.

Hitler had never made any secret of his distrust of the Hungarians. Prime Minister Miklos Kallay's remark that Hungary had nothing against the Russian people and was merely fighting Bolshevism seemed to confirm some of the Führer's worst fears. Furthermore, Romania and Hungary continued their squabble. According to a memorandum by Hitler's State Secretary, Ernst von Weiszäcker, Hitler's Chief-of-Staff General Franz Halder had revealed that complaints had been received from the Romanians about the weak military showing of Hungary, who had been impelled into the cauldron of Stalingrad by the spectre of losing Transylvania.

Antonescu returned to this particular grievance during his audience with Hitler. The commitment of Romanian forces must be conditional on the Hungarians playing their part. Already, 700,000 Romanians had participated in the campaign of the previous year and they had lost a quarter of them.

If Stalingrad was an object of ferocious hatred to Hitler, to Stalin it was an icon. From within the factories and shops and apartment buildings, a citizen army was to be recruited, fuelled by a defiant order: 'Ni shagu nazad!' (no retreat). Stalingrad, so went the order, was to be defended street by street, block by block. On 25 August, the Regional Party Committee heralded a state of siege 'of our beloved town, our homes and our families. Let us barricade every street; transform every district, every block, every home into an impregnable fortress.'

In a bid to sack and destroy, the largest possible German force was concentrated around the city, a process that was only made possible by denuding forces elsewhere. The Don was buttressed by the satellite forces. The most serious weakness lay with the under-equipped Romanians, whose divisions could only produce one anti-tank company, and that with outdated guns, and were short of ammunition generally.

The first day of the attack on Stalingrad had allowed the Germans to be front row spectators of what they believed was the immolation of the city. The operation amounted to the cold slaughter of 40,000 innocents; the elderly and women and children being cut down by the assault of the Stukas of VIII Air Corps. On 23 August, 1942, they were bombed both on the roads leading towards the Volga ferries and bridges and aboard the battered tugs, ferries and steamers, crowded by those seeking to escape east. At this point, Hitler could perhaps be forgiven for believing that Stalingrad, once bathed in blood, would fall like a ripe plum and that the Red Army would be pulled back to the eastern bank of the Volga.

16th Panzer Division had outrun the support of the other divisions and reached the city outskirts. From then on it was a new sort of war. Those who attended Hitler's staff conferences recalled how in the triumphant days of 1940 he used to spread his hands in great wide arcs above the maps to signify the lightning advances of his armies. But no longer. Progress was slow and painful, with no arrogant stride across the steppes. Panzers were bogged down by snipers, barbecued by Molotov cocktails.

General Paulus and the men of his desperately weary 6th Army continued to butt their way through the factory districts, with a dogged persistence that was partly due to Paulus being told that Stalingrad was the price of any further promotion. To Nazi journalists marshalled in the battle area, he was outwardly reassuring: 'Stalingrad will fall now, anytime.' In reality, though, he was far from happy. Both he and General Weichs were worried about the security of the flanks of Army Group B; 6th Army and 4th Panzer Army were both at the head of a long exposed salient, manned by the satellite forces. The situation in the south was particularly dangerous, with a flank completely uncovered except by 16 German Motorized Division far off in the Kalmuck Steppe.

A flanking position was taken up by Romania's 6th Corps near a group of lakes in the area of Tsata. Its lot was defeat by Red Army forces of no great strength and it was severely over-extended on an open steppe deprived of local provisions and shelter.

The northern flank of the salient from Stalingrad extended westwards to a bridgehead at Kremensk. The area to the west had the protection of the northern Don flank, entrusted to General Peter Dumitrescu of the 3rd Romanian Army, Colonel-General I Gariboldi's 8th Italian Army and General Gustav Jany's 2nd Hungarian Army. All were in advanced states of vulnerability: Germany was unable to supply them with the weapons and equipment they badly needed, particularly when it came to opposing Soviet tanks.

*   *   *

Any participation in BARBAROSSA had been opposed by Mussolini's generals. Not for the first time, the Duce's pride had been hurt when he had been informed through the German Ambassador of the invasion one hour-and-a-half after it had been launched. Nevertheless, a personal message had been sent from the Italian leader to the Führer: Italy considered herself at war with Russia as from three o'clock that morning. Furthermore, Mussolini had offered an Italian expeditionary force for the front. In fact, 200,000 Italian troops were despatched – forces which would have been of far greater use in the shaky North African theatre.

As the situation on the Russian front deteriorated for the Germans, Hitler used all his powers of persuasion in begging the Duce for additional forces. The two senior Axis partners met at Salzburg. Hitler had proclaimed: 'Our aim is to wipe out the entire defence potential remaining to the Soviets, and to cut them off, as far as possible from their most important war industry.' Predictably, Hitler spoke of much else besides. Mussolini, exhausted by the torrent of verbiage, agreed to provide nine extra divisions.

*   *   *

The chief preoccupation of the Romanians was with lack of resources. They were constantly nagging the Germans for replacements for the obsolete 37 mm guns with which they had been supplied. The result was six German 75 mm guns per division. The other equipment provided was French, captured by the Germans in the heady days of 1940.

General Dumitrescu sensed that some major Russian initiative was imminent, citing to Paulus the marked increase in the number of Don crossings to the Russian rear and statements from deserters. There had also been some local attacks. These, he believed had the sole object 'of finding the soft spots and to pave the way for a major attack.' But all attention was on the intended final assault on Stalingrad, and his warning seemed to receive little or no attention.

With the advent of September there was already a drop in the temperature and the looming spectre of winter. But Hitler was deaf to any warnings about the weakness of his flanks, intoning the obsessive mantra: 'Where the German soldier sets foot, there he remains. You may rest assured that nobody will ever drive us away from Stalingrad.' Paulus was ordered to keep going, to battle his way through to the Volga, regardless of the cost.

Hitler's determination had its effect. Morale among Soviet troops slackened and there were wholesale defections, which even the presence of NKVD contingents could not prevent. The Commander of the 62nd Army, assigned to defend Stalingrad, General A I Lopatin, in a state of despair and nervous collapse, was dismissed. On 12 September his place was taken by the pugnacious, abrasive, General Vasily Chuikov who, on the very first day of his appointment, told General Andrei Yeremenko, Commander of the South East Front: 'We shall hold the city or die there!'

He had earlier had a nasty surprise. German assault groups a mere 800 yards from his headquarters had smashed into 62nd Army's positions, fighting their way to the Volga, threatening the central landing stage, the lifeline of the besieged army. There Chuikov had called on fresh blood from the 13th Guards Division, who braved the enemy by crossing the river in small boats and barges. Within the city, Chuikov had organized resistance, not just house by house, but room by room.

Paulus continued to parrot his confidence in victory. It would come at any time. An officer of the 24th Panzer Division described Stalingrad as 'an enormous cloud of burning blinding smoke . . . a vast furnace lit by the reflection of the flames.'

The city's agony stretched over two months, highlighted by Paulus's further offensive on 4 October, which opened with an assault on three Soviet strongpoints. These were the Tractor Factory, the Barricades arms plant and the Red October steel works. Red October was a complex of foundries and calibration shops, manufacturers of small-arms and metal parts. The waters of the Volga licked hungrily at the fuel which rolled swiftly down the hill from the oil tanks, becoming one roaring hell of flame which engulfed a large rowing boat and passengers making for the eastern shore. The Russian-held area was reduced to two tiny enclaves, one 13 km (8 miles) long and 1.5 km (1 mile) deep. A further isolated outpost lay in the far north.

By this time Hitler had moved his entourage from Rastenburg to the Ukrainian headquarters, Wehrwolf, at Vinnyitsa, 700 miles from the front. Distance served to breed illusion, and the Führer chose to ignore the bleak fact that he was committing virtually all his resources to Stalingrad.

Faced with uncomfortable truths he adopted his usual practice: sacking those who dared mention them. List had been the first to go and for a time Hitler had chosen to command Army Group A in person. Then on 29 September, Halder, after a series of scenes which had left him white and shaking, was relieved as Chief of Staff for being defeatist. Hitler had stormed: 'We need National Socialist ardour now, not professional ability. I cannot expect this of an officer of the old school such as you.' Halder took his leave of the man he later described as 'a political fanatic.' He was replaced by General Kurt Zeitzler, whom Hitler believed to be more pliant than his predecessor.

*　　*　　*

Zhukov used the time of Stalingrad's agony well. Some 35,000 runs into the city were made across the Volga with 122,000 men landing on the west bank, travelling clandestinely by night. By mid-November, more than a million men and 28,000 pieces of land and air weaponry were in place. Infantry divisions and armoured brigades had mustered for training.

At 0720 on Thursday, 19 November, the skies were torn apart by a fearsome artillery and *katyusha* (multiple rocket launchers) barrage, followed two hours later by the Russian T-34s, drowning the noise of the artillery fire whose bursts had raked the lines. Operation URANUS had begun.

Within hours, the Russians had sliced through the Romanian 3rd Army between Serafimovich and Kletskaya on the Don, just north-west of Stalingrad. From the south, further Soviet forces wrestled with the German 4th Panzer Army and Romanian 4th Army. The fronts were ripe for piercing. Amid blizzards shrouded in thick mist and consequently with sparse air support, General Nikolai Vatutin's forces advanced some 75 miles in three days.

The Romanian 3rd Army contained five corps (one Panzer) comprising 155,492 Romanians and 11,211 Germans. The frontier, due to a shortage of barbed wire and mines, was inadequately fortified and reserves of artillery ammunition were running dangerously low. Nevertheless, resistance by the Romanians and Germans was fierce; Vatutin battled through to Kalach on a bend in the Don where he linked up with Yeremenko's forces.

The Russians encircled four Romanian divisions. In severe trouble was General Mihail Lascar who, as Commander of 1st Mountain Brigade, had previously been awarded the Ritterkreuz for capturing Russian positions at Balaclava at considerable cost, in the previous January, during the attempt of Manstein's 11th Army to break through in the Crimea. The Lascar Group at Stalingrad comprised disparate forces with no overall Corps Headquarters. Their field telephone lines, command bunkers and light anti-tank guns had been destroyed; nevertheless they were able to see off the infantry. In the overall battle for Stalingrad, it was but a small triumph but it worked wonders for the morale of the men of Lascar Group, tired, underfed and unspeakably cold. The Group awaited XLVIII Panzer Corps to relieve it, but by then that Corps had other priorities. The two Soviet forces had linked at Kalach, only 40 miles west of Stalingrad. By the evening, Paulus reported that 6th Army was surrounded: the teeth of the pincers had snapped shut.

Henry Shapiro, the United Press correspondent in Moscow, went by train to a point some 100 miles north-west of Stalingrad. He then travelled by car to Serafimovich, on the Don bridgehead, which the Russians had captured in heavy fighting in October and from which Vatutin had now hurled his troops towards Kalach on 19 November.

Shapiro wrote:

> By the time I got to Serafimovich, the Russians were not only consolidating the 'ring' round Stalingrad, but were now making a 'second ring'; it was clear from the map that the Germans at Stalingrad were completely trapped, and couldn't get out. . . .
>
> Well behind the fighting-line, there were now thousands of Romanians wandering the steppes, cursing the Germans and desperately looking for Russian feeding-points, and anxious to be formally taken over as war prisoners. Some individual stragglers would throw themselves on the mercy of the local peasants, who treated them charitably, if only because they were not Germans. The Russians thought they were 'just poor peasants, like ourselves.'
>
> Except for small groups of Iron Guard men who, here and there, put up a stiff fight, the Romanian soldiers were sick and tired of the war; the prisoners I saw all said roughly the same thing – that this was Hitler's war, and that the Romanians had nothing to do on the Don.

Shapiro went on to give an account of an entire steppe strewn with dead horses and wrecked gun carriages and tanks and guns 'and no end of corpses, Romanian and German.'

While the beleaguered Paulus, depending on a single thousand-watt transmitter and precariously delivered handwritten notes for communication with the outside world, reported 'murderous attacks on all fronts', the last Romanian outposts fell between the river Chir and Kletskaya on the Don. Antonescu intervened with a request to pull out. By now, every highway shook under the roar of columns of Russian tanks and trucks. A few lucky Romanians reached elements of General Ferdinand Heim's XLVIII Panzer Corps and were shepherded south towards freedom beyond the banks of the Chir. The cost to the Romanians had been appalling – the 3rd and 4th Armies devastated, the 4th being left with only three battalions.

Yet the Romanians fought on, bereft of the superior equipment and armour they had craved from Germany. The pressure on the three women pilots of the Escadrilla Sanitara (now renamed 108 Light Transport Squadron), had been relentless. Russian bombs rained down on the airstrip at Kotelnikovo, to Stalingrad's south-west. Two days later, Mariania Dragescu had been returning to Kotelnikovo with two wounded when her engine cut out over the combat zone. Amid the debris of battle, she brought the aircraft down and forthwith started repairing the filter before taking off again.

One week later, at Plodovitoye, south of Stalingrad, Dragescu, in the teeth of an air raid, had to veer sharply away and Nadia Russo's aircraft suffered rudder damage. There had been at least two bombing raids a day; casualty evacuation from the new landing strip had to be fitted around them.

The Romanian Army Chief of Staff, General Ilie Steflea, complained in vain to the Germans about lack of resources. But the Germans were in the hands of a Führer deaf to all reason – but not sufficiently deaf to the bluster of Hermann Göring that his Luftwaffe would come to the rescue of 6th Army. Göring's claims would almost have been comic if Paulus's predicament had not been so tragic: 6th Army, boasted the obese Reichsmarschall, would be fed and armed by air. At the same time as the wounded were being evacuated, the Russian hordes would be bested. Then the relief forces would arrive and Stalingrad would finally fall. Apart from anything else, where were the available aircraft? Most of them were tied down in North Africa where Hitler was also in trouble. By November, 1942, the entire Luftwaffe air transport force amounted to a mere 750 Junkers Ju-52s. No more than 140 tonnes of supplies got through to the dying 6th Army, including a plane load of brown paper and twelve cases of contraceptives. In short, the intended relief was a fiasco.

Hitler ceased to be seduced by the bombast of his Luftwaffe chief. Instead, he switched Manstein from the Leningrad front and put him in charge of the newly created Army Group Don, comprising Hoth's heavily reinforced 4th Panzer Army, General Karl Hollidt's Army Detachment and what little remained of the 3rd and 4th Romanian Armies.

Dumitrescu had the sorry task of assembling these remnants from stragglers and the army's rear echelons.

Manstein's orders were to 'bring the enemy attacks to a standstill and recapture the positions previously occupied by us.' It was the ultimate fatuity – Hitler in fantasy land. At the most, there could only be damage limitation. Manstein's aptly named plan, WINTERSTURM (Winter Storm) provided for Hoth's Panzers to slice through the Russian lines and provide Paulus with an opportunity to break out. But events were moving fast; not for the first time, the Russians struck in a sector held by the weak troops of one of Germany's allies.

Colonel-General Gariboldi's Italian 8th Army, deployed on the middle Don between 2nd Hungarian Army and Hollidt's forces, caught the full brunt of an attack by three Soviet Armies on 16 December.

The Italian 8th Army, as well as a Blackshirt battalion, included contingents of the Julia, Tridentina and Cuneese Divisions, trained as Alpine troops, who fared reasonably well in the Russian winter. It was far from being enough. The fighting was short and savage. The newly formed Russian 1st Guards Army broke though on the Italian 8th Army's left, speeding to the main base at Kantemirovka by 19 December, capturing supply trains, munitions and ammunition dumps. The Italians, also savaged on their right flank, gave up. Abandoning their equipment, they fled.

As for the Hungarians, they had been served little better than the Romanians when it came to resources. Throughout, Hitler had made no effort to disguise his ongoing distrust of Hungary, an atmosphere inflamed by Ribbentrop who had proclaimed in the middle of December that there was a regrettable and needlessly defeatist attitude in Hungary on the direction of the war effort. Hitler's reaction was to send a telegram to Horthy, requesting him to instruct the Hungarian troops on the Don to put up a stout defence if attacked.

General Ferenc Szombathelyi, Chief of the Hungarian General Staff, echoed Hitler's request with an order that positions must be held without a retreat. Horthy, however, was in possession of reports from 2nd Army that they lacked sufficient equipment and had been assigned too long a sector of the front with too few reserves, and so well understood their predicament.

The fortunes of the Hungarians that January were studded by unmitigated disasters. By the 14th, the Hungarian 12th Light Division was in full flight, a débâcle which was followed by the rapid collapse of units in the face of the Soviet two-pronged attack. On the 17th and 18th, the 19th and 23rd divisions were reported to have given up without a fight.

In his diary entry for 8 May, Josef Goebbels reported that Hitler now graded the Romanians first, the Italians second and the Hungarians last in the order of effectiveness on the Russian front.

By now, German occupied territory had been so drastically overrun as to threaten, not just Army Group Don's lines of communication, but also the capture of Rostov and so those of Army Group A, still clinging to the Caucasus. Suddenly, Rostov had assumed an importance dwarfing even Stalingrad. More than a million-and-a-half men would be at risk. In Stalingrad itself, the sick, frozen, demoralized Germans had been forced to eat the brains of dead horses to survive. At the end of January, 1943, the 6th Army shuffled to almost certain death in the Russian prisoner-of-war cages. Only 5,000 would ever see Germany again.

The ultimate irony of this disaster lay in Hitler's desperate attempt to strengthen Paulus's resolution by promoting him Generalfeldmarschall. Paulus now became the first German officer of that rank ever to be taken prisoner.

To the end, Hitler had remained inflexible in his refusal to countenance withdrawal, radioing Stalingrad: 'Surrender is forbidden. Sixth Army will hold their positions to the last man and the last round.' But Stalingrad had ceased to exist, except as a single mass grave. It was thus small wonder that Hitler's allies, so many of whose men had bled on the Volga and the Don, began to look to the business of securing for themselves a future beyond a Third Reich which had suddenly taken on the complexion of defeat.

PARTISAN WARFARE : YUGOSLAVIA

Despite the capitulation of Paulus and 91,000 men at Stalingrad, Hitler's writ had yet to run. But the ominous signs had already been there, not the least of which was the approach of Fascist Italy's terminal decline. At a meeting at the Wolfsschanze between Hitler and Ciano on 18 December, 1942, the Führer had demanded fresh efforts to maintain supplies to North Africa but Ciano's mind had been elsewhere, raising the question of some form of 'accommodation' with Soviet Russia, a delicate circumlocution for Germany cutting its losses and getting out, concentrating strength on safeguarding, not only North Africa, but the Balkans and the West. Not surprisingly, the idea had been anathema to Hitler, with his obsessive hatred of Bolshevism. In no way could positions elsewhere be buttressed by taking the heat off the Eastern Front. Ciano's suggestion sowed a seed of suspicion. Word was passed to Canaris of the Abwehr: Italy would repay watching.

In fact, to many observers, that country was already melting out of the war. On 23 January, 1943, British forces occupied Tripoli. Mussolini, however, was still in power. Goebbels, Hitler's Propaganda Minister, was careful to eschew any doubts from his diary entry: 'The Duce has again assured the Führer and in a most emphatic way that he will march with us through thick and thin and that he will always remain faithful to the Axis.' The truth was that, however loyal the Duce might be personally, those on whom he depended for his power had been plagued with anxieties since the victory of General Montgomery's 8th Army at El Alamein in November, 1942.

Predictably, scapegoats had to be found, if only to assure Hitler that Fascist Italy was still capable of waging a war. Count Ugo Cavallero was dismissed as Chief of Staff, because of the failures in North Africa. Unfortunately for the Duce, his successor, General Vittorio Ambrosio, was one of the chief conspirators in moves to be rid of the Duce himself.

The uncertainty of the generals proved infectious. Even more fatal to Mussolini was the hardening opposition among his ministers. Along with all this, he was prey to deep depression and there were bouts of self-loathing at his own sycophantic dependence on the Hitler he had once so despised.

The catalyst was provided by the Allied invasion of Sicily, Operation HUSKY, during the night of 9–10 July, 1943. Conscious that the fates were gathering, Mussolini sought a meeting with Hitler at Feltre, near Treviso. The Duce sketched the predicament of his country, increasingly threatened by the might of Britain and the United States. Hitler undertook to supply Mussolini with air and army reinforcements, although he could ill afford them, and then returned to his Obersalzberg retreat, the Berghof, straight into a major crisis.

His closest aide, Martin Bormann, handed him an intelligence report that had been compiled by Himmler, containing clear evidence of a planned *coup d'état* to topple Mussolini and install Marshall Pietro Badoglio, whom Himmler described as 'a leading Freemason in Italy', to form a war cabinet. The next day, Hitler learnt that the Fascist Grand Council had met in Rome. In normal circumstances, this was a rubber-stamping body over which Mussolini, resplendent in his grey-green uniform of the Fascist militia, presided. But this had been anything but a normal meeting.

At a severe disadvantage with a painful ulcer, the Duce had launched into a long rambling discourse of evasion and justification for years of bombast, hyperbole and plain untruths. The reaction was one of embarrassment, followed by a straight-from-the-shoulder condemnation by Count Dino Grandi, formerly one of his closest colleagues. The accusations came thick and fast – 'the restrictive and idiotic formula of the Fascist war'; 'A dictatorship on Italy which is historically immoral'; 'You have destroyed the spirit of the armed forces' – with all the force of hammer blows. At the end, Mussolini, his eyes smarting with pain under the bright lights, begged for an adjournment until the next day. But even this concession was denied him: Grandi agreed to just ten minutes. On reassembly, the Council voted that power should return to King Victor Emmanuel, who granted the Duce an audience on 25 July.

At the door of the Villa Savoia, the King shook hands gravely with his former leader. It might have been the conclusion of a normal meeting but moments before Mussolini had learnt from the King that he was the most hated man in Italy. He had proffered his resignation, not believing even then that it would be accepted. But the King had told him: 'I have to tell you that I unconditionally accept your resignation as Head of the Government.' Humiliation was just beginning. The ringleaders who had plotted against Mussolini were determined that there should be no resistance and no possibility of the former leader marshalling forces that could prove loyal to him.

As Mussolini walked from the royal palace to his official car, a force of *carabinieri* closed in. He was hustled into an ambulance which sped towards Podgora barracks and then to the island of Ponza 'to safeguard his person against public hostility.' In fact, Italy's Fascist dictator for twenty-one years was under arrest.

*   *   *

Beyond Italy, the previous loyalties of the Axis had become progressively strained, not least in the notoriously unstable Balkans. Croatia had been a special anxiety. The terrorist Dr Ante Pavelic depended for his existence on German bayonets and the muscles of the dreaded Ustachi, many of whose followers had been trained near Padua in Italy and Yank Pusta in Hungary. As early as October, 1941, reports smuggled out of Croatia had appeared in the British press of scarcity of food, requisition of crops and the plunge in morale which had followed the loss of all Dalmatia to Italy and other parts of Croatia to Italy and Hungary. In addition, Pavelic was a dedicated student of the Third Reich's mechanics of repression. There had been the insistence that Croat citizens must be Aryan and innocent of 'previous activities against the liberation activities of the Croatian people.'

Jews had been made to provide the government with an inventory of property and any legal transactions involving Jewish interests had been nullified, including the sale of their property. Jews in Zagreb were also forbidden to travel beyond the city limits, to shop at Aryan establishments or to buy anything before 10 o'clock in the morning. A further decree had provided for the imprisonment of up to five years for any persons who 'concealed having relations with Jews.'

Pavelic had a formidable roster of detested enemies: Serbs, Jews and Communists. Above all, Serbs, who were attacked with jackboot rhetoric:

> Knife, revolver and explosives are the instruments with which the Croatian peasant will regain the fruit of his labour, the worker his piece of bread, and the Croat his freedom. . . . They are the musical instruments on which the Croatian people will play the requiem mass of the foreign Serbian rule.

The objects of his detestation returned the compliment. Pavelic and his Ustachi were cordially detested by most Croats, who regarded them as jackals of the Italians. But there were enough time servers to keep them in business, certainly enough of their thugs to bring terror to the streets.

The Ustachi, furthermore, were killers in a hurry. The invasion of Yugoslavia, was barely over before the atrocities began.

Just how closely Pavelic was prepared to ape his German masters can be gathered from a comparison of Croat and German measures.

In the case of the Germans there was Incident Report 108, issued in Berlin by the chief of Sipo (Central Security Department of the SS) and the SD (SS Security Service) on 9 October, 1941. Sub-titled 'Serbia', it stated: 'The mopping up action of the German Army in the area around Sabac has led so far to the taking of 22,000 male prisoners. . . . As a punishment measure for twenty-two soldiers who were shot at Topola a few days ago, 2,100 Jews and Gypsies will be executed.'

As for the Ustachi, it had set about a clutch of Serbian villages in the district of Bjelovar. An Orthodox priest and a school teacher had been seized along with 250 peasants who had been forced to dig a long trench in which they were buried alive. With an attention to bureaucratic detail worthy of the *Einsatzgruppen*, the incident found its way into the Ustachi archives, filed under the terse heading *Ustachen Werk bei Bjelovar* (What the Ustachi did at Bjelovar).

In overall charge of massacres such as these was Zagreb's Chief of Police Eugen Kvaternik, a professed admirer, not just of the Germans, but of G G Yagoda, the former head of Stalin's secret police, the OGPU, and son of Marshal Slavko Kvaternik, who had been one of the chief organizers of the assassination of King Alexander at Marseilles.

In a bid to escape persecution by the Croatians, Serbs took to abjuring their Orthodox faith and demanding baptism from the local clergy. As a device for survival in the market town of Glina in August, 1941, it proved futile. On a hot afternoon, a crowd of peasants, farmers and shopkeepers from the fertile districts of Banija and Kordun on the borders of Bosnia, barely 50 miles from Zagreb, had crowded into the Orthodox Church only to realize that they were victims of a trap, when the doors were slammed shut and bolted.

They remained there sweating until dusk, when Pavelic's strongmen, distinguished by the crude U-shaped badges on their caps, clattered in from their trucks and began an orgy of butchery; victims were frequently despatched by a knife delivered in a swift slice to the base of the neck. The church icons were also desecrated and those who darted for refuge behind wrecked altars and the pillars were dragged out and swiftly despatched. A volley of rifle shots took care of those who had scaled the scaffolding to reach the belfry. When it was all over, one hundred and sixty corpses were flung into ditches by the Ustachi. There was only one survivor and he melted away into the forest to join the scattered band of the resistance.

Repression in Croatia accelerated. Nevertheless, Hitler and his military circle had cause to worry. Resistance inside dismembered Yugoslavia was growing apace. Furthermore, intelligence from the Balkans and neutral Turkey had reached agents of the British Special Operations Executive (SOE) that there was a growing level of guerrilla activity in the wild mountainous landscape of Serbia and it was decided to bring this particular pot to the boil. From its base in Cairo, through the British naval command in the eastern Mediterranean, SOE organized a British submarine, operating from Malta, to land on the Dalmatian coast, near Petrovic. Its occupants included a British agent, Colonel Bill ('Marko') Hudson, a tough South African mining engineer fluent in Serbo-Croat, who made contact as soon as he could with the two leading figures in Balkan resistance.

The first was Josip Broz but, of course, no one called him that. To everyone he was Tito; as a name, it was a portrait of the man in miniature. The word meant 'This, that' and it summed up a personality supremely in control and accustomed to having orders obeyed: 'Do this, do that.' Tito was in the romantic tradition of revolutionaries: a strikingly handsome seventh child of Croat peasants who grew to inherit a body to match. And there was the charisma of a guerrilla fighter with a string of aliases: Engineer Slavic Basic, Engineer Kostanjic, Tomanek or (to his Communist Masters in the Comintern) Walter. Anyone who tried to pigeonhole Tito was unwise; a fervent Communist and rabid anti-Nazi, certainly. But first and last a Yugoslav patriot, leader of the Partisans, by common consent the Second World War's most effective resistance movement.

But for Tito, there was not just one war. The drama of resistance had another leading player, the second man whom Hudson was to contact. The Serbian Colonel (later General) Draza Mikailovic, was the leader of the Chetniks, named after the 19th century Serb resisters to the Turks and for the most part royalist and fiercely anti-Communist in their sympathies.

Differences between Tito and Mikailovic sprang from the latter's political ideology. For Tito, the war's aim was a socialist Yugoslavia. On the other hand, the leader of the disparate Chetniks wanted to preserve what Tito sought to destroy: a Yugoslav community of Serbs, that, holding no Socialist allegiance, would wait for the delivery of the Allies and the return of the old certainties of Royal Yugoslavia. Between Tito and Mikailovic there could be no common ground.

Pavelic and his Ustachi now switched their assault to the Partisans. His own air force was formed under the command of Pukovnik (Colonel) Vladimir Kren who went to work fast, reactivating airfields at Banja Luka, Mostar, Sarajevo, Zagreb and Zemen. Kren next went in search of pilots; a sizable number of Croatians were released from the POW camps to which they had been sent at the time of the German invasion.

On 26 June, 1941, Breguet 19 and Potez 25 light bombers flew in from Sarajevo with Fizir FP2 light biplanes which raked the lines of the Partisans who replied in kind and downed two of the bombers. The pilots reacted to hits by making immediate attempts to crash land; no parachutes were available. Indeed, the crews operated without flying suits or helmets.

But virulent hatred was reserved for the Serbs. When it came to brutality, the Ustachi did not scruple at poaching on the preserves of their German masters. Franklin Lindsay, an officer of the American OSS (Office of Strategic Services) who later was parachuted into north-west Yugoslavia to make contact with Tito, learnt from a Partisan that the Ustachi smashed open freight cars to murder Serbs who were being transported through Croatia to Nazi labour camps.

As 1941 wore on, Croatia came to resemble nothing so much as a primed bomb with a running fuse. The lawless excesses of Pavelic's regime caused widespread alienation, notably from the Church from whom he had hoped for support. Rebellious former loyalists were ruthlessly purged.

Hemmed in by bodyguards, travelling in a bullet-proof car, Pavelic went in fear of his life, while his wife was sent to Italy to recover from a nervous breakdown. As early as September, 1941, resistance had been on the loose in Zagreb. Fifty men, dubbed Communists and Jews, were executed for being 'intellectual instigators' of a string of bomb explosions in the town's central telephone exchange in which a German Major, twelve German soldiers and several Croats were wounded.

Reprisals were draconian. Despite rigid censorship within Yugoslavia, which allowed only a trickle of news to reach the outside world, it was revealed from Istanbul that sixty-six executions, either by shooting or hanging, were carried out in Croatia over five days, including those of two men who were executed merely for failing to report to the authorities.

By the following summer, reports were reaching London that Axis control throughout Croatia was slacking drastically, despite the presence of an estimated 180,000 Italian troops and 15,000 Germans to buttress the 16,000 Ustachi, of which 6,000 were in Zagreb. In July, resistance struck: Sturmbannführer Helm, Gestapo Chief in Zagreb, was assassinated.

The SS ran amok, raging through the streets and firing at random, tossing hand grenades into the doors and windows of restaurants and public buildings; deaths mounted to more than 700. Pavelic had abundant reason for fearing for his skin; by late October reports were reaching Turkey that a bomb had been lobbed at him by a turncoat follower and had narrowly missed. The Diplomatic Correspondent for *The Times* of London wrote: 'Political confusion and insecurity in Croatia have reached a point where nothing would surprise the public – or even the Germans.' That confusion and insecurity unleashed all pent-up hatreds against the Ustachi.

At Dugo Selo and Puscha, points east and west of the city, a German officer and his orderly were killed; a senior Ustachi administrator was kidnapped and murdered. The Ustachi, with the aid of German and Italian troops, rounded up Catholics and National Croats, who were dubbed 'Communist' conspirators and promptly executed. Offers of large rewards and respect for anonymity in return for information on agitators and saboteurs were blithely ignored by the Croats. Opposition took on a classic pattern of resistance: the two rail entries to Belgrade were cut, with reports of derailment of expresses at Popovacha and Sisak.

Within 35 miles of Zagreb, destruction of the lines to Fiume and Split became commonplace. Croat bands were active further afield; assorted Communists and Catholic nationalists mustered opposition to the Italians throughout Dalmatia and in the mountain fastnesses nudging the German border.

Berlin, faced with Croatia falling apart, acted by giving command in the Balkans a new face. Pavelic, it was agreed, must be removed, along with other members of an obviously incompetent cabinet. Choice for the new head was Dr Vladko Macek, a former deputy prime minister and head of the Croat Peasant Party. A staunch patriot, he steadfastly refused to take office while foreign troops occupied Croatia; faced with his intransigence, the Germans sent him back to detention. Hitler had no other course but to summon Pavelic and order him to reconstruct his government and carry out dismissals where necessary.

Himmler's Gestapo agents stormed into Zagreb, along with two additional German divisions, including light tanks and armoured cars. The latter bypassed the capital and plunged into the interior with a remit to stamp out anarchy. German repression spread to the streets of towns with mass arrests; buses and trams were halted and passengers searched while entire streets were cordoned off. A bunch of Pavelic's bureaucrats were entrusted to young Austrian-trained SS men, adept at obtaining 'confessions' from the intransigent where necessary. Ustachi politicians and police were charged with espionage both for the Chetnik forces of Mihailovitch and the Communist Partisans.

It was adrenaline for the resistance. Predictably, what had begun as pinpricks of opposition grew into a tangible menace for Hitler. Besides needing to draw on Yugoslavia's mineral resources, the Führer needed his pathway to Greece. As for forces, until the collapse of Mussolini the Germans had been able to depend on twenty Italian divisions.

With the Duce gone, another seven German divisions were mustered for Yugoslavia and four more drawn from the unhappy King Boris of Bulgaria, already under pressure from Hitler to honour previous pledges as an ally and help out on the Russian front. Doing battle with Partisans was altogether a different prospect from tackling conventional forces. What was needed was a special unit delighting in using special methods: a role, in fact, for the notoriously adaptable Brandenburgers.

By the autumn of 1942, the Brandenburgers, who had greatly distinguished themselves on the Eastern Front, fighting courageously behind the Soviet lines, were granted divisional status. But the power of their original masters, the Abwehr, had begun to dwindle and, increasingly, they found that they were being controlled by OKW as a line formation. So it was that when Brandenburgers were being called for to fight in Yugoslavia, only the 5th Brandenburg Regiment was still operating in the Special Forces role. Consequently it was that regiment that was despatched to join a force consisting of some 100,000 men, made up of Waffen-SS divisions, the 1st Alpine Division, 40,000 Italians and various contingents of Croats in addition to the Brandenburgers. A massive operation, with air supply for any outlying detachments who might find themselves fighting in largely inaccessible mountain terrain, was launched against the Partisans in the middle of May, 1943.

Tito planned to move south-east away from the enemy. But his escape path was blocked and encirclement looked imminent. Fortunately for him, there was an alternative plan for a breakout elsewhere, to the west and north of which he now took advantage. It was aided by diversionary attacks from the Partisan Fifth Division in central Bosnia under the command of Arso Jovanovic, one of the tight inner circle of Partisan leaders. Tito and his forces managed to break out but the losses were heavy.

*　　　*　　　*

As the months wore on, the pressure on the liberation forces in Croatia intensified under the sheer weight of German reinforcements. In a series of incidents, dive bombers of the Luftwaffe targeted the town of Senj on the Croatian coast as well as several villages at the foot of the Papuka mountains to the east. The presence of two Wehrmacht divisions revealed that the Germans were making use of some new allies, including Russian prisoners of war and an assortment of Tartars and Cossacks from the north Caucasus. General Andrei Vlasov, one of their leaders, was a former rising star of the Red Army, who had turned into a fervent anti-Stalinist, throwing in his lot with the Germans after being captured on the Volkov front in July, 1942.

Predictably, Pavelic lost no time in joining this wave of repression, issuing a decree which reached London and was published by British newspapers. It read:

> All acts of sabotage will be punished by shooting and, in serious cases, by hanging. These security measures are directed against persons proved to have joined in attacks or acts of sabotage, as well as those officially known to be active Communists or rebels. *The security measures are also applicable to the husband, wife, parents or children of the above.**

The final sentence revealed just how much Pavelic had absorbed from his Nazi masters. For this was a grim echo of *Sippenhaft* (Clan Decree), a practice beloved of the SS to massacre the innocent under the plea of justified removal of what Himmler decreed to be 'bad blood'.

Gottlob Berger, Himmler's recruiting agent, cast envious eyes on Yugoslavia and, at the risk of violating his superior's racial preoccupations, went hunting for Croatian volunteers. The raising of additional SS resources had its obvious attractions for Hitler. He consented to the formation of the SS-Volunteer-Division Prince Eugen which took into its ranks four battalions of a Ustachi Active Unit (*Einsatzstaffel*) which had originally consisted of ethnic Croatians.

From the very first, Prinz Eugen was committed to ferocious warfare with the Partisans. Later, in Bosnia, the Kama Division was set up under the leadership of SS officers and recruited from nationals as part of the 5th Waffen-SS *Gebirgskorps* (Mountain Corps).

Colonel Pericic, Brigade Commander of 1st Mountain Brigade, operating with SS units around Popovaca in Bosnia, reported on 26 September, 1942, on events which had taken place ten days earlier:

> . . . an SS unit of eighty men marched out of Popovaca to Osekovo, with a mission to obtain cattle. A short while after the arrival in Osekovo, this unit was attacked by Partisans. Under pressure, the SS unit had to draw back to E station. There it had four badly wounded and several lightly wounded personnel. The leader of the unit telephoned Popovaca that he had been forced to retreat and that he had killed everybody that he had seen in the course of the withdrawal because it was impossible to tell the local population from the Partisans. He admitted that during this action he had personally killed 100 people.

---

* Author's emphasis.

Such operations carried out by Prinz Eugen became more frequent. A post-war report of the Yugoslav State Commission on War Crimes of the Occupying Power and its Collaborators read:

> On 28 March this Battalion overran villages . . . and carried out horrific barbarism, burning and plundering. These animals murdered in a single day in the above-named Dalmatian villages 834 people, including grown men, women and children and burnt 500 houses down and plundered everything that was to be plundered. The German soldiers drove men, women and children into one place and then opened fire on them with machine guns. They threw bombs among them, robbed them of their possessions and afterwards burned the corpses . . .

The broadening of the concept of the Waffen-SS – the seeking of voluntary recruits within Croatia – was ultimately to prove counterproductive. As the dire reputation of Prinz Eugen spread, voluntary recruitment slumped. Spurred on by Hitler, who desperately needed as much manpower as he could muster, particularly in the face of the increasing success of the Partisans, Himmler ordered Berger to employ still stronger methods to obtain volunteers. In fact, Himmler was to go even further. Since volunteers were not forthcoming, there must be conscription. Compulsory military service was introduced. Thus the original identity of the Waffen-SS, which had been underpinned by the racial philosophy of Himmler, was jettisoned along with the belief of many within the Axis that total victory could any longer be assured.

*　　*　　*

Life was not exactly happy for the Allies, either. Those on the receiving end from Ultra – the special security classification given by the British to information gained from breaking the code of the German enciphering machine Enigma – were assembling evidence which showed that Mihailovic's links with Italian, Ustachi and even German commanders was far too friendly for comfort.

Neither were the Chetniks themselves revealed as wholly reliable. Indeed, self-styled Chetniks, holding no allegiance to Mihailovic, were known to be working for the Serb quisling government in Belgrade. Amid the tortured tangle of Yugoslavia's serpentine intrigues, only one prediction could be made with any certainty: there would be no early or tidy end to the war in the Balkan region.

– 13 –

KURSK : THE TURNING POINT

Ion Antonescu supposed it had been balm of sorts. On 1 July, 1943, Generalfeldmarschall Manstein had presented him with the Gold Crimea Shield in Bucharest, marking the anniversary of the surrender of the last of the Russians at Sevastapol. But there were other matters that preoccupied the Marshal in the haze of a Romanian summer and they had little to do with the presentation of baubles.

His erstwhile rival, Horia Sima, who had been spirited to Germany at the time of the abortive rebellion by the Iron Guard, had been attempting some spectacular empire-building. At the end of 1942, he had managed to reach Italy on a false passport, determined to contact Mussolini and propose the setting up of an Iron Guard bureau in Rome. Since the Duce's own followers were exhibiting dubious loyalties, the last thing the Italian dictator needed was even a hint of a rival authoritarian movement. In any case the risk of antagonizing Antonescu, to say nothing of Hitler, would have been sheer madness. There were the supplies of oil to consider.

At this point, enter Himmler. The Reichsführer-SS demanded Sima's extradition forthwith. Mussolini complied and Horia Sima ended up in Dachau while Antonescu took care of any of his sympathizers at home.

Of even greater concern than the abortive fantasies of Horia Sima, was the plight of the Romanian armed forces. Those on the Eastern Front represented the largest contribution by any of Germany's allies, eventually reaching 700,000 men.

There had been the euphoria of the opening campaigns when the 3rd and 4th Armies and a motorized division had advanced confidently with Hitler's 11th Army. Disillusion had soon followed. By December, 1941, the push into the southern Ukraine had claimed 130,000 killed and wounded. Rear area formations, ill-trained and inexperienced, had born the brunt. At Stalingrad, the Russians had not been slow to sense the weakness; the cost to the Royal Romanian Army had been 173,000 casualties.

Hitler had behaved characteristically when he and Antonescu met at Rastenburg early in January for what amounted to a post-mortem. The Romanians and the Italians, the Führer declared, were to shoulder most of the blame for the disaster at Stalingrad. Antonescu was no sycophant and rigorously defended the record of his forces in the field. Up till now, he told Hitler bluntly, the Eastern Campaign had been a conspicuous failure. If it was to be pursued with any chance of success, this should be after seeking some compromise peace with the Western Allies.

Hitler not only rejected any such suggestion but declared that Romania, despite its losses, should step up its manpower, particularly as Germany was guaranteeing its borders. The meeting, however, concluded with both sides agreeing that they must continue in partnership. Furthermore, there was a German commitment to make fresh armaments deliveries to Romania. Compared with other protestations of loyalty that Hitler was receiving, he found those from Antonescu the most reassuring.

But the partnership was already threatened from within. The Marshal's foreign minister and distant kinsman, Mihai Antonescu, made overtures to the Italians and Bulgarians, arguing with them that unless there was a settlement with the West, they all faced occupation by the Red Army.

Antonescu also cast an anxious eye on the hated Hungarians who seemed to receive favourable treatment from the Reich when it came to the supply of arms.

However, Antonescu had no monopoly of dissatisfaction. Slovakia had begun with a minor role in BARBAROSSA. The total Slovak armed commitment under the command of General-in-Chief and Defence Minister, Ferdinand Catlos, had stood at around 90,000, with initially only two infantry divisions – sixty per cent of the army's size at the time of the Polish offensive. Late in 1943, with the Red Army launching its offensive to liberate the Northern Caucasus, Slovak forces had been forced to retreat. The Schnell – Fast or Attack – Division withdrew as part of Germany's 17th Army. During the retreat, a company led by Lieutenant Pavol Marcely switched sides and joined the Red Army.

A commission from the Wehrmacht in Bratislava had desperately striven for an optimistic note, citing Catlos's observations:

> More and more the spirit of the front line soldier seems to make an impression on the Slovak people. . . . The positive attitude to the fight against the common enemy did not subside even when the Eastern Front had to go on the defensive. . . . The Slovakian people were proud that Slovakian soldiers

were holding their ground so bravely, even in the difficult winter. . . . Co-operation with Germans was extremely good.

This, however, was in sharp contrast to the showing of a below-strength First Infantry Division which fought the Red Army near Melitopol, east of Odessa and north-west of the Sea of Azov. This had resulted in a massive defection of 2,731 Slovak soldiers to the Red Army.

*   *   *

Meanwhile, Hitler had been impatient to get on with his war in the east. The eyes of the self-appointed genius of the Wolfschanze had fastened on an area which extended north from Belgorod, lying north-west of Kharkov to the area of Orel. In the middle was the Kursk salient or bulge.

Kursk itself was an industrial city with valuable coal-mining, engineering and manufacturing centres. Intelligence sources had informed Hitler that there was enormous offensive Soviet strength at this point, with a massive input of field forces. Hitler's plan for the territory was code named ZITADELLE (Citadel).

On 1 July, an assembly of senior commanders was told by the newly invigorated Führer: 'I have decided to fix the starting date of Zitadelle as 5 July.' There were dissenting voices and not because of the daunting short notice. There was the shadow of events in the Mediterranean area where a landing in Italy by the Allies was expected. Once that happened, available forces would have to be switched to fill the gap.

But Hitler, deaf to such voices, was totally mesmerized by ZITADELLE. If the Russians, he argued, were allowed to slice their way through the salient they would have a clear route to the Ukraine. The operation order was terse: 'The objective of the attack is to encircle the enemy forces in the Kursk area by means of a well co-ordinated and rapid thrust of two attacking armies.' In a word, encirclement. It was a well-tried recipe and it had worked before. Why not again?

The Wehrmacht, however, was unwittingly sharing its plans. A group of anti-Nazi officers, based in Berlin, relayed information about operational plans of ZITADELLE to 'Lucy', cover name of a spy ring operating through Switzerland. The details reached Stavka, the Soviet high command. There had been ample time for the forces of the Red Army to build up. Until his final choice of date, Hitler had delayed the operation three times – a fatal error, which would incur a fearful penalty.

Manstein had command of General Model's 9th Army in the north and of General Hoth's 4th Panzer Army in the south, each army consisting of eighteen divisions of which seven in the north and ten in the south were armoured. It was an impressive tally but it left out of account

Hitler's procrastination. The Russians had already received advanced warning through 'Lucy' and were able to put in hand an immense programme of defensive work. By the opening of the battle in July, they were protected by a belt of minefields, liberally sprinkled with brilliantly camouflaged anti-tank strongholds, no less than twelve miles deep. In the face of inevitably slow progress, Hoth eliminated 2,000 Soviet tanks and took 32,000 prisoners. But the density of the minefields – a German corps would lift as many as 40,000 mines in a single day; the strength of the Soviet counter-attack forces and, above all, the unspeakable weather, which turned the battlefield into a quagmire, soon brought things to a grinding halt, particularly in the north.

Above all, this was a battle of tanks. The tactical rule book – that the purpose of the Panzers was to exploit enemy weakness rather than pitch tank against tank – was quite literally blown into oblivion. At Prokhorovka, which lay well to the north-east of Belgorod, slaughter came to the German Army – slaughter on a scale recalling the very worst battles of the First World War. There was no land and no sky, only a yawning nothingness, created by clouds of dust and smoke. From that dreadful reek, the shadowy juggernauts thundered into the fray. Across the open steppes the Russian tanks, the T34s and KVs, had struck across the flank of the Panzers, which included Tigers and Panthers, charging at they knew not what, even destroying their own side in the process. At long last, the fighting stopped. Knocked out Soviet and Nazi tanks littered the steppes; the silver grey grass was stained with oil and blood from both sides, while the sky was jet from the smoke of belching fires.

Hitler unexpectedly summoned Manstein and Feldmarschall von Kluge, commanding Army Group Centre, to his headquarters in East Prussia to announce he was calling off ZITADELLE.

The defeat for the German Army at Kursk was monumental and Soviet propaganda was not slow to exploit what it termed the last gasp of the Panzer arm. In fact there were more than a few gasps left but the truth was that strategic initiative had been snatched from Hitler never to be regained.

Elsewhere, the portents were grim. British, American and Canadian troops had landed in Sicily. Italian resistance had collapsed; the Allies were already advancing down the country roads. Even as Hitler spoke of the suspension of ZITADELLE, the Russians, strong and re-equipped with thousands of load-carrying vehicles supplied by Britain and the United States, launched two simultaneous assaults between Bryansk and Orel. Here was fast-moving mobile warfare of the kind that the Wehrmacht had excelled in three years before. But those days were gone for the German Army; transport losses proved irreplaceable. The

Germans marched towards ultimate defeat, the Red Army to miraculous recovery.

In Moscow, impatient queues formed for newspapers. All the headlines were exultant. Perhaps the most memorable was splashed in bold type across the front page: THE TIGERS ARE BURNING.

*　　*　　*

Other problems already threatened. Joint Romanian–Hungarian resentment and mutual suspicion hardened. Then came the fall of Mussolini, followed swiftly by the new Italian government of Badoglio, impatient to shed its Fascist clothes and open negotiations with the Allies. Hitler knew that, for all his protestations of loyalty, Antonescu had been badly shaken by the defeat at Kursk. For how long could his loyalty be depended upon and, an equal source of anxiety, his supplies of the vital oil from the Ploiesti oilfields?

In November, 1942, when the situation had looked grim at Stalingrad, Generaloberst Jodl, the Wehrmacht Chief Operations Officer, had commented on the situation on the Eastern Front, declaring that 'no success gained by the enemy there can be directly disastrous unless we should lose the Romanian oilfields.'

The portents were not encouraging. All Wehrmacht reserves of motor fuel were approaching total exhaustion. Romania was sucking in supplies of oil for domestic consumption – increasing from 1,811,000 to 2,098,000 tons between 1941 and 1942. Refinery production had slumped. The Germans rushed in specially trained contingents to make good the damage to the Russian refineries which the Red Army had destroyed in the summer of 1942 in the wake of the German strike into the Caucasus.

It was obvious that there would be Allied air strikes against Ploiesti, possibly from the Americans in North Africa rather than from the fully stretched Russians. To Americans connected with the oil industry, Ploiesti was almost home town and boom town. As early as 1857, the United States, along with Britain, France and the Netherlands, had built and managed the eleven refineries there. The defences of the town, nestling at the south of a valley among the Carpathian foothills, were reinforced and they were formidable indeed.

In charge of this sprawling mass of storage tanks, power plants and pumping stations was Generalleutnant Alfred Gerstenberg who, as well as being an experienced airman, knew something about air defences. The Luftwaffe, as it happened, owed him a considerable debt. In the years leading up to the Nazi assumption of power, he had helped prepare it for war by commanding a secret flying school at Lipetsk, south of Moscow.

Airmen there had covert training in defiance of the Treaty of Versailles. In October, 1940, Gerstenberg received his reward which was to become Air Attaché in Romania with a remit to make Ploiesti impregnable.

Gerstenberg had the considerable advantage of a direct line to Hermann Göring, with whom he had flown in the First World War. The contact yielded a generous supply of technicians and, as valuable, battalions of highly trained flak gunners. Ploiesti went on to bristle with the latest technology including a highly sophisticated radar system and an operation control centre primed at Otopeni near Bucharest. In addition, there were two decoy 'Ploiestis', placed at sensible distances from the real thing.

The defensive force, consisting of fighters, was in the hands of Oberst Bernhard Woldenga, who had begun his career as a master mariner and latterly became a trainee pilot with the Hamburg America Line, which at one time had contemplated setting up an airline. As a Luftwaffe pilot, he had flown on the Polish front, in the Battle of Britain and in Greece and Russia. For the defenders of Ploiesti, however, he had an added attraction. During his service in North Africa he had come up against United States B-24 Liberators, considered as the most likely aircraft to be used against Ploiesti.

The 6th Bulgarian Fighter Regiment, stationed near Sofia and commanded by Colonel Vasil Vulkov, was firmly under the control of the Germans' Luftflotte 4 but represented the weakest of the air resources available for the defence of the oilfields. Its squadrons had a very mixed bag of aircraft – Polish single-seater fighters, a sprinkling of Messerschmitt Bf-109s and a number of Czech Avia 534 biplanes.

At 0700 hours local time on 1 August, 1943, 177 B-24D Liberators took off for one of the major Allied air raids of the war. The aircraft of Operation TIDAL WAVE flew from bases in Benghazi, Libya, on a journey of 1,900 miles with their 4,000 pound bomb loads, making for the mountains of Albania and Yugoslavia and thence across the Danube in Bulgaria.

Lieutenant General Lewis H Brereton, a veteran of the Philippines and now the commander of what had been the Middle East Air Force, re-designated 9th Air Force, had decided on low-level formation flying, of necessity shorn of fighter escort, for maximum accuracy – a tactic designed to catch the enemy off-guard.

The Americans were first detected by German radar on Crete. The control centre in Athens was alerted as were the flak defences on Ploiesti. The four bases around Ploiesti were at maximum readiness, as the 389th Bomber Group peeled off to home in for a successful attack on the assigned target of Campina. Elsewhere, however, the situation was less happy. Two of the groups, 376th and the 93rd, fell victim to faulty map reading, flying towards Bucharest, lying well to the south of Ploiesti. By the time the error had been discovered and the crews back on their route, the Germans had opened up, their flak gunners sending the exploding shells into the oncoming B-24Ds, with cannon and machine guns also unleashing their coloured streams of tracer. All at once, the raid resembled a bizarre, nightmare obstacle race, the Americans flying at a low level, astonishing even Gerstenberg as he watched them ducking and weaving to avoid collision and entanglement in the balloon cables, as oil fires meanwhile carpeted the area in rich, acrid smoke.

The Romanians put up fifty-nine sorties and claimed twenty confirmed or probable kills for the loss of just two aircraft. Romanian AA guns claimed a further fifteen. The claimed tally led Woldenga to comment: 'The Romanian pilots, although not all got into combat, showed great courage.'

Conspicuous among these was Sub-Lieutenant Carol Anastasescu of Escadrille 62, pilot of one of the two Romanian aircraft lost:

> There were four bombers in Indian file. I came in from the right and slightly above, aiming for my target's starboard engines, and passed clear under him. I had hit him but he had not caught fire. I attacked three or four more times, and the last time I saw smoke emerging. When making my next diving pass, I looked down and saw my original target explode on the ground.
>
> I hit a second bomber, but I don't know the result, because as I was pulling out I heard a crack at the root of the left wing, by my left leg, a little below the fuel level. The lever was damaged, but I didn't seem to be wounded. I disengaged when I saw a flame shoot from the fuel lever near my leg. I tried to put my left leg out but burnt my palm, and I felt a searing pain when I opened the cockpit ready to jump.

But he was too low for a safe jump. Through the pain, came cold fear that the aircraft would blow up. Then he saw a bomber peel away and make straight for him so he opened up with all his forward facing armament. 'My aircraft was billowing smoke, I couldn't suppress the fire, and the pain was becoming insupportable. At that moment my only desire was to end it all quickly. . . . I aimed my aircraft for his port engines. I felt an intense heat and . . . I woke up in hospital.'

He had come down on the Vega refinery where there were emergency services to pull him free from the wreck which, incredibly enough, one report deemed as recoverable. The fate of the US bomber remained unrecorded, although Anastasescu claimed that he had collided with it and killed the crew.

At the end of it all, the Germans claimed that Ploiesti's Romanian anti-aircraft gunners, by common consent the best technical arm of the

Romanian armed forces and German-trained, had indeed shot down fifteen Liberators. This figure was later disputed as was that for American kills, which at one time was put as high as forty.

Ploiesti still stood but it had been severely crippled, for the next eight months at least. The largest of the refineries, Astra Romana, had sustained serious damage. Those at Brazi, five miles to the south, and at Campina were inoperable. But Gerstenberg had trained his damage control teams well and the refineries were soon back in production. Even so, with the situation as it was on the Eastern Front, Hitler could not afford such loss of resources as resulted from TIDAL WAVE. And there was always the spectre of the return of the Liberators.

*   *   *

Hitherto, Hitler had regarded Romania as something of a single vast oil well, gushing forth riches, enabling him to prosecute his war in the east. It was an attitude which, along with that country's loyalties, he could no longer take for granted.

As early as March of the previous year, the Führer had received a complaint from Josef Goebbels and from Walther Funk, his economics minister, that Romania had not been supplying enough oil and food to the war effort. Bulgaria too had been told, in the delicately polite language of diplomacy, that if the country was deficient in its contributions, relations between it and Germany 'might deteriorate.'

In his diary entry, Goebbels had been blunt, declaring that King Boris '. . . is said to be playing a somewhat double-faced game. He is a sly, crafty fellow, who, obviously impressed by the severity of the defensive battles on the Eastern Front, is looking for some back door by which he might eventually escape.'

Boris had in fact always been uneasy. Circumstances, rather than ideology, had propelled him into becoming one of Hitler's jackals, a position he had found increasingly uncomfortable. Not the least of his anxieties had involved Bulgaria's declaration of war against the United States. The crucial date had been 7 December, 1941, when the Japanese attacked the United States fleet at Pearl Harbour.

Both Germany and Italy pressed Boris, pointing out that Article 3 of the Pact placed upon each member the obligation to give full assistance to any member who became victim of an aggression – in this case by the Americans, because the United States had been the first to declare war on Japan originally.

There could be no question of temporizing; Ribbentrop, it was made clear, was banging on the door. By way of a futile face saver, Bulgaria's Prime Minister, Bogdan Filov, announced in the *Sobranije* that Bulgaria, in fulfilment of her obligations was 'declaring a symbolic war on the United States.' The reassurance was offered that Bulgaria was a great distance from America and would therefore never have to fulfil its obligations. Whoever was reassured by this caveat, it was not Boris. After the *Sobranije*'s affirmative vote late in the afternoon, Boris had left his palace for the cathedral of Alexander Nevsky where, a deeply troubled figure, he was seen at prayer.

He had much to pray about. Not least there was the public consternation at the declaration of war on the United States, symbolic or otherwise.

Even more menacing was the aggressive posture of the country's right wing. This had been adhered to originally by students and intellectuals under the leadership of the charismatic Ivan Dochev, who had been shrewd enough to invest the movement, the Legionnaires, with a cloak of respectability by electing as two of its senior members, General Nikola Jekov, the former Commander-in-Chief of the Bulgarian forces, and General Christo Loukov, a former War Minister, both of whom had done little to hide their pro-German sympathies.

There were other forces at work. It was as if the revelation of the Wehrmacht's defeat at Stalingrad had acted as a push button for armed resistance. Since Bulgaria was an ally of the Reich and not an occupied country, there were less obvious targets for subversives. But already Moscow was looking ahead to a Bulgaria that would be ripe for postwar conversion. The Communist Party was ready to take to the streets.

There were mere pinpricks at first, the familiar devices of blowing up trains and exploding fuel barrels. Then came the payment of individual scores, suspected turncoat Communists were 'punished' with a single bullet. Colonel Atanas Pantev, a former police director who had made hunting Communists into something of a mission, was despatched by four terrorists outside an apartment building.

Among the most prized victims of the Communists was General Loukov, whom picked assassins, from an organization dubbed the Liberty Front, had shadowed for weeks, before forcing their way into his home and gunning him down in front of his wife and daughter.

The successive advances of the Red Army, along with Hitler's mounting miscalculations on the Eastern Front, were for Boris the stuff of nightmares. At Stalingrad, when the 6th Army had been encircled and destroyed, four armies allied to Nazi Germany had been swept from the map. The grab for the Caucasian oilfields had not come off. By the late summer of 1943, it became clear that the Wehrmacht had been unable to regain the territory lost during the winter and a disaster of Stalingrad proportions loomed at Kharkov. Hitler's desire to hold that city was not simply military machismo. He confided to Manstein: 'Its fall would produce an unfavourable effect on the attitude of Bulgaria and Turkey.'

Inside Bulgaria, agents of the SD watched Boris closely, as they also watched various officials whose belief was that a German defeat was inevitable and that there should be a shift in policy whereby the country came to terms with the British. Furthermore, it was widely agreed that this could only be achieved by driving out the Germans.

There followed a succession of invitations to Boris for meetings with Hitler at Berchtesgaden and at Rastenburg. At one of these, in late March, the King was subjected to close interrogation by a glacial Ribbentrop, who wanted to know why a certain Bulgarian envoy had travelled recently to Istanbul and had a secret meeting there with a former American ambassador. The screws were turned a little tighter in a subsequent meeting at which Hitler revealed his anxieties about the situation on the Eastern Front. Germany badly wanted extra troops. One way of securing them, Hitler suggested, was that Bulgaria should assist by stepping up its contribution to the occupation forces in Serbia and Greece.

As usual, Boris was studiously polite but noncommittal and was careful to point out that the German arms which had been promised to him were undelivered. Although the matter of further participation by Bulgarian forces remained open, the King's anxiety remained and in this he was not alone.

Mihail Antonescu, looking to the interests of Romania, made contact with the Bulgarian minister, Stoyan Petrov-Tchomakov, and revealed that he had even been talking to the Hungarians which, considering the bad relations between the two countries, was a fair indication of how desperate was the situation. However, the Bulgarian noted that Romania's ability to grasp realities remained limited. Antonescu stressed to him: 'We must look to the individual interests of our own countries. None of this, of course, will change our relationship with the Germans.'

Other moves by Bulgaria included an approach to the operational base of America's Office of Strategic Services (OSS), based in Switzerland, and to Britain. The former evinced little enthusiasm; the latter produced a sharp slap-down to the mere suggestion that there should be any contact with Bulgaria. An August, 1943, aide-memoire presented to the US Department of State declared:

His Majesty's Government cannot have any dealings with King Boris, whose fate they regard as a matter of indifference, any more than they can have with the present government. . . . Any attempt to give him support in the hope of detaching Bulgaria from the Axis would probably fail and we

16. SS Obergruppenführer und Generaloberst der Waffen-SS Karl Wolff. A former Adjutant to Himmler and Commander SS and Police in Italy from September, 1943. His clandestine negotiations with the Allies, behind Himmler's back, brought about the early surrender of all German forces in Italy on 2 May, 1945. Seen here at the post-war Nuremburg trials. *(Photo: Topham Picturepoint)*

17. Adolf Eichmann, Head of the Jewish office of the Gestapo and responsible for implementation of the 'Final Solution'. *(Photo: Topham Picturepoint)*

18. Otto Skorzeny. Brigadeführer der Waffen-SS, whose highly publicised commando exploits did much to raise German morale. *(Photo: Associated Press/Topham Picturepoint)*

19. Josip Broz, known as Marshal Tito. Commander of the left-wing guerrilla forces fighting the Germans in Yugoslavia and implacable enemy of General Mihailovich, leader of the right-wing Chetnik guerrillas. *(Photo: Associated Press/Topham Picturepoint)*

20. A dejected and dishevelled Mihailovich awaiting trial after his capture by Tito's men on 13 March, 1945. *(Photo: Topham Picturepoint)*

21. A subdued Mussolini surrounded by his German 'liberators" outside the *Campo Imperatore* Hotel on the Gran Sasso d'Italia. (*Centre rear:* Skorzeny and General Soleti of the *Carabinieri*, brought in on Skorzeny's advice to ensure Mussolini's protection from his Italian guards). (*Photo: Topham Picturepoint*)

22. The final ignominy. The bodies of Mussolini and his mistress, Claretta Petacci, hang head down beside that of one of another executed Fascist. 28 April, 1945. (*Photo: Topham Picturepoint*)

should ... merely compromise ourselves in the eyes of our Balkan allies and the world, besides laying up for ourselves incalculable difficulties in our plans for the future of South Eastern Europe.

On 3 August came an invitation from Hitler for a one-day conference at Rastenburg. Eleven days later, an aircraft, flown by Hitler's personal pilot, Hans Baur, picked up the King and General Nikoa Mihov, the War Minister. It was later alleged, but never confirmed by independent evidence, that, prior to leaving, Boris had telephoned his sister Evdokiya, declaring his belief that Hitler would finally demand troops for the Eastern Front. Furthermore, Boris allegedly made it clear that he would not only resist but would finalize plans with his father-in-law, Italy's King Victor Emmanuel, to quit the war.

If true, these allegations would give a convincingly sinister explanation to what subsequently occurred. The meeting between Boris, Hitler, Ribbentrop, Keitel and the Führer's Chief-of-Staff, Kurt Zeizler, had been tense. Hitler had indeed demanded that Bulgaria should join in the war with Russia, shouting down the King's argument that Bulgarian neutrality was in everyone's interests, including that of Germany.

Boris emerged from the conference a stricken man. Hans Baur in *Hitler's Pilot* wrote: 'On the return flight the weather was wonderful, but although the King, who had in the meantime, become an enthusiastic flyer, greatly enjoyed the flight, he was unable to conceal his depression. He had staked everything on 'our Führer', and now he was compelled to realize that his card had been trumped.'

On his return to Sofia, and in a sharp change of mood, the King made for his mountain retreats at Stark Bistritsa and Chamkoriya, during which he made a successful assault on the 9,596 foot Mount Musala, the highest mountain in the Balkans. Three days later, he was complaining in a telephone call to his sister of difficulty in breathing and felt pressure on his chest. A gall bladder attack was cited in the original diagnosis, but when there was no improvement, the government insisted on the best medical brains in Europe and these were flown in from Germany. A clamp down on all news from the royal palace succeeded only in fanning rumours.

Eventually, two terse press notices were issued. The first, admitted that the King was 'seriously ill'. The second referred to a condition which 'continues to be serious.' As it turned out, this was an understatement. There was fear of complications with the brain and a neurologist was called in from Berlin. Lung congestion persisted and there was a spread of inflammation, according to the official bulletin. At 4.22 on the afternoon of 28 August, 1943, King Boris died at the age of forty-nine.

When the news broke, there was a flood of speculation in the world's press which paraded a variety of conspiracy theories and murder plots, ranging from the possibly plausible to the plain bizarre.

In a news story of 18 September, *The Times* of London cited 'information from a reliable source' that Boris had been assassinated by a Macedonian terrorist, introduced into the Bulgarian secret police with the connivance of Peter Gabrovsky, the former Minister of the Interior who controlled the police and who took his orders from Himmler. It had been revealed that Boris had been in touch with an Allied diplomat in Istanbul, formerly stationed in Sofia, who acted as a conduit to the Russians, who let it be known that his overtures for peace would be successful.

One of the most melodramatic theories was provided by the former Minister to Sofia, Sir George Rendel, who in his book *The Sword and the Olive* suggested that the call Boris had allegedly made to his sister before his departure for Rastenburg had been tapped by the Germans. 'King Boris then arranged to return to Sofia by air, but, as was usual with him, since he was a bad air traveller, prepared to take a drug to help him on the journey. By Hitler's orders another drug was substituted, and the aircraft flew unusually high. King Boris stood the journey and, on landing, suffered a sharp and fatal heart attack.'

Members of his family were convinced that the King had been poisoned. Boris's Queen, Giovanna, whose memoirs were published in the Italian magazine *Oggi* during 1961, declared: 'My husband did not die a natural death. Prince Cyrill, on trial by the Communist regime in Bulgaria after the war, stated that: "My brother was eliminated because he refused to send troops to Greece".'

All theories raised more questions than they answered. With Boris gone, Bulgaria was bereft of the one figure with the diplomatic skills that just might have engineered his country's escape from the war. On 14 September, Filov, who became one of the three regents for the infant King Simeon, was replaced as Prime Minister by Dobri Bozhilov, a former Finance Minister who had been one of the prime movers behind a special tax imposed on Bulgarian Jews.

As for King Boris, his end, however caused, spelt not simply the death of one man, but the collapse of a dynasty.

- 14 -

THE ROT SETS IN

King Michael of Romania, virtually a prisoner in his own kingdom, produced at the dawn of 1944 a cruelly accurate assessment of Ion Antonescu, his dictator and tormentor: 'Once erect and brisk – now bent and round shouldered with care.' If Michael had but known it, that description equally fitted the physically deteriorating Adolf Hitler. After the arrogance bred of earlier successes, catastrophes had followed thick and fast for both men: the Soviet victory at Kursk, the defection of Italy, and, for Antonescu, the American bombing of the Ploiesti oilfields, as well as the ongoing bickering with Hungary.

Yet the Romanian Army, tired, ill-equipped, demoralized and in thrall to its German masters, remained on the Eastern Front. The Mountain Corps was engaged on anti-partisan operations under the German Crimea Command, while the Cavalry Corps on the Caucasus was subordinated to the German Group Wetzel.

The Russians kept on coming. After the capture of Gomel to the north of Kiev, in November, 1943, the Soviets had readied their forces for the recapture of Kiev itself, hoping for a rich haul of prisoners. The intention was to entrap enemy forces strung along the lower Dnieper. Hitler had already begged Antonescu to keep his surviving divisions at the Kuban bridgehead on the Caucasus, which the Führer had envisaged as a springboard for further forays against the Russians.

But Antonescu's problem was not so much manpower as the weaponry to make it effective. With characteristic bluntness, the Conductator made it clear that any contribution of military muscle by Romania would be out of the question unless the Cavalry Corps and Mountain Corps were re-equipped with tanks, howitzers and half-tracks.

Such provision was beyond the Germans before summer. The interim encouraged dangerous and mutinous introspection in the Romanian forces; some officers had become vocal in their disaffection, declaring openly that they would rather be campaigning in Transylvania.

Nor was the Caucasus Hitler's only worry. The threat to the Crimea peninsula nagged. The Wehrmacht's 17th Army, buttressed by German naval units and the Luftwaffe, was keeping the lid on Soviet pressure; the Russians were prevented by the presence of the Germans from using the area as a springboard for landings in Romania and Bulgaria. That old spectre – the possible destruction of the Romanian oil fields – returned to dog the Führer. He reasoned that if the Crimea was evacuated and German control of the Black Sea relinquished, hitherto neutral Turkey would inevitably be driven into the Allied camp. In fact, Romania's newly appointed Ambassador to Turkey, Alexandru Cretzianu, was instructed by Mihai Antonescu to act as main intermediary with the Western Allies.

But the hard-pressed, demoralized Romanians clinging on in the Caucasus, knew nothing of this. All they did know was that the Soviets had remained the enemy. Early in February, the Soviet 47th Army's Operation SEA had launched a direct assault against Group Wetzel and on Novorossiysk, which lay to the west of the Kuban in the north-east corner of the Black Sea coast. It had been accompanied by a major seaborne landing in its rear at Ozereika and a diversionary landing at Stanichka, just south of Novorossiysk.

Such a foray was at first exhilarating for the Red Army. The Russians had wilted under the triumphant romp of the Wehrmacht through the Kuban and the Caucasus. But then a bridgehead had been established at Ozereika, after a fierce naval bombardment by two cruisers and three destroyers and against determined resistance from the Romanian 38th Infantry regiment. It had proved a puny affair and the bridgehead was annihilated within three days by the 10th Division and German reinforcements. At Stanichka, German coastal artillery had failed to get the Russians in its sights and they pressed their advantage. The roar of massed Soviet guns crashed across the bay at Novorossiysk. Forces that had failed to press the advantage at Ozereika were switched to this new theatre. Around 17,000 Russians poured ashore and the reinforcements via the bay were unstoppable.

It was not until July that the armour promised to the Romanians arrived. Much of it was below standard; the cream had already been sold to the Hungarians. On 10 September, Red Army forces began the assault that would clear the Kuban bridgehead finally. Six days later, Novorossiysk was theirs and the agonized phased withdrawal from the beachhead to the Crimea began.

But there was no let up there, certainly not for the 4/24th Romanian Division, locked in front line combat around Melitopol to the north east of the Crimea peninsula, eventually bundled across the Lower Dnieper, along with the German XLIV Corps.

Two thirds of the Division's combat strength bled on the arid, sand-swept space of the Nogay Steppe, between Zaporozhe, lying to the north of Melitopol, the Sea of Azov and the Dnieper estuary where the 4th Ukrainian Front (Army Group) of Colonel-General Feodor Tolbukhin, a former commander at Stalingrad and a survivor from the old Bolshevik days of the Russian civil war, had launched his attack on the German 6th Army.

Generaloberst Erwin Jaenicke, faced by overwhelming numbers and the unreliability of the Romanian forces, pressed for withdrawal by sea. Support came from his superiors, Generalfeldmarschall Ewald Kleist and General Kurt Zeitzler. Support, too, from Antonescu, who pointed out that the Soviet landings made at Kersch on the east of the increasingly isolated peninsula made any question of holding the sector increasingly impractical. The Führer was having none of it and wrote to Antonescu on 29 November: 'The Red Army and Navy lack the resources to mount a successful conquest of the Crimea.' Hitler went further. He pledged to defend the Crimea by every possible means with a counter-offensive across the Dnieper which would re-establish land links with the peninsula.

Antonescu countered with what he saw as the inevitability of Russian forces sweeping on into the Ukraine. Hitler's riposte was to declare that by June the Ukraine could be recaptured but that would only be possible if the Crimea was held in the meantime. The Führer, sensing that Antonescu was wavering, pressed the advantage with a concession: it might be possible to evacuate the Crimea in part, while marginally building up Romanian strength there. Such a concession was vital: the German divisions could not have held the peninsula beyond a matter of months. Not for the first time, Hitler's mesmeric powers presaged disaster. Early in April came the fall of the main supply port of Odessa, followed within weeks by the Russian artillery muscle on the Perekop Line, straddling the narrow strip at the Crimean peninsula's neck. Second Guards and 51st Armies were released by Tolbukhin. Outflanked, the 10th Romanian Division crumpled, abandoning the Perekop position.

General Andrei Yeremenko, Commander of the Special Baltic Front, broke out of his bridgehead, finally taking Kersch in a head-on dash for Sevastopol, whose capture two years earlier had been one of Manstein's principal triumphs. Now it was being defended by five German regiments with artillery salvaged from a single corps; the Romanian Mountain Corps was the sole Axis formation holding fast. For Yeremenko, there was nothing between Kersch and Sevastopol. For the Germans there was no prospect but evacuation. Jaenicke was unwise enough to press the truth on Hitler, protesting at the Führer's mantra: 'Defend to the last man.' The result was only too predictable: Jaenicke was dismissed.

It made no difference. The Red Army ruled the skies and three armies faced the Germans and the Romanians – half a million men with around 600 tanks. The 51st and Independent Coastal Armies of the Red Army attacked Sapun Heights, a key position south of Sevastapol. While the 51st Army came from the east, Yeremenko struck from the south. On 8 May, Sevastapol had fallen and Hitler had at last given leave to withdraw. Romanian divisions that had not already been mauled at Stalingrad and Odessa were in headlong retreat, except for the Mountain Corps. But now there was no option beyond withdrawal.

There were vital roles for Romania's Air Force and Navy. With the Luftwaffe, Air Force Headquarters set up an air bridge between Odessa, terminal of the coastal convoy route to Sevastapol, and the Crimea. It would be ready to evacuate at least 3,000 wounded ahead of the loss of the peninsula and, indeed, had been carrying out an evacuation role since the previous October, when the Soviet advance to the mouth of the Dnieper had cut off seven Romanian and five German divisions. Romanian gunboats and torpedo boats and the warship *Admiral Murgescu* had been harassed by merciless artillery, air and submarine attacks. A total of 24,855 Romanian and German troops embarked in twenty-five convoys without serious loss.

Nicolae Mujicicov, a midshipman on the destroyer *Regele Ferdinand*, which left Constanta for Sevastapol on 9 May, recounted:

> Towards the middle of the night of 10/11 May, we found ourselves off the Chersones Peninsula, the embarkation point for our troops. The sea was calm. . . . Muffled sounds reached us from the land, and the flash of explosions and the paths of tracer and flares where our troops were clinging to life in the last defence line. . . . We were immediately caught by some powerful, land-based searchlights. We repeatedly managed to escape the beams, but became a target for artillery fire . . .
>
> Once dawn broke on 11 May, Soviet aircraft began to attack. Wave after wave followed each other in quick succession. Formations of from ten to fifteen assault planes were interspersed with others of medium bombers or torpedo planes. Between 0600 and 1030 our destroyers, being the most prestigious target, came under attack about thirty-three times in rapid succession. The most serious of these came from the assault planes, which dived in with all their 20 mm cannons and machine guns blazing, dropping bombs of various sizes, often with delayed action fuses, and anti-personnel grenades. The cannons and machine guns of the assault aircraft peppered the sides and superstructure and killed and wounded many of the crew. One volley hit our First Officer, Tiberiu Sirbum, and Lieutenant Mircea Voda at the submarine detection apparatus. Newly appointed Midshipman Alexandru Cristodorescu was mortally wounded and died in my arms. One

bomb of considerable size hit the port stern about 1.5 metres below the waterline, ending up in an oil tank. . . .

Each attack came in from one side only and concentrated particularly on the middle of the vessel, causing especially heavy losses among our exposed ant-aircraft gunners there, who were immediately replaced by others from the unengaged side. . . .

Midshipman Mujicicov recorded that the most serious damage came from a large bomb that did not explode but punched a hole below the water line with the loss of a quantity of fuel oil, some of which was retrieved from the damaged tank with canvas buckets. To continue was out of the question; the commander, with radio reception down, decided to withdraw the mission.

The destroyer arrived back off Constanta at 1205 on 12 May, entering through the southern gap in the mine barrages. A Soviet submarine was lurking there, but nothing befell us. At 0200 we were met by a tug at the port entrance. It was not a moment too soon – the turbines had finally given out through lack of fuel! We had not eaten or slept properly for some two days. Our losses were 11 dead and 28 wounded among the crew. . . . That afternoon, at 1700, Antonescu himself boarded the *Regele Ferdinand*, which was listing heavily to port and personally congratulated the crew . . .

*   *   *

By now, the Red Army had cut through the Germans and into Northern Bukovina – a Soviet advance which had stirred Hungary to attempt leaving the war. Romania's overtures to the Western Allies were well advanced, as Hitler well knew. Nevertheless, he could not afford to turn on his wavering ally, knowing that if Romania was occupied by Nazi forces the outcome could only be a fierce guerrilla war within the country.

As for Antonescu, his loyalties were divided. His hatred of the Bolsheviks was potent, but at the same time contacts within the Allied camp had made it clear that Romania would be expected to turn its guns on the Germans, a course that Antonescu, who had his own code of honour, was reluctant to adopt.

Such ambivalence bred fresh suspicion in the Führer, but suspicion had become part of the very air he breathed at the Wolfschanze since on 20 July he had narrowly survived an assassination bid by his own officers. Furthermore, the suspicion was infectious. Before he set out on what was to be his eleventh – and, as it turned out, final – meeting with Hitler on

125

5–6 August, Antonescu stiffened his forces in Bucharest, in case there was a German-inspired coup.

The interview between the two dictators could scarcely be described as cordial. One of Antonescu's main preoccupations was the situation on the Bessarabian front, the area he had hoped to recover at the time he had entered the war. Could Hitler hold it now? Hitler assured him he could to which Antonescu made the blunt rejoinder that such an assurance was of dubious value, judging by the fate of the Crimea and the Ukraine.

The Führer's reaction was as characteristic as it was predictable. That, he declared, had been the fault of Manstein and of Kleist, both by this time dismissed. There was probably no other man alive who would have dared utter Antonescu's next words to the Führer: 'I think the responsibility lies elsewhere.' As the discussion wore on, the reality emerged plain and stark: there could be no absolute guarantee of the Bessarabian front nor air defence against the Western Allies.

Indeed, *The Times* of London of 12 November, 1943, had reported panic among the population of Bessarabia at the rapid advance of the Soviet forces.

> Specially fearful are those newly settled in the Bessarabian districts. Farms stand abandoned in Romania proper. Trains are stormed at every station. Thousands who find it impossible to obtain standing room in them have taken to the roads. Clerks, factory workers and others struggle along beside herds of cattle and peasants' carts.

Crowds of some 30,000 had besieged the Swiss consulates especially in Bucharest, seeking visas to enter Switzerland.

If relations had been cool at the onset of that final meeting, they became positively arctic. Hitler had already declared to the Conductator that he no longer considered Hungary's occupation of North Transylvania valid under the Vienna Awards; a meaningless concession, as it now turned out.

The Führer, steadfastly refusing to accept any personal responsibility, then attacked Romania for its lack of economic co-operation. For Antonescu, who had put his country at considerable risk for Nazi Germany, this was an intolerable slight. Time and again he had given in to the Führer's wheedling and persuasion that his country should identify itself ever closer with Nazi Germany.

At Germany's behest, around 45,000 Romanians, including female *Volksdeutsche* volunteers and conscripted teenage boys, had been sucked into the SS and numbers were steadily increasing. But there was no build-up of enthusiasm among the ranks of the Romanian Army. On the contrary, there was little stomach left for the war and some of the country's senior figures, backed by King Michael, were looking at ways of severing their links with Nazi Germany. The portents of defeat had long been in place.

Hungary, as Romania's traditional enemy, had progressively trimmed her sails towards the Allies. A comparison of the Hungarian and Romanian press had proved instructive over the last few months: Budapest newspapers began carrying Winston Churchill's speeches in full, whereas in Bucharest the Axis line was rigidly followed. The attitude of Bulgaria, the next door neighbour, had appeared to be softening towards the Russians while in the south, Yugoslavia had never ceased to be a hotbed of resistance.

There was no serious movement for assassination of Antonescu, as there had been for Hitler back in July. Any hint of that would have been to invite immediate occupation and attendant repression. Instead, there evolved the National Democratic Bloc under Michael and royalist army officers, headed by General Constantin Sanatescu, Head of the King's Military Household, who, along with others, began plotting a democratic path out of the war.

Romania's immolation on the field of battle continued, typically at Jassy on 20 August from where the Soviets intended to knife through to Bucharest and Ploiesti. Here a massive ten-hour artillery barrage pulverised the 5th Infantry Division's forward defences. The Soviet 27th Army followed up with lines of tanks and assault guns and the Division was rapidly annihilated. It was one defeat among many but it helped to push capitulation forward. The fighting was still on – indeed at least sixteen German divisions were in the country when, on 23 August, the King went on the radio with his announcement:

Romanians! In the difficult hour of our country I have decided for the salvation of the Fatherland, on the immediate cessation of hostilities and I call upon a Government of National Union to fulfil the determined will of the country to conclude peace with the United Nations. Romania has accepted an armistice offered by the Soviet Union, Great Britain and the USA. From this moment all hostilities against the Soviet armies and the state of war with Great Britain and the US will cease. I receive with confidence the appeal of these nations. The United Nations guarantee the independence of Romania. They have recognised the injustice of the Diktat of Vienna, under which Transylvania was torn from us.

Anyone who opposes the decision we have taken, and who takes justice into his own hands, is an enemy of our nation. I order the Army and the whole nation to fight with all means, and at the cost of any sacrifice, against him. All Romanians must rally round the Throne and the Government. He who does not assist the Government, and resists the will of the nation, is a traitor to the country. At the side of the Allied armies, and with their help, we will cross the frontiers unjustly imposed upon us at Vienna.

At the side of the Allied armies . . . Romania had not just surrendered but had changed sides.

Outwardly, the young King had appeared impotent to act, helpless before the overbearing Antonescu who treated him as a child. But in fact the slowly maturing Michael had planned his coup in conjunction with the opposition parties, including Communists and Socialists. In an interview for the British magazine *The Spectator* in June, 1997, with the writer Simon Sebag-Montefiore, the former King recalled his key encounter with Antonescu which had been carefully prepared with General Sanetescu:

> On 23 August, 1944, I summoned Antonescu and he arrived . . . late as usual. I said he must make an armistice at once. He flatly refused to do so without Hitler's permission, so I nodded at the head of my Military Household and I told Antonescu, 'If you don't want to do it, let somebody else!' Antonescu became furious: 'I am not leaving the country in the hands of a child!' So I spoke the agreed sign: 'There is nothing else for me to do.' At which three NCOs and a captain burst in and led him up to the King's safe where my father used to keep his stamp collection. I locked him there. Then we formed a new government.

Although many were still taken by surprise at the switch in sides, German suspicions had begun to mount – not least when the telephones at their headquarters in Bucharest were disconnected. Now the key figure of the hour was, according to witnesses, the overbearing Baron Manfred von Killinger, the Ambassador to Bucharest who lost no time to reaching the palace to hector the young King over his defection. It was a role to which Killinger was well suited. Berliner Inga Haag, wife of a member of the joint military German-Italian Commission to both Romania and Hungary during the reign of the Axis, met Killinger at this time and today recalls: 'He was an ardent Nazi, an aristocrat who had donned a Sturm Abteilung uniform – the Brown Shirts – during the early days of the Nazi movement. He was a thoroughly unpleasant individual of decidedly limited intelligence.'

Despite Killinger's ineffectual blustering, the King stood firm, but at the same time guaranteeing that German troops evacuating the country would not be attacked.

As might have been expected, Hitler's reaction to the new government was to release the full force of his spite and fury with a concerted attack on Bucharest. But Generalleutnant Alfred Gerstenberg's assault on the Romanian capital was soon stalled. Enter the Brandenburg Division, that hitherto reliable standby in a major crisis. As we have already seen, the Brandenburgs had expanded from Company, through Battalion to Divisional status. In addition a number of specialist units had been formed, including the Parachute Battalion, raised the previous February. Mastermind of the Brandenburger's latest adventure, was one of the Third Reich's most colourful personalities, a man Hitler called 'my favourite Commando.'

Like many of those who sought power with the SS, Otto Skorzeny was an early Austrian member of the Nazi Party, who in 1943 had been assigned to the RSHA under Walter Schellenberg, Chief of Amt IVE responsible for counter espionage. Skorzeny's new responsibility was Parachute Battalion 500 of the Brandenburgers, whose men were to seize three airfields, immobilize the aircraft there and fight their way into Bucharest.

The result does not figure in the annals of Brandenburg glory; the coup was too far advanced for that. The full armed strength of Romanian paratroopers and FARR security echelons was unleashed on the Brandenburgers, who were either mown down or obliged to surrender.

By then there were other priorities: not least the whereabouts of Antonescu. Skorzeny was notorious for melodramatics, the grand gesture. The former Conductator, he decided, must be kidnapped. Plans were laid for Antonescu to be seized by special forces operating from Bulgaria. But the coup leaders, fearful that their prize might be seized by those still loyal, had handed him over to the Red Army who lost no time in spiriting him to Moscow.

For the moment – and only for the moment – Skorzeny was out of the limelight. In his place stood Artur Phelps, a former general in the Romanian Mountain Corps who in 1940 had been enlisted by the head of the Romanian *Volksdeutsche*, Andreas Schmidt, to poach would-be *Volksdeutsche* from the Romanian Army. The industrious Phelps's success enabled the establishment of the 7th SS Mountain Division, which went on to carve a particularly brutal name for itself in Yugoslavia.

Phelps was ordered to take command of all paramilitary organizations of the *Volksdeutsche* in southern Transylvania. But even his energy could not help. There were no eager recruits now; those that could be found either surrendered willingly enough to the Romanians or hastily melted away.

The last major pocket of resistance was the Ploiesti oilfields which the Germans hammered ceaselessly and fruitlessly. Here Soviet troops were able to steal a march, by arriving just ahead of the Romanians. By 30 August, only a single constricted pocket, some seven miles to the north of Ploiesti was still in German hands. When that was lost, the threat to Bucharest from the north had been removed; Soviet and Romanian forces could now make for Transylvania.

*   *   *

Viewed at its close, 1944 was a year that accorded Joseph Stalin some grim satisfaction. It had opened, on 13 January, with the final offensive to relieve Leningrad. Two weeks later, streams of red, white and blue rockets signified the city's liberation after 900 days; deaths, through disease and starvation, have been put at 1.5 million local inhabitants and servicemen. But the Red Flag flew with pride once again. Accompanying events had some depressingly familiar features. Generalfeldmarschall George Kuchler, commanding Army Group North, had advocated withdrawal and then been forced into it by the weight of the Soviet advance. Predictably, he was sacked. His replacement was the fiery Generalfeldmarschall Walther Model, the so-called 'Führer's fireman' because Hitler switched him to all the battle fronts in turn, in a vain attempt to stem the Russian tide. But it was too late. Model clung on for a month and then withdrew. Leningrad could not be held.

And, of course, Romania was far from being the Führer's only nightmare.

– 15 –

SKORZENY

Salzburg had become a ghost town with cafés and bars closed, streets and sidewalks deserted. The silence was shattered with the rumbling convoys of trucks with their armed, field-grey SS troops, keeping open the path to the ancient castle of Klessheim. Here Hitler's most senior advisers, Keitel, Jodl and Himmler, gathered for a crisis meeting on 18 March, 1944.

Everywhere, battlefronts were shuddering under the march of the enemies of the Reich, unstoppable in their march to the Rhineland border, to the very threshold of East Prussia. Operation OVERLORD, the invasion of Europe was only months away. Parts of Italy had been liberated. Marshal Tito in Yugoslavia had his ever-growing force of Partisans and was receiving British supplies by sea. There was also Partisan incursion into Croatia while Soviet forces coursed towards the Bulgarian border. In Slovakia, discontent seethed; dissidents, through the underground Czechoslovak Communist Party, were in touch with Moscow.

Yet Hitler was wrapped in a cocoon of delusion. His reaction to the slightest breath of criticism was to scream '*Feigling!*' (Coward!). Who but a coward could fail to recognize the great opportunities within the grasp of Germany? The Führer urged: 'One more bold counter-offensive. That's all that's needed.'

Ever a man of obsessions, all his hatreds and suspicions were now focused on Hungary. And he had good reason. As with Hungary's detested neighbour Romania, loyalties were strained. The war in Russia had proved a disaster for the Hungarians. At the end of 1942, their troops near Vorenezh had suffered such severe manpower and equipment short-ages that the average battalion had been required to hold a front 3.5 kilometres long. The annihilation of the 2nd Hungarian Army on the Don had cost 148,000 casualties.

From now on, it was a question of too little too late. Hitler had delayed in plugging the Romanian-held portions of Transylvania into which the Hungarians could have marched, bolstered with German muscle. As it was, the Russians had reached the Iron Gates, the centre to the Hungarian plain. In the absence of any opposition, the Soviet forces burst into the Carpathian mountain girdle barring the way to central Europe. General Miklos-Dalnoki, commanding the woefully under-equipped 1st Hungarian Army, battled his way to Timisoara and Arad in a desperate bid to gain the mountain passes. But the cause was hopeless. The race to the Carpathians had been lost. Horthy decided on peace with the Russians. Indeed, cautious approaches through the Vatican and through intermediaries in Stockholm, had dated from the winter of 1943.

In February, Ribbentrop had delivered another bombshell to Hitler, warning the Führer that the administration of Miklos Kallay in Hungary was in touch with the Allies.

Hitler had barely had time to digest this when he was studying a letter from Horthy himself, asking for nine light Hungarian divisions to be returned home. The Führer next learnt that orders had been given for the sabotage of German military freight trains passing through Hungary intended for the armies of Manstein and Kleist. Clearly, Hungary had progressed from being merely obstructive to downright dangerous.

Hitler reckoned nonetheless that he still needed Hungary as the supplier of grain, oil and bauxite. He had toyed at first with the idea of garrisoning Budapest with Romanian and Slovak troops but was persuaded that this might only lead to unproductive squabbling among the two Axis partners.

The final plan, concocted by the Abwehr, was to invite the seventy-six year-old Regent of Hungary to Klessheim for discussions on how to resolve current military problems. Horthy, Hitler reasoned, would incur intense suspicion at home if he refused a meeting. He would surely arrive with some of his top military advisers; Hungary's defences would thus be weakened severely, making a planned invasion by German troops that much easier.

Horthy's acceptance was the cue for Hitler, in consultation with Jodl, Ribbentrop and Himmler, to refine Operation MARGARETHE, which had been mooted as early as the previous September for the occupation of both Hungary and Romania.

The Hungarian delegation arriving at Salzburg on 18 March was received with full diplomatic courtesies. Horthy remained suspicious; he might well have been even more so had he known that the conference room bristled with microphones and tape recorders; Hitler was determined that the Regent would not wriggle out of any undertakings he might give.

The contrived mood of informality was short-lived. Horthy's behaviour, ranted the Nazi leader, was intolerable, particularly after what had occurred in Italy. There had been sabotage and collaboration and the blame was clearly shared with the Hungarian premier, Miklos Kallay, who must be dismissed. Germany must have its own government in Hungary. Hitler piled threat upon threat until Horthy decided that he could face no more. He retorted: 'If everything has been decided, my presence is no longer necessary.'

As he prepared to leave, there was a touch of pure theatre. As if on cue, the air raid sirens of Klessheim sounded their combined wail. Enemy action, proclaimed Hitler, was imminent. All telephone links with the outside world had been cut, and, of course, it would be quite impossible for the Hungarian delegation to leave. The party was invited to stay for lunch. The charade worked; Hitler made it clear to Horthy that the invasion was under way and that it was too late to draw back.

The Regent caved in. It was nine in the evening before Horthy was able to regain his train. He and those who had come with him left behind everything that Hitler had demanded. A pro-German government would be appointed; Hungarian troops would be subservient to the Wehrmacht.

Even before he left Austria, Horthy was left in no doubt as to what this meant for his country. Aboard the train with him was the Chief of Police Otto Winckelmann and Dr Edmund Veesenmayer, already carrying the title of Special Envoy for Hungary. A creature both of the Foreign Office and the Abwehr, Veesenmayer had a bizarre history. Back in 1940, he had strutted with the title of Plenipotentiary for Ireland which had involved concocting schemes for the Irish Republican Army (IRA) to be pressed into service with an attack on England. Veesenmayer was of particular interest to Himmler, however, as the author of a report from Belgrade which had called for the deportation of Serbian Jews. Such dedication and expertise, the Reichsführer-SS believed, should be harnessed to the new developments in Hungary. On arrival at the station at Budapest, Horthy encountered a cruelly cynical touch: he was greeted by a German guard of honour.

For Himmler here was also an opportunity for yet further extension of power. A month before the invasion, the Reichsführer-SS sent Werner Lorenz to Budapest with the remit to supply yet another round-up of 'volunteers' for the SS, as well as making preliminary arrangements for the evacuation of Germans in Hungary, should the advance of the Red Army make it necessary.

The SS presence grew steadily more menacing. Press reports from Istanbul were soon recording a ruthless campaign against the Jews, who were dragged handcuffed from their homes and offices, loaded like cattle in trucks to be driven off to an unknown destination. The enforced separation of Jewish families brought with it hundreds of suicides. The furnishings of one of the largest synagogues in Budapest were tossed into the street, the interior converted into stables for the Wehrmacht. Armed patrols of SS roamed the streets unimpeded.

Wehrmacht motor columns roared into Budapest from Vienna. Surrounding airports were seized. As Hitler had insisted, Kallay was dismissed and Germany was granted control of the Hungarian economy and communications system, together with rights of free movement for the Wehrmacht. Budapest newspapers were heavily censored; items from Stockholm, Lisbon and other neutral capitals vanished. Then came the turn of the political parties of the Left. A decree was issued by the Minister of the Interior which dissolved the parties of Social Democrats, the Independent Smallholders and the Peasant Union.

As for Horthy, still holding his position but even more Hitler's creature, there was an ominous silence in the first ten days of German occupation; an expected radio broadcast by the Regent was not forthcoming. In fact, Horthy was biding his time, superficially docile to the occupiers but all the time in touch with Moscow, whose forces moved ever closer. On 15 October, 1944, he struck, dismissing the pro-German cabinet, later announcing that he had signed an armistice with Russia.

Hitler reasoned that drastic measures were clearly needed. In fact, gangster methods. Re-enter Otto Skorzeny. The lanky, sabre-scarred Austrian already had an impressive track record when it came to the unorthodox. His abortive attempt to kidnap Antonescu was comfortably dwarfed by an earlier, infinitely more colourful escapade that had followed in the wake of Mussolini's overthrow the previous July.

The Duce had been spirited out of Rome by order of the Badoglio government and had been moved frequently from one prison to another. The authorities had anticipated an attempt at rescue by Hitler who had indeed envisaged a swift, daring initiative. He had declared: 'I will never permit my friend Mussolini to be handed over to the Allies.' The Führer's plan had been to snatch the former Duce from the Campo Imperatore Hotel where he was being held, atop the Gran Sasso d'Italia, the highest range in the Abruzzi Apennines which could only be reached by funicular railway. It had been work for a ruthless and resourceful troubleshooter. Hitler had consulted Himmler on a likely candidate; the Reichsführer-SS had come up with 'Scarface' Skorzeny.

Skorzeny has always been credited with the success of that brilliant operation. It was, in truth, a Wehrmacht job, planned and controlled by General Kurt Student, the head of the airborne forces. The troops involved were from the 1st Battalion of the 7th Fallschirmjäger Regiment, commanded by Major Mors. No 1 Company, commanded by Oberleutnant Freiherr von Berlepsch, was tasked to fly in in gliders and make the snatch. Because of the good work done by the SS in locating Mussolini, Student agreed that Skorzeny, and fifteen Waffen-SS men from the Special Purposes Regiment Oranienburg, might accompany the glider-borne company.

Although he had no official standing in the operation, true to form, Skorzeny pushed himself into the room where Mussolini had been found and then begged Hauptmann Gerlach, the pilot of the light aircraft which was to take the former Duce on the first stage of his journey to Hitler's headquarters at Rastenburg, to allow him to accompany Mussolini. Gerlach agreed with great reluctance. The little aeroplane was already overloaded but there was no time to be lost in argument. In the event, Skorzeny's extra weight very nearly proved fatal. With great skill, Gerlach launched the Fieseler Storch off the edge of the plateau and just got it airborne, though seriously damaging the undercarriage in the process.

To Student's fury, little mention was made of the key role of the Fallschirmjäger in the wave of propaganda which followed – the credit went to Skorzeny and the Waffen-SS.

The Duce, a pale unshaven figure in a crumpled blue suit, had been delivered intact to Hitler's headquarters at Rastenburg.

Skorzeny was clearly a man for a tight corner. In September, 1944, he was given a fresh assignment. There came the summons to the Wolfsschanze; Skorzeny was instructed to join forces with Winckelmann, the police chief, and with Otto Friessner, the commander of the German front, and restore order in Budapest.

No one needed to spell out to Skorzeny the crisis facing Germany. The map table at the Wolfsschanze told him everything. The flags stuck there were Russian, not German, clustered like flies beside the horseshoe contours denoting Germany's eastern border and each representing a Russian army. One hundred and twenty enemy divisions were strung along the Carpathians; they could surge in a vast tidal wave over the Danubian plain. The Germans would be trounced.

Skorzeny was jerked out of his preoccupations by Hitler thrusting into his hands the large crackling sheet of Third Reich official stationery bearing the Swastika in gilt relief in the left hand corner and the legend 'Führer and Chancellor of the Reich.' Skorzeny made out in Hitler's lurching spidery hand:

Sturmbannführer Skorzeny of the Reserve Corps has been charged directly by myself to execute personal and confidential orders of the highest importance. I request all military and civilian services to bring all possible help to Sturmbannführer Skorzeny and to comply with all his wishes.

The personal and confidential orders were spelt out starkly: Horthy was to be snatched from the Burgberg – Castle Hill – in the heart of Budapest and his government overturned. Since the Regent was heavily guarded, the castle would have to be taken by storm. Hitler assured Skorzeny that he would be supplied with the necessary back-up.

Only when he had been bustled out of the Wolfsschanze, did Skorzeny have a chance to ponder his task; snatching Mussolini from the Grand Sasso had been perilous enough, but at least his quarry on that occasion had been a largely discredited individual in failing health surrounded by troops of dubious loyalty. The Hungarian Regent, on the other hand, was a powerful head of state, heavily guarded in a comfortable government building on the Burgberg, known as the Citadel.

It scarcely improved matters that, soon after Skorzeny arrived in Budapest, posing as Dr Solar Wolff, representative of a Cologne firm of tool-makers, he encountered SS-Obergruppenführer Erich von dem Bach-Zelewski, Himmler's Chief of Partisan Warfare, considered by Hitler to be a worthy aide to Skorzeny in the proposed Horthy kidnapping.

The Obergruppenführer's pride was a giant 650 mm mortar with which he was eager 'to blow the Citadel off the hill.' Skorzeny realized swiftly that, had such a crude tactic been adopted, desertions by the Hungarian Army would surely have been unstoppable. In addition, the SS divisions would be at the mercy of the approaching Russian armies. Skorzeny was emphatic: the mortar could only be used as a last resort.

Certainly, there was call for desperate measures. Along with the advance of the Red Army, Colonel General Nadai, a representative of the Hungarian government, had flown to Naples, seeking a meeting with the British and American representatives. The meeting, as it turned out, proved abortive. But there was no stopping the Hungarians. A few days later, a delegation went to Moscow to see if an accommodation with Stalin was possible.

There were grounds for supposing it was. A letter sent to General Bela Miklos, one of Hungary's most respected military leaders, fell into Skorzeny's hands. It urged Miklos:

Abandon the Germans! Join with the Soviet Union in attacking the Wehrmacht. The defeat of Nazi Germany, militarily and politically, is only a matter of time. Every other satellite except Hungary has already broken with Hitler.

From the military theatre the news continued grim, notably from the South-Eastern Front. Faith that had been placed in thirty Romanian and

Bulgarian divisions proved misplaced. They turned against Germany. If the Hungarians followed suit, then the front would surely collapse.

On the surface, everything in Budapest appeared normal; military loyalty seemed stuck fast. The capital was still noisy with German rolling stock trundling up to the Carpathians to feed the divisions. Hungarians and Germans continued to meet daily on the Burgberg. The German Embassy occupied a place of honour among the government palaces. But the reality was that there was clearly a need for a fast and successful outcome of the Führer's remit. But how?

Skorzeny told his American biographer, Glenn Infield, after the war that his plans crystallised when meeting Edmund Veesenmayer who remarked on the role being played by Horthy's dark, wilful, handsome son, Miki. The younger Horthy was in his thirties and widely regarded as a playboy, leaping nimbly between the bars and beds of high-society in Budapest. It was generally accepted that he was a political innocent; German Intelligence had gleaned that he was persuaded that his father's dynasty would be safe in the Russian embrace. Furthermore, hints were dropped that emissaries of Josip Tito would be pleased to meet him and act as negotiators to bring this about.

A bogus meeting with these emissaries was set for Sunday, 18 October. The plan – codenamed with twisted humour MICKEY MOUSE – called for the seizure of Miki. This posed the interesting question: if the son were in Third Reich hands, would Admiral Horthy give up his plans to abandon Hitler, if it meant getting his son back safely? It was considered worth a try.

Skorzeny arranged for two of his officers to rent an apartment in the building where the 'meeting' was to be held. Miki was duly contacted and the 'meeting' set up. The plan was that a group of German Commandos, in the guise of Wehrmacht uniformed *Feldgendarmerien* (Military Police), would be positioned nearby and that, once Miki was safely inside the apartment block, they would rush the building and spirit him away. However, Skorzeny had not bargained for a contingent of Hungarian troops lurking in a truck from which they had the building under observation. As soon as the Commandos rushed the block, the Hungarians opened fire. From the vantage point of a broken down Mercedes, not far away, a certain Dr Solar Wolff, who had been on the way to a perfectly innocuous dinner engagement, watched the proceedings, only ducking down when the bullets pierced the doors and shattered the windscreen of the car.

All at once, there appeared to be Hungarian troops everywhere. The chances of the Germans being able to quit the apartment building with their quarry unscathed lessened by the minute. At that point, the solid, law-abiding Dr Wolff ceased to exist.

Skorzeny stood up, conscious that one of his comrades was lying next to him. He snatched a grenade from the man, hurled it towards the Hungarians and yelled: 'Don't let them get into the open.' The solid marble portal of the building crashed, slicing into the Hungarians. When the chaos had cleared, a group of prisoners was ushered downstairs. Miki Horthy, who had arrived in the firm belief that he was meeting Tito's men, was among them.

What happened then was Nazi gangsterism at its crudest. The Regent's son was slugged unconscious, rolled into a carpet and rushed to the airport. His destination was Mauthausen concentration camp near Linz in Austria and eventually Dachau in Bavaria.

The initiative was now seized eagerly by two men. The task of bringing pressure on Horthy was entrusted to Edmund Veesenmayer who joined forces with Rudolf Rahn, another of Hitler's special envoys to Budapest.

Armed with the news of the successful kidnapping of Miki, Rahn planned to confront the Regent. He was outsmarted. Horthy had already broadcast the news of his surrender, declaring:

It is clear today that Germany has lost the war. . . . Hungary has accordingly concluded a preliminary armistice with Russia and will cease all hostilities against her. I have issued the corresponding orders to the military command.

The Regent, however, was prepared to display some conciliation to his former ally; at least up to a point. He offered to suspend the capitulation for a few days so that four German divisions could withdraw from Budapest. In fact, senior Hungarian generals had already looked the other way; two of them, Miklos Bela and Varos Dalnoki, had lost little time in deserting to the Russians.

It was a clue for the tireless Bach-Zelewski to plead the case once again for his beloved mortar. It should be hurled at Horthy's defences at the Citadel on the Burgberg without further delay. But Skorzeny, despite his usual instinct to think on his feet, opted for persuasion. The Regent was told that if he resigned and transferred power legally to Ferenc Szalasi, the Hungarian Fascist leader, who was waiting in the wings, and agreed to go into exile, Miki would be returned to him and he would be given refuge in Austria. If he refused, then the Citadel on the Burgberg, which had been cut off from the town by Hungarian troops and mined, would be attacked and flattened.

Wehrmacht hardware, which included Tiger tanks, carrying troops from the Maria Theresa cavalry division, bolstered by forces of a parachute division and the Jagdverbande Mitte (formerly Jägerbataillion), roared towards the castle as part of Operation PANZERFAUST.

However, throughout the night, telephone communication had been maintained between a desperately weary Horthy and the German Embassy; the Regent gave in and signified his approval of the premiership of Szalasi. By then the armoured force had been on the road for half an hour. There was some confusion; not all the Hungarian troops had received the orders that they were not to oppose the Germans. But it took little effort to break down what resistance there was.

Horthy's exit from Germany, accompanied by Skorzeny, was pathetic. Before he left, he begged Rudolf Rahn to spare the life of his son. Skorzeny, according to his own account, treated the former Regent with gentle courtesy. He was, Skorzeny explained, to be sent under safe conduct with 'guest of honour' status to Hirschberg Castle in Bavaria. With just a hint of steel, the SS man volunteered the information that Hirschberg was a very secure castle indeed.

Horthy, on his last drive through Budapest, received scarcely a sign of recognition. He left behind him a German puppet government in the hands of a fanatical anti-Semite. Persecution and deportation of the Jews of Hungary would resume – part of an ongoing process in Hitler's vassal states, destined within months to become one vast charnel house.

16

NEMESIS : THE FINAL SOLUTION

Nemesis was the glum spectre over Hitler's satellites; the advancing Red Army and resistance within were seeing to that. At last the Jews within these countries dared to hope for liberation. Right from the start of their long nightmare, there had been no lack of institutions dedicated to the destruction of the Jews, operating with the blessing of Himmler's operatives.

In 1942, for instance, Reinhard Heydrich remarked that undertaking deportations of Jews from Slovakia was 'no longer too difficult' – implicit recognition that the Slovak authorities had needed scant prompting. The *Ustredny Hospodarsky Urad* (Central Economic Office, UHD), attached to the Prime Minister's office had been busy ousting Jews from the economy and overseeing 'Aryanisation'. Greatly encouraged, the German Ambassador to Bratislava, Hans Ludin, had asked for the deportation of 20,000 young Jews – needed, it was explained, to build 'new Jewish settlements'. Some anxiety had been expressed. This, it was felt, would mean that those who remained would be economically unproductive. A figure of 60,000 deportations had eventually been reached.

Furthermore, the Tiso government had been willing to pay for the privilege of being rid of its Jewish encumbrances. It was agreed that 500 Reichsmarks per head would cover the cost of 'vocational training'. The Slovaks had consented to pay a fee equivalent to $1.8 million.

From March to November, 1942, around 60,000 Slovak Jews had been deported for Auschwitz, and the area of Lublin. The Hlinka Guard had made itself busy throughout, taking on as one of its prime responsibilities the guarding of the concentration and transit labour camp at Sered, which the Slovakian government had already put to good use. Here a reign of terror prevailed, with a string of transports deporting 4,500 Jews to Poland, 300 of them on a Day of Atonement.

Some Jews had been more fortunate. The precepts of Aryan supremacy so beloved of Himmler were broadly interpreted when money was in prospect; negotiation – euphemism for bribery – served to slow down the authority's enthusiasms for deportation or 'resettlement'.

Escape became possible. Up to the March, 1944, German occupation of Hungary, more than 10,000 Jews, stripped of all their resources, crossed the Hungarian border. They had conveniently become converts to Christianity and possessors of impeccable Aryan credentials.

But no means all Jews were willing to buy their way to freedom; there were those more than willing to fight for it. As early as 1942, when the deportation programme seemed unstoppable, armed cells of resistance had sprung up. Disparate groups of Agrarians, Nationalists and Communists hammered out a banner of the Slovenskö National Council, or SNR. There were splits from the start, the Army insisting on sharing its loyalty between the SNR and the Czechoslovak government-in-exile.

Strange bedfellows emerged; the underground Czechoslovak Communist Party and the middle-class 'Flora' group, formed around a celebrated Slovak politician, Dr Vavro Srobar, looked towards a single Czechoslovak nation. The Agrarians also envisaged one republic, but with some autonomy for Slovakia. Inevitably, for the Communists, none of this was acceptable. Under the leadership of Gustav Husak, the future President of Czechoslovakia, they pressed the cause of Slovakia becoming a republic of the Soviet Union.

The Partisans fighting in the mountains viewed such differences with impatience. They controlled significant areas of eastern and central Slovakia and there seemed no reason not to strike. A decision was taken to cut through the increasingly unproductive squabbles of the SNR, to say nothing of the exiled Czech government in London.

On 28 August, 1944, Slovakia erupted. The aim of the insurrection was to oust the Hlinka Guard and free the state from dependence on the Nazis. Alexander Mach, the Minister of the Interior and Deputy Prime Minister, was soon admitting in a broadcast:

> The country is virtually in a state of war, temporarily imposed upon it by underground forces and parachutists. The Government is therefore compelled to proclaim martial law and is determined to clear Slovakia of subversive elements with its own forces rather than appealing for help to Germany.

To reinforce the imposition of martial law, the Slovakian police, Hlinka Guard and Slovakian *Volksdeutsche* SS combed the villages, dragging out anyone suspected of being an agent of the guerrillas. The rebels were reinforced by Partisans and escaping prisoners from the Czech Protectorate, from Poland, Austria, Hungary and Bulgaria.

On the day that the revolt broke out, the 178th Slovak Tatra Division in north eastern Slovakia took the town of Zilina for the rebels. Near Batovany, a bitter battle raged where a vastly outnumbered Jewish unit from the Novöky labour camp fought valiantly. The gates of Sered were opened and the younger prisoners made good their escape to join the rebels.

In the east, where rebels battled against 108th Panzer Division, radio contact was made with the Russians with appeals for supplies, armed strikes, reinforcements and, most crucial of all, for a Red Army offensive across the San river.

But within days they were surrounded. The home-based Slovak Army could not sustain the uprising. Rescue response came from the First and Fourth Ukrainian fronts; portions of the Czech Army in exile in Russia were also airlifted in.

The Germans, not prepared to tolerate sweeping Partisan gains or Tiso's increasingly obvious inability to control this recalcitrant puppet, attacked from all sides. From Hungary came 108th Panzer Division, 86th SS Regiment and Battlegroup Schaeffer. They by no means had everything their own way. Panzers from the Czech Protectorate faced defeat at the town of Zilina, while SS divisions were soon in trouble at Trencin and Povazska Bystrica.

General Catlos, Slovakia's armed forces Commander-in-Chief, continued nevertheless to parrot Mach's assurances that the presence of German troops was due solely to activity by rebel parachutists. However, it was becoming steadily apparent that, save for pockets in the east, Slovakia was falling to the Nazis.

The German armed presence included a couple of divisions from ethnic minorities, the 18th Horst Wessel, which was *Volksdeutsch*, and the 14th Galician from the Ukraine, along with additional SS units. There were also troops of Einsatzkommando 14, under the command of SS Obersturmbannführer G F Deffner who commandeered the local prison to detain insurgents, illegal workers and specifically those under suspicion for having been involved in the uprising. The Hlinka Guard hustled prisoners into trucks bound for isolated areas where there were previously constructed anti-tank ditches.

Some prisoners, sensing what was planned for them, attempted to avoid the Hlinka Guard firing squads by jumping into the ditches, often hiding under bodies of those who had previously been shot through the back of the neck.

The rebellion lasted until the end of October, 1944, by which time German forces marching on three sides had crushed the opposition and captured the rebel headquarters at Banskö Bystrica. President Tiso awarded a special Merit medal to those who had displayed 'courage and loyalty'. It carried a profile of himself and the optimistic title *I Prezident Republiky* (1st President of the Republic) while the reverse had the motto *Za Boha, Za Narod* (For God and the Nation).

On the day that Banskö Bystrica fell, Tiso ordered a Mass of thanksgiving to be celebrated in the presence of senior German officers. A proclamation was issued by the Slovak government:

> At this moment of joy we think with sincere gratitude of the Führer of the greater German Reich and his heroic Army. We appeal to the population of the liberated territory to fulfil loyally all orders of the government and the authorities and to assist the German Army. We assure you that the government will again help the innocent population, which suffered under the terrorist regime of the Czecho-Bolshevik usurpers. . . . The Slovak State lives and shall live on.

Western Allied concern for the insurgents was lukewarm; Slovakia was reckoned to be within Stalin's sphere of interest.

The rebellion's end saw no end to the ferocious anti-Jewish pogrom, a state of affairs highly satisfactory to Heinrich Himmler who even at this stage of the war saw no reason to curb his addiction to power. In Bratislava to attend to unfinished business, the Reichsführer-SS made clear to leaders of the Jewish community that none of their people could be exempt from deportation. Sered, the scene of so many escapes in the confusing open days of the uprising, was once again in full operation under a new commandant. Alois Brunner had become a staff member of the SD in Vienna. His track record was impressive. In 1938, the same year in which he had joined the SS, Brunner had been put in charge of the Vienna *Zentralstelle für Judische Auswanderung* (Central Office for Jewish Emmigration). His SS colleagues regarded him with fear and dislike. The fact that he was dark and swarthy with a slightly hooked nose bred instant suspicion among the racial purists who referred to him scathingly as 'Jew Süss'. No one, though, could deny his energy.

In September, 1944, he was in Bratislava, working closely at Sered with the Hlinka Guard. With the rank of SS-Hauptsturmführer, his arrival was a whirlwind. Existing staff, including members of the Slovak police, were dismissed and replaced by his own henchmen. No longer was there anywhere for Jews to hide. New orders covered all Jews, irrespective of citizenship, profession, age or sex, including Jews to whom exemptions had been granted by Slovak or German authorities or enterprises, also Jews of mixed marriages who had no children, or whose children were above eighteen years of age.

From Brunner himself, came a crude addendum: '*Alle, die Juden beschützen stinken*'. (All those who protect the Jews stink.)

143

Behind Brunner lurked an even more powerful figure. In 1933, the year Hitler assumed power, a young Rhinelander, Adolf Eichmann, a travelling salesman for the American company Vacuum Oil, had lost his job. It was a predicament not uncommon at the time but Eichmann had been able to call on useful friends. In Austria, where the family had moved, an acquaintance, Ernst Kaltenbrunner, had already persuaded the young Eichmann to join the National Socialist Party and eventually the SS.

When Austria banned the Schutzstaffel, Eichmann moved to Germany, underwent some military training and served for a while at the concentration camp at Dachau. But this had been Nazism for a journeyman; it promised scarcely the whiff of power. That was to lie in Berlin and, more specifically, in the central office of the *Sicherheitsdienst* in Berlin, headed by Reinhard Heydrich. Eichmann made himself an assiduous student of racial matters, focusing his researches on the appropriate SD offices and gaining the essential prerequisite of approval from Heinrich Himmler.

He was therefore ideally equipped by 23 June, 1938, when all existing German police forces came under the umbrella organization of the RHSA. This included the Gestapo as Amt IV. Section IVB dealt with the political activity of religious sects, but more notorious was its sub-group, IVB4, the Gestapo Jewish Affairs Office, entrusted eventually with the 'final solution' of the Jewish problem under Eichmann. From the four-storey building at 116 Kurfürstenstrasse, Berlin, he became responsible for the execution of Nazi policy towards the Jews in Germany and the sixteen countries comprising all the occupied territories. From his office went out a stream of orders to his representatives, giving place and time of departure of trains to the extermination camps and the number of deportees aboard.

Active in this work in Bulgaria was SS-Obersturmführer Theodore Dannecker, while in Romania Hauptsturmführer Gustav Richter had long been busy with implementing deportations across the river Bug to Poland.

With the removal of Horthy, the hour in Hungary belonged to the stocky, moon-faced anti-Semite Ferencz Szalasi and his green-shirted, jacked-booted acolytes of the Arrow Cross, groomed with enthusiasm by Veesenmayer with his direct line to the higher reaches of the RHSA.

Repression of the Jews was not long in coming; a torrent of restrictions poured from the Interior Ministry in Budapest. The noose was tightened in stages, beginning with the inevitable order to wear the yellow star in public. Progressively, Jews were edged out of jobs in the media and the arts and then forbidden to operate businesses of any kind. Private cars and even the use of taxis was banned to Jews; valuables, savings, cash and radios were required to be registered.

The smooth running of ghettoization and deportation was in the hands of the Hungarian police where district commands, set up by the superintendent Major General Göbour Faragho, were administered by four colonels whose staff were concerned solely with organising the fate of the Jews and had unlimited powers of arrest, interrogation and search.

They went about their work with an enthusiasm rivalling even that of the Germans. Under interrogation in 1961, after his capture by the Israelis, Eichmann revealed that, although directives from Himmler excluded men over sixty, children and those unfit for manual labour, the top police officers 'didn't want any age limit, they wanted to evacuate everybody, lock, stock and barrel.'

Two days after Szalasi assumed power, Eichmann returned to Hungary where he been personally in charge of deportations. Plans for earlier deportations had been halted at the behest of Horthy who had been approached by the Pope and the King of Sweden, both of whom had gained intelligence on the extent of the pogrom within Hungary. But with the removal of the Regent, the deportations, organized with the help of Hungarians, resumed.

Eichmann now reckoned that he had a free hand. On 2 November, the Russians had a toehold in the outer suburbs of Pest. All Jewish labour companies were shunted west of the Danube, moving to the South-East Wall, a defence under construction to protect Vienna. Then followed a mass expulsion. 25,000 Jews, mostly women, were forced to march in the vilest weather conditions to the Austrian border.

The Attorney General at Eichmann's trial revealed: 'Anyone who found the walking difficult was shot by the guards who beat and tormented their victims every step of the way. Those who had no strength left, collapsed and died. Hundreds committed suicide or died of typhus. All that was issued to them to eat and drink, was hot water and a little bread once every two days.'

> They died like flies and the whole route was strewn with corpses. The number of those who fell by the way is estimated as between six and ten thousand. The horrors attained such proportions that even the escorting Hungarian officers and soldiers began to mutiny and requested that they be sent to the front. . . .

The number of deportations to Auschwitz would have been a lot higher had it not been for the efforts of diplomats within the Swedish and Swiss legations in Budapest, most notably the Swede Raoul Wallenberg.

Wallenberg, then 32 years old, went to Hungary at the behest of the US War Refugee Board set up by American President Franklin Roosevelt to seek aid for the Jews within the neutral countries. The Germans were anxious to maintain good relations with the Swedes, who had nominated Wallenberg for a special mission and provided him with diplomatic status. Status, however, was not something legally possessed by the so-called *Schutzpass* which Wallenberg waved so confidently in the faces of Hungarian officials.

For all it carried the holder's photograph and was emblazoned with a design resembling Sweden's national flag in gold and blue and displayed with an impressive variety of official stamps and signatures, it had no legal validity whatever. But Wallenberg was relying on his knowledge of the Germans' inbred respect for officialdom and authority and it worked. Some 12,000 *Schutzpassen* were handed out wherever Jews congregated, and many were let go. Pliable Hungarian and German officials were heavily bribed to leave entire apartment blocks of Jews alone. These proved an ideal hunting ground for the Arrow Cross whose ranks forced their way into Jewish families, carrying out snatch arrests.

Ferenc Fila, an Arrow Cross journalist and particularly virulent anti-Semite, summed up the pervading sense of anarchy: 'In the besieged city order had loosened. Anyone with a machine gun hanging from his neck could be judge and executioner.'

*   *   *

While the Jews were suffering in Hungary, the Bulgarians paid dearly for their jackal alliance with Nazi Germany. With inevitable defeat looming, the government introduced draconian curfew orders in March, 1944. From 6 pm onwards, the streets had been forbidden to civilians, with a special police permit to be held in the hands at all times. Furthermore, the holder was required to walk in the middle of the road. Penalties were severe, with Radio Sofia announcing the shooting of two government officials unwise enough to pocket their permits. A special 'fighting police' contingent, consisting of 'picked police troops' and 'volunteers with proved patriotic ideas', who showed every sign of being inspired by the SS, sprang into existence with the remit to 'crush revolts, fight the enemies of the state, suppress all Partisan and terrorist bands and restore order.'

As for the Jews, Eichmann's Obersturmführer Dannecker had long been in cahoots with Alexander Belev, the Bulgarian Commissar for Jewish Affairs, who in the late 1930s had been a member of the fascist *Ratnitsi Napreduka na Bulgarshtinata* (Guardians of the Advancement of the Bulgarian National Spirit), which had maintained links with similar organizations in Germany, including the SS. At the end of the previous February, the Dannecker-Belev Agreement drew up a blueprint decreeing 'the deportation of the first 20,000 Jews from the new Bulgarian lands, Thrace and Macedonia, into the German eastern regions.'

This, however, had far from slaked Dannecker's thirst for Jewish blood. In a report to Eichmann that there were at most 14,000 Jews in Thrace and Macedonia, Belev undertook to make up the shortfall – 6,000 Jews from Bulgaria proper, a provision not in the original agreement.

News of the proposed deportations coursed through the Jewish community; the mood soon bordering on panic. The greatest fear was focused on Kiustendil, a city some 50 miles from Sofia, containing 980 Jews, where a makeshift camp was to be set up prior to deportation. On 4 March, a curfew for all Jews was slapped on the city. Preparations for the moves east, it was learnt, would begin in six days.

But there were Jews prepared to act. Community leaders started raising cash to be earmarked for the bribery of officials within the Commissariat for Jewish Affairs, the KEV. Word spread way beyond Kiustendil; the tide of protest lapped at the door of Dimeter Peshev, the city's representative in the *Sobranije* (parliament), who had remained ignorant of the full extent of the deportations. Peshev sought support from members of the political opposition who had never concealed their distaste for Bulgarian anti-Semitism. What was more, Peshev believed that he held a trump card – the Dannecker-Belev Agreement had spelt out measures ordering Jewish deportation from 'the new Bulgarian lands' but not those from the pre-1941 boundaries before the takeover of Thrace and Macedonia.

Peshev and a clutch of his colleagues, choosing a time when the *Sobranije* was in session, engineered a confrontation with the ex-Ratniski member Peter Gabrovski, the Minister for Internal Affairs. At first, Gabrovski attempted to bluff it out. He had, he declared, no knowledge of any deportation plans. In which case, Peshev countered blandly, the *Sobranije* would learn how the plans for the deportation of the Jews from the boundaries of the old Bulgaria ran counter to the original decree. And the plans for Kiustendil were well known.

The implications were obvious: if the bulk of the *Sobranije* discovered that it had been deceived, the result might well spell the fall of the government in an acceleration of protest. The government caved in with the 'postponement' of the deportation of Jews from the areas of the former Bulgaria.

It was four hours to midnight. The round-up of Jews, which had already begun ahead of schedule, was thrown into reverse. But there was no escape for the Jews of Thrace and Macedonia; a total of 11,384 Jews from both places perished in Treblinka and the other death camps.

The victims were helped on their way by eager agents of the KEV. At post-war crimes trials, those from Thrace who survived spoke of eviction from homes without warning, of spells in camps with minimum food, water and toilet supplies. At the railway stations, long queues formed, invalids on stretchers and pregnant women were forced onto the departing trains. But the face of the war changed rapidly, with such ominous landmarks for Bulgaria as the death of King Boris and the Allied invasion of Italy which, for the Allies, had had the desired effect of drawing the teeth of massive German forces. The influence of a Germany rapidly on course for defeat considerably lessened the plight of the Jews. Dannecker's assignment headed for failure.

While Dannecker was experiencing his frustrations in Sofia, SS-Hauptsturmführer Gustav Richter, as *Juden Berater* (Jewish Adviser), had long been Eichmann's dedicated creature in Romania. At his happiest when enmeshed in the deepest thickets of bureaucracy, Richter had sought local official recognition for his activities.

On 12 September, 1941, he got together with Deputy Prime Minister Mihai Antonescu and Radu Lecca, the Commissioner for Jewish Questions, who had been prominent in helping to establish anti-Jewish laws and the inevitable accompaniment of looted property from Jews as early as 1941. Within a year, he was ready to implement the deportation of Jews already held in concentration camps before deportation east.

Like Dannecker, Richter came up against the resistance of those Romanian Jews who had found a voice and had persuaded a hitherto pliant government to change its mind. All of which had proved a severe embarrassment for Eichmann, who had informed Himmler in a confident letter that the Romanian Jews would be deported to Lublin. Those fit for work would be employed while the rest would be handed over for 'special treatment.'

Eichmann's hopes had been dashed. Antonescu, under increasing pressure, had informed the Germans that, instead of deportation, it would be open to the Jews to buy their way out and emigrate to Palestine. But already an estimated 120,000 Jews, who had experienced forced marches, to say nothing of cold, sparse food, lack of hygiene and enforced heavy labour, had been crammed into concentration camps in Transnistra which Antonescu had carved out of the Ukraine and now took on the role of a super dustbin for the Jews incarcerated there. To add to the confusion, the Jews native to the province became unwanted refugees, shunted back and forth, frequently ending up at the demarcation line between German and Romanian forces. Unable to cope, the Germans pushed the refugees back into Romanian territory. There they were allowed either to rot or be finished off by Romanian and German troops.

Time was running out for the likes of Gustav Richter. But not as yet for Adolf Eichmann.

17

THE AXIS DISINTEGRATES

The machinery of terror fashioned by Eichmann ran on, despite the spectre of Germany's defeat. Along with it, politicians strove frantically to rid their countries of further alliance with a cause hopelessly lost. Dobri Bozhilov, Bulgaria's Premier, who had succeeded Filov within months of King Boris's death, lived on the edge of fear. Feverishly, Bozhilov had stepped up negotiations with the Western Allies while at the same time seeking to avoid the fate visited upon Italy and Hungary, when those countries had tried to slip the Nazi noose. To the Soviet Union, with whom Bulgaria had never been at war, he was vociferous in proclaiming neutrality; an awkward stance while German air and land forces remained in the country and Bulgarian troops continued to occupy parts of Yugoslavia and Greece.

Such a plea did not appeal to an increasingly impatient Stalin. Neither were the people of Bulgaria, suffering through their stomachs, in the mood for sympathy. Since 1941, there had been centralized control of grain and crops, much of which had been requisitioned for sale to Germany. There was bread rationing and there were meatless days. By 1944, official food prices in Sofia had soared to 563 per cent of their 1939 values, while on the black market the figure had reached 738 per cent.

Bozhilov's diplomatic gyrations failed. In his place, the following July, came Ivan Bagrianov whose initiatives ran aground in the face of the coup against Antonescu in Romania. There came the time when the Russians were prepared to wait no longer and demanded a Bulgarian declaration of war against Germany. It was the lot of yet another Premier, Konstantin Muraviev, to concede on 8 September. On the same day, Soviet forces poured into Bulgaria, from the Romanian frontier, making for the Black Sea port of Varna while others pushed on for Yugoslavia.

The advance into Bulgaria was unstoppable. Some 340,000 troops of the First, Second and Fourth Bulgarian Armies became attached to the

Third Ukrainian Front of Marshal Fyodor Tolbukhin, making for Hungary and Austria. The arrival of the Russians sounded the death knell of the old Bulgarian Army.

Euphemistically named 'Assistant Commanders' – in fact, political commissars – arrived to remove some 800 officers; Colonel Ivan Kinov, a Red Army veteran, became the new Commander-in-Chief.

The overthrow of Antonescu in Romania had been followed by a brief period of euphoria. Preparations for King Michael's *coup d'état*, helped in part by the activities of his emissary, Prince Barbu Stirbey, and through negotiations with the Allies in Cairo, had resulted in reassuring noises in Moscow where Foreign Minister Vyacheslav Molotov proclaimed: 'The Soviet Government declares that it does not pursue the aim of acquiring any part of Romanian territory other than Bessarabia, or of altering the social structure of Romania as it exists at present.'

But for the Romanians, the speed of events put any contemplation of the future in abeyance. With the rapid collapse of the German front, Malinovsky's mechanized columns had arrowed towards the oilfields of Ploiesti before the Germans had been able to destroy them. The German defences reeled until Romania's 4th Parachute Battalion helped to immobilize anti-aircraft gun emplacements and German civilian personnel on the airfields surrounding the capital.

The next day the airfields were secured; the hour belonged to Grup 9 Vanatori's Captain Buzu Cantacuzino. Romania's highest scoring air ace, he had the unique distinction of chalking up fifty-six kills among the crews of United States Air Force, Red Army and Luftwaffe opponents. Over Bucharest, he added to that title by downing a brace of German Heinkel He 111s.

Despite the reassuring words of Molotov early on, the Russians, who eventually took Bucharest on 31 August, 1944, had soon made their presence felt. Their arrival there was described by A T Cholderton, Special Correspondent of the London *Daily Telegraph*:

One Russian supply column driven into Bucharest comprised rough four-wheeled carts drawn by ponies or heavy cart-horses requisitioned locally. Most of these troops were boyish-looking though there were some older men among them. They were dusty, tired, fit, and proud-looking, because after fighting bitterly for years they had entered a defeated country. Red Army mobile units choked the Bucharest suburbs, the men taking advantage of the log jam, to buy wine in a city where there were no spirits to be had because the Romanian authorities had locked up all supplies.

Cholderton had landed at shattered Bucharest airport after a flight from Istanbul. The government, anxious for the presence of a Western observer, had placed a Lockheed at his disposal – a considerable risk, since the skies were not clear of German aircraft. He found a country in limbo, neither at war nor peace:

> The armistice is not yet signed as the new Romanian government are without direct news from their armistice commission in Moscow and because Russian generals are without orders to halt on any given line.

Communist propaganda posters sprouted throughout Bucharest. Brigadier Burenin, the Red Army Commandant for the city, ordered a takeover of all wireless and telegraphic communication systems. Nevertheless, there was optimism. Nationalist sentiments which had been allowed to slumber for the last four years were reawakened; not least the prospect of reconquering Northern Transylvania. For the Russians, it was not a priority but a ploy to divert Axis attention and reserves away from the proposed assault of 6th Tank Army and 27th Army on Debrecen, Hungary's second city, lying east of Belgrade and to the right of the river Tisa.

Optimism was short-lived. Romania had finally signed its armistice with the Soviet Union, Great Britain and the United States on 12 September. As well as being required to wage war on Germany and Hungary, the cost would be 300 million dollars worth of goods and raw materials in reparations to the Soviet Union. In terms of territory, nothing had been gained for Romania: the country was required to resume the Romanian–Soviet frontier of June, 1940.

Even worse for the Germans, Finland, which had helped Germany achieve the siege of Leningrad, announced its readiness to make peace. Hitler was now robbed of his Axis partners at both the southern and northern ends of the eastern front. The Russians had been determined to crush the Finns. On the front line between the two forces on the Karelian Isthmus, the Red Army had launched an assault which, on the morning of 9 June, had been audible to the citizens of Helsinki, 170 miles away. Marshal Mannerheim, the Commander-in-Chief, was forced to fall back and fought tenaciously to hold a newly created line. Breakthrough for the Russians proved tough, for the Finns were at home on their own rugged territory.

There had also been fighting at Maselkaya, to the north of Lake Onega, the Finnish 11th Corps breaking under the waves of assault of the Soviet 32nd Army. Finnish forces had managed to pull back yet again, this time halting on the so-called 'U Line' arching inland from the eastern shore of Lake Ladoga. By mid-July, both sides were stuck in stalemate. For Mannerheim, it was enough. He entered into negotiations with the Russians.

Matching the unstoppable progress of the Soviet juggernaut in the south, had been the guerrilla war in Yugoslavia, fought by the Partisans whose ranks had grown significantly since the country was first occupied in 1941. In the wild, forested mountainous terrain, the Army of National Liberation had harried the enemy mercilessly, blowing up railways and cutting telegraph wires with an impunity matched by the cutting of the throats of their enemies. The German defences had been worn down at high cost over much of Dalmatia, Croatia and Slovenia.

With the capitulation of Italy and its change of sides, the race had been on to get to fourteen Italian divisions of various strengths and secure their arms. The first of Hitler's jackals changed its spots quickly enough, although many of the turncoat forces stoutly retained their Italian identity with pro-Tito Partisans, now known as Garibaldi Natisone or Venezia. The change of allegiance expanded the National Liberation Army strength to some 80,000.

There had been cautious but nevertheless positive shifts in the image of the Partisans among the Allies, who previously had regarded Tito's followers as shadowy and slightly suspect figures. Dealings had been with the bearded, steel spectacled Mihailovic and his Chetniks. For Mihailovic, the main enemy remained the Communists, a source of contention with Tito that had dated from at least July, 1942, when he had sent Moscow a denunciation of the Chetnik leader as traitor and collaborator.

It was the beginning of a slanging match between the two. On 27 March, 1943, Mihailovic had radioed the government-in-exile in London:

> Can a convict like Josip Broz, who is listed with the Zagreb police under No 1034, alias leader of the Communists under the name of Tito, be compared with the Yugoslav Army as a national fighter? . . . The plunderer of churches and convict Josip Broz, a locksmith's assistant?

Three months later, Brigadier Fitzroy Maclean parachuted into Partisan territory in Yugoslavia as a special envoy to Tito at the behest of Winston Churchill. Maclean's report on 'Comrade This and That' had been favourable. In addition, information gathered by liaison officers with the Chetniks and presented to the British GHQ in Cairo had revealed that many Chetnik leaders had received arms and payments from Germans, Italians, Serbs and Croats to fight the Partisans.

Although many Chetniks deserted to Tito, others gave their allegiance to the Croat Legion (*Hrvatska Legija*) which had been formed at the time of Hitler's invasion of Russia. An appeal by Pavelic to rally to Germany's side in the 'crusade against Bolshevism' had received a swift response. Within weeks an infantry regiment had been raised with two battalions, all sporting the grandiloquent motto 'By the grace of God and the deeds of heroes.' In addition to renegade Chetniks, the Legion, comprised some 5,000 officers and men, including German officers and NCOs, all decked out in German uniforms. But the Croat Legion apart, Tito came to have a particular score to settle with Pavelic followers.

On the face of it, Para Battalion 500/600 was an orthodox enough name for an arm of German airborne forces, which in the spring of 1944 had plenty to occupy it at Cassino and Anzio in Italy and in the dying months of the Russian campaign. But in truth there was nothing remotely orthodox about Para Battalion 500/600; it owed its existence not to Reichsmarschall Hermann Göring as Commander-in-Chief of the Luftwaffe but to Himmler, the tirelessly insidious accumulator of power.

Until the autumn of 1943, Göring's air force had stood alone and unchallenged. The Reichsführer-SS, in addition to taking over the Reich intelligence services, had raised with the Waffen-SS an army of more than thirty divisions answerable only to itself and to him. Himmler reckoned it was time to turn his attention to the Luftwaffe.

He envisaged an SS battalion of paratroopers, many of whom would be drawn from men who had served sentences in military penal establishments, who, Himmler reasoned, would be open to appeals to their patriotism and, more to the point, the prospect of freedom. All ranks were ushered into training at the Kralyyevo Para School, honed for action against Partisan forces in Yugoslavia, Greece and Albania. Within six months came news of a special mission for the Para Battalion, personally sanctioned by the Führer.

The purpose of the operation codenamed *Unternehmen Rösselsprung* (KNIGHT'S MOVE) was stark and simple: paratroopers would land on the partisan headquarters at Drvar in western Bosnia and seize Tito – ideally, alive. The date was to be 25 May, which happened to be Tito's official birthday. Details of the operation were wrapped in high secrecy, the paratroopers being briefed on the object of their mission only two hours before departing from Zagreb airport.

The forces involved were to be the 7th Volunteer Mountain Division 'Prinz Eugen', raised from *Volksdeutsche* in Croatia, Serbia, Romania and Hungary, detachments of a Brandenburg battalion who were Intelligence and Counter-Intelligence specialists, together with assorted Croatian units. German XV Mountain Corps was to encircle Drvar. The battalion would be dropped into the constricting ring which was an area known to be held by at least 12,000 Partisans. The plan was for the initial attack to be made at 0700 hours and the second wave, made up of reinforcements, would land at midday, for there were not enough DFS 230 gliders available for more than a single assault.

Because of constant harassment by the Germans, Tito and his staff had been forced to move headquarters several times, which had seriously disrupted armed operations. In the Partisan area of Drvar, the Partisans, armed with heavy weapons, were installed in a small but well equipped hut. It lay in a valley from which soared the Jasenovac mountains to the north and high wooded hills to the south. Tito usually visited it in daylight hours, preferring to work and sleep in a village a few miles away. The morning of the attack proved an exception; he had decided to stay the night at Drvar so that he would be on the spot for his birthday celebrations.

At precisely 0700 hours on D-Day, 314 paratroopers catapulted from their transport aircraft, Drvar and the surrounding area having been bombed an hour earlier. The ground was then clear for the gliders, each of which on landing skidded across rocky ground within yards of the hut. Tito's escort battalion of men and women Partisans were ready. Fire power barbecued the flimsy gliders even before they came to a halt. Those in the first wave of the parachute attack were all killed but many of the Partisans fell to the second wave.

The day was carried however for Tito by extensively prepared field defences. At no time did any of the SS manage to enter Tito's hut, although a bodyguard unwise enough to show himself was shot dead.

Replacements from the Partisans seemed inexhaustible; the SS para-troopers had no relief forces at all. Nevertheless they still presented a real danger and Tito realized that the best way out of the hut was by an emer-gency exit which consisted of a hole beneath the floorboards from which dangled a rope. The escape route reached a stream which, if followed, passed a sawmill beyond which was a plateau happily obscured from the area round the hut by trees and bushes; from these it was possible to cross into orchards lying further along on the other side.

Most of Tito's personal staff got away, dogged by fear at the possible appearance of the German motorized units, bolstered by air support, known to be in the area. Tito himself, aided by the British mission to Yugoslavia, was flown to the British-occupied island of Vis off the Dalmatian coast. There he set up yet another headquarters from which to control the Partisan war.

Nothing could disguise the truth that KNIGHT'S MOVE had been a conspicuous failure. The Germans and their partners had but one gain. Tito had been anxious to mark elevation to the rank of Marshal by having an especially striking uniform made for him by a local tailor. The Germans bombed the man's shop, badly gashing the uniform in the process. The remnants were eagerly seized on by the propagandists of Dr

Goebbels and featured prominently in the newspapers but it was, quite literally, an empty triumph; Tito and his companions had melted into the forest.

Tito's status had now grown to the extent that he was steadily being recognised as the undisputed leader of the Yugoslav resistance. On the other hand, the exiled King Peter, dreaming of the day when his country would be rid of the Germans and he could return, was presiding over what was widely regarded as increasingly irrelevant government-in-exile. It was put to him that the doyen of the Partisans must be included in any new cabinet. In fact, Peter was being thrust aside as an irrelevance; the Yugoslav monarchy was shrinking to a footnote.

Hitler might have fulminated over the fall of Mussolini. Ante Pavelic, the Croatian Poglavnik, did not. Here was a heaven-sent opportunity to wriggle out of the Rome Agreement, originally concluded between the Duce and the Ustachi-run Independent State of Croatia (NDH), and to take control of the former Italian-occupied Dalmatia. But the mood there had swung to the Partisans away from the Ustachi.

By November, 1943, so-called Partisan National Liberation Councils had sprung up throughout Yugoslavia, but their role could only be shadowy in territories of Serbia, Macedonia and Slovenia where the Germans still held sway. Partisan power was, however, far stronger in Croatia and the plight of Pavelic's Ustachi looked progressively grimmer. There was panic in Zagreb. A power struggle was unleashed within rival factions of the Ustachi, some of whom were anxious to do a deal with Russia while others were determined to soldier on with the Nazis.

In the following July, the Poglavnik struck. Two cabinet colleagues, Mladen Lorkovic, who had been Foreign Minister from 1941–43, and Anste Vokic, the War Minister, were arrested on charges of plotting a pro-Allied coup, imprisoned and subsequently murdered by the Ustachi.

The 3rd Ukrainian Army of Marshal Fedor Ivanovich Tolbukhin, in conjunction with Tito's forces, opened their assault on Belgrade on 20 October. Here the fighting was hand-to-hand and stretched to a full week. A Soviet ultimatum to surrender was rejected, and within forty-eight hours the Germans were obliterated, at the cost of 15,000 dead. Russian units were given the name of 'Belgrade' divisions. Their sappers swept in, in a bid to clear the heavy fields of mines while shattered enemy equipment littered the roads. Pavelic was already laying plans for escape, intent on fleeing both from his old Axis partner and the Russians.

General Francisco Franco, the Spanish Caudillo, was however, not intent on flight. In December, 1943, remnants of the Volunteer Legion – colloquially, the Blue Legion – commanded by Colonel Antonio Garcia Navarro, had been formed for anti-Partisan duties on the

Estonian–Russian border and ordered in blizzard conditions to hold six-and-a-half miles of front at Kostovo.

The Legion, much of which had already been withdrawn, had only been able to muster the equivalent of one rifleman for every foot of snow. With the slim forces available there was no hope of repelling the attack which erupted on Christmas Day amid a disintegrating northern front. The order to retreat soon followed: a long, slow march through freezing wind and snow. Harassed by Partisans, the march soon became a slow stumble in the execrable weather. Even when the men of the Legion had reached Luga, to the south-west of Leningrad, there had been no respite; they were moved north-west to the Narva coast of Estonia to repel possible Soviet landings.

Amid all the striving by opportunists to be done with Hitler, there remained no more pathetic figure than the miserably deflated Benito Mussolini, leader of a mere fantasy, the reborn Fascist state known as the Salo Republic on Lake Garda. Hitler's oldest partner was approaching his final agonies.

– 18 –

THE DEATH OF MUSSOLINI

The Junkers 52, which brought Benito Mussolini from Munich after his dramatic air rescue from the Grand Sasso, had touched down on the airstrip at Rastenburg in bright sunshine on 15 September, 1943. But the weather failed to match the occasion; Adolf Hitler was greeting a fallen dictator. The scene might have been that of two old friends greeting each other in mutual misfortune. The Führer's eyes were full of tears. A shrunken Mussolini, in dark overcoat and trilby hat, appeared deflated and listless in the face of shattered dreams. The two men holding hands, stood for a while in silence.

Hitler's stance of commiseration did not last long; he could not afford to sustain it. The cold truth was that an armistice between Italy and the Allies had been announced the previous week. When the two former Axis partners were at last alone, Hitler bluntly spelt out the fate of Italy following the overthrow of the Duce. What, Hitler asked him sharply, did he propose to do? Mussolini replied that he felt like retiring, if only to avoid a civil war in Italy. Hitler brushed the suggestion aside – any such course would send a message to the world that the Duce no longer believed in the inevitability of a German victory.

The Fascist cause in Italy, Hitler urged, must be revived speedily. A government based in Rome was of course out of the question; one must be established in northern Italy. If it were not, the alternative was clear: the Italian Army could either fight Germany, its late ally, or its men face deportation as prisoners of war to Germany. The consequences to the Italians would not stop there. If the German Army was forced to fall back to the Po or even the Alps, it would scorch the earth in the process.

Hitler did not let up, fully aware that Mussolini's physical and mental state was such that he would be unable to resist. The former Duce must head a new Fascist grouping, its members to consist of those of proven loyalty. Traitors must be punished with merciless harshness.

Furthermore, the northern provinces of Italy – Alto Adige, Venezia Giulia and the Trentino – must be occupied by Germany to act as a buffer against possible attack through Yugoslavia. The provinces were also the known haunts of Partisans and a civilian population of dubious loyalty. Furthermore, the Führer hinted broadly, there would be further demands.

In feverish voice and slurred words, Mussolini broadcast a 'proclamation' on his return to Munich, which reconstituted the government as *Partito Fascisto Repubblicano* with himself as Premier and Marshal Graziani as Minister of Defence, with other posts for loyal adherents.

During his broadcast, Mussolini attempted vainly to recover the fire of the old days and rally adherents as he once did from the balcony of Rome's Piazza Venezia. But it sounded hollow and unconvincing. In exasperation, Goebbels recorded in his diary: 'He is not a revolutionary like the Führer or Stalin. . . . He lacks the broad qualities of a worldwide revolutionary and insurrectionist.'

The fact was that the first of the jackals had lost all interest. With Rome no longer an option, his base for the new born Fascist state, the so-called Salo Republic, became the isolated Rocco delle Caminate, near Gargnano, on the shores of Lake Garda in the extreme north. But there was no privacy. A reconnaissance battalion and a flak battery of the SS Leibstandarte were provided for 'protection.'

Domestic arrangements bordered on the bizarre: on the personal orders of Hitler, Mussolini's wife Rachele was able to join him and, so was his mistress Claretta Pettaci, who was installed in a villa a few miles away. Meanwhile, the humiliations mounted. Mussolini had little stomach to seek vengeance on those who had voted or connived at his downfall before the Grand Council which included his son-in-law Count Ciano, dubbed by Goebbels 'the poisonous mushroom'. But Hitler insisted.

Ciano had left Rome with his wife Edda and their children and, despite warnings of the danger, had arrived in Munich the previous August. Vainly, Ciano attempted to obtain a visa for South America. But he reckoned without the hatred of the Germans and in particular Ribbentrop. He was arrested.

The trial of Ciano and five others, which began on the morning of Saturday 8 January, 1944, was conducted by members of a black-shirted tribunal sitting in front of a black cloth sporting the symbol of Fascism. There were no concessions to old loyalties. Among the accused, subsequently shot along with Ciano at Verona jail four days later, was seventy-eight-year-old Marshal de Bono, who had taken part in the march on Rome which had put the Duce in power. Ciano struggled free from his bonds at the last moment to face his executioners with the cry of 'Long live Italy.'

Any hopes that Mussolini might have had for a freshly constituted party proved illusory. From the very beginning, there were moves to undermine the new Fascist Republic which most Italians, long grown cynical, viewed as more than slightly ridiculous, even contemptible.

In fact, disillusion and with it, distrust of Mussolini, had become deep-seated far beyond Italy. In the months before the defection of Italy to the Allies, warning bells had sounded in Germany. In March, 1943, a key role had been assigned to a veteran whose proven loyalty to Hitler and the National Socialist movement stretched back well before the Führer had successfully jockeyed for power during the death throes of Weimar Germany.

Karl Wolff had been with the freebooters of the Freikorps between December, 1918, and May, 1920. It was the springboard for a career that could only be described as meteoric. By 1931 he was a member of the SS and ADC to Franz Ritter von Epp, a fire-eating martinet who, as one of the earliest Nazis, became Hitler's 'Statthalter' or Governor in Bavaria.

Wolff was, above all, Himmler's man, something not entirely un-connected with the fact that, at six foot with blond hair and blue eyes, he fitted the Aryan ideal to perfection. Approval from Himmler – who called his protégé '*Wölfchen*' – meant preferment. Wolff was assigned to prepare an operational SS and Police Command in Italy that would shadow Marshal Badoglio in the event of the latter's defection. It had proved only a beginning. By September, Wolff held the title of *Höchster SS und Polizeiführer*. The 'Höchster' (Highest) was significant; officials were usually designated with a mere 'Higher'. Aside from General-feldmarschall Kesselring, the Commander-in-Chief of the German forces, Karl Wolff had become the most powerful man in Italy. And the upward progression was not yet over.

On 20 July, 1944, the bomb which had been placed by Claus Schenk, Graf von Stauffenberg, under Hitler's table during a map conference at Rastenburg, had exploded but failed to kill the Führer. From then on, the Army had become Hitler's object of pathological distrust and hatred. Predictably, Himmler, the tireless power seeker, discerned yet a further role for his SS. Wolff was appointed military plenipotentiary in Italy.

With the new post came the chance to fight his own personal war. This was not with conventional armed forces but with the numerous groups of Partisans which had rallied to the banner of no less than six wildly disparate parties as Committees of National Liberation. United in a new found detestation of Fascism, the Committees had grown and flourished in all provinces, towns, villages and factories.

Fascist loyalties so ardently sworn a short while ago were forgotten. Communists vowed to abide by the florid terms of the oath of the Soviet Partisans: 'For the towns and villages burnt down, for the death of our women and children, for the torture, violence and humiliation wreaked on my people, I vow to take revenge. . . .' Once Mussolini had been toppled, pressure on Badoglio was stepped up for a speedy conclusion of an armistice with the Allies.

But then had sprung what appeared to be a new dawn for the Germans. The forces of Kesselring had conducted a skilful retreat through Sicily and the length of Italy. No matter his reverses on the eastern front, Hitler had relished seeing these forces dig in firmly south of Rome, hindering the advance of the Allied troops. Occupation by the Germans boded ill for the CNL leaders. Those captured were shot, while the more fortunate made for the mountains.

But it was no passive retreat. Immediately, squads of Partisans were formed into small, armed detachments which, together with town and village dwellers, attacked the offices of Nazis and Fascists, not simply out of vengeance but in pursuit of vitally needed funds so that the various groups could stay in business.

Liaison with the Allied forces had grown steadily stronger. Instructions streamed from the headquarters of General Sir Harold Alexander, commander of 15th Army Group. An indication of what was expected of the Partisan groups, growing steadily more professional, could be gathered from a directive issued to those in the Spezia zone on 3 July, 1944:

> It is the duty of all patriots in this zone to do everything in their power to hinder the completion of the German defences and to destroy as much as they can of the defences already completed. . . . Destroy all you can, carry their tools away and make them useless . . .
>
> The leaders of the patriot groups in this zone must detail at least two men to note down exact information on the German defences in their area and to make them on as large scale maps as possible. . . . The patriot leaders must make sure that the men who gather all this information cross the lines and reach us.

Kesselring described in his memoirs what this meant for the German soldier serving in Italy:

> . . . The Partisans almost always wore no emblems, hid their weapons or, again in violation of international law, went about dressed as Germans or Fascists, thus freeing themselves from the obligations a uniform carries with it.
>
> In consequence, there was considerable irritation on our side, for the German soldier in the infested areas could not help seeing in every civilian of either sex a fanatical assassin or expecting to be fired at from every house.

The whole population had, in any case, helped in or connived at elaborating a warning system which placed every German soldier's life in danger.

Only in a very few exceptional circumstances did the bands accept fair fight. Once they had stealthily done their mischief or, if a sense of inferiority made them break off a fight, they melted away among the civilian population or as innocent as country hikers.

Partisans were willing to put up with every imaginable discomfort. Their common lot was cold, damp, lice, scurvy, hunger and thirst. Medical supplies were a luxury and it was not uncommon for wounded men to be shot lest they fall into German hands. When Partisans were captured, those over the age of fifteen were invariably executed.

Documents which fell into Allied hands at the end of the war testified to the increased embarrassment caused to the Germans by the Partisans and to the drain that their numerous activities caused to Nazi-Fascist manpower. A letter to Kesselring, dated 2 April, 1944, from Marshal Graziani, Commander of the Republican Fascist Army, implored him to cut down German requests for Fascist soldiers and labour. Graziani wrote:

> One of my most urgent problems is to increase as much as possible the number of formations engaged in fighting the rebels; this fight is a necessary and quite indispensable preliminary to the re-establishment of the authority and prestige of the state.

By that summer the German forces were again in decline. Mussolini's Fascist pocket steadily diminished. Early in June, the Allies took Rome. The Nazi line fell back, after losing Florence in August, to the Gothic Line which stretched from La Spezia to Rimini. Reprisals against the Partisans grew fiercer.

Although the notorious massacre of the village of Lidice in Czechoslovakia back in 1942, following Reinhard Heydrich's assassination by Czech agents, had achieved almost instant worldwide notoriety and condemnation, even more savage acts by German SS and Fascists in northern Italy in the last full year of the war passed unremarked amid the general carnage. At Vadio, on the Prato–Bologna road, 1,400 people were massacred. At Vinca, after the male population had fled, a mixed force of Germans and Italians hanged 172 women and children.

As for Mussolini, the seat of his puppet government, now situated on the banks of Lake Garda in the Villa Feltrinelli, the air was not simply heavy with the sure knowledge of military defeat, but domestic hatred flared with the constant squabbling between the Duce's wife, Rachele, and his mistress Claretta. By escaping to his office, Mussolini indulged in his dreams of a reconstituted, truly Socialist republic for Italy. Meanwhile, the Allies were advancing on the heels of the retreating German Army which was falling back through northern Italy to Switzerland and Bavaria.

There came the day when all dreams were shattered. On the evening of Thursday, 19 April, 1945, accompanied by an escort of troops led by SS Hauptsturmführer Otto Kisnatt of the SD and SS Untersturmführer Fritz Birzer, Mussolini arrived at the Milan Prefectura to discuss terms for an honourable surrender. Over the next five days, arguments raged over whether it was worth making a last stand or surrendering.

Events, however, were speedily rendering such discussions irrelevant. On the following Wednesday, 25 April, Mussolini had a final meeting with Cardinal Idelfonso Schuster, the Archbishop of Milan, who, unknown to the former Duce, was already in the throes of negotiations both with the Germans represented by Oberstgruppenführer Wolff and the Allies, and with representatives of the CLNAI (Italian Committee of Liberation for Upper Italy). From them Mussolini learnt that his role no longer counted.

Wolff and his adjutant, Standartenführer Eugen Dollmann, who was also involved, had been only too aware of the way that the war was going, and had been anxious to save their own skins. Wolff had made it clear to an assistant of Allen Dulles of the Office of Strategic Services, the US intelligence network based in neutral Berne, that he would help the Allied cause in return for favours. Not the least of these was ensuring that his name did not appear on the list of war criminals.

At his eventual meeting with the professorial, pipe-smoking Dulles, Wolff had been left in no doubt of the conditions with which he would have to abide if discussions were to have any hope of success. He had been told bluntly: 'If there is the slightest hint that you are speaking on behalf of Himmler, this conversation will last no more than a few seconds. Is it clear that only unconditional surrender will be considered?' Wolff had nodded dutifully, adding only that he needed the approval of the Wehrmacht, which meant that of Kesselring, who had given him the impression that he would not be averse to an honourable settlement.

On his return from the meeting, Wolff received a message which made his stomach lurch. Obergruppenführer Ernst Kaltenbrunner, the head of the RSHA, ordered him to report forthwith at Innsbruck near the Austrian-Italian border. The mere name of the towering, scar-faced alcoholic Kaltenbrunner was enough to inspire fear in even the most self-assured members of the SS. Wolff reasoned that a summons from such a sinister source could have only one meaning – somehow Kaltenbrunner, who was known to be totally Hitler's creature, had learnt of the peace overtures. The price of such treachery would be certain death.

But worse followed. A call from Himmler had been friendly. Then in the manner of someone inconsequentially discussing the weather, the Reichsführer-SS let it be known that Wolff's wife and children had been brought under 'the personal supervision' of the Gestapo. Wolff meanwhile was required to remain in Italy. There were subsequent calls, during which Himmler would give cheerful news of those detained.

Soon Wolff had another worry. The negotiations with Dulles were thrown into doubt when Hitler plucked Kesselring from Italy in March, 1945, and flew him north to replace Rundstedt as Commander-in-Chief West and prop up the crumbling German front. Kesselring's replacement, General Heinrich Gottfried von Vietinghoff, a career officer, was at this stage an unknown quantity to Wolff. In something approaching panic, the SS man confided in Baron Luigi Parelli, a conduit to Dulles, that he was in favour of calling off the entire negotiations.

Parelli was unsympathetic: 'Do you prefer to be arrested as a traitor or indicted as a war criminal? One of these is your fate, anyway. I suggest we carry on.' That meant keeping in touch with the Allies via a hidden radio transmitter. Even more dangerous were the tentative overtures made to Vietinghoff.

When he eventually learnt of Wolff's ceasefire initiatives, Mussolini indulged in a new dream, focusing all hopes on a last stand in the Alps – plainly impossible, since US troops were only some 40 miles away. Perhaps Fascism could survive without him if he were finally to make an escape to Switzerland or Spain.

In a final speech to his dwindling band of Blackshirts, he recovered something of his old fire and bombast. But to the bulk of the Partisans it meant nothing; they demanded that the Duce should be handed over to them. Mussolini gave immediate orders to depart for Como, a point for departure across the frontier into Switzerland.

A squad of Blackshirts forced a path through the crowd. Mussolini, machine gun slung over his shoulder, sat in the back of an open Alfa-Romeo, followed by another containing Claretta Petacci with her brother, his wife and children. To ensure that Mussolini would not attempt escape, two lorry loads of 2/2 Flak Abteilung of the Waffen-SS afforded protective steel.

At Como, the Duce pinned his hopes on one of his most loyal supporters Alessandro Pavolini, who had undertaken to bring him 3,000 loyal Fascists for the last stand in the mountains. Even if the 3,000 had existed, bringing them to Mussolini would have proved impossible. The Milan suburbs had erupted and armed workers were in control. The Allies were advancing as surely as the Germans were pulling back. When Pavolini did eventually succeed in reaching Como by armoured car his news was dire.

Mussolini lost no time in civilities. 'How many?', he demanded anxiously. Pavolini hesitated with considerable embarrassment.

'Well, tell me. *How many?*' The other shrugged: 'Twelve.'

An equal humiliation was the news that the Blackshirts in Como had signed a surrender with the Partisans. The only hope remaining was Austria. Mussolini himself took the wheel of the Alfa-Romeo. Once again, the retinue consisted of Claretta and her family. A belligerent Pavolini vowed that he would shoot his way out of any road blocks erected by Partisans. Incredibly, Mussolini's confidence surged anew: 'With 200 Germans we can go to the top of the world.'

At first, the convoy was unmolested and the road ribboned ahead, seemingly empty. The lack of any visible sign of Partisans and the eerie silence bothered Pavolini who, scenting danger, suggested that Mussolini transfer from the Alfa Romeo to an armoured car. Pavolini's instincts were right. At a spot six miles from the village of Menaggio, which lay directly on the route to Lake Lugano and the Swiss border, was the ironically named Rocca di Musso where the rock rose vertically from the edge of the road and there was a sheer drop to the lake. A better place for an ambush could scarcely be imagined.

The convoy was brought up short by a vast tree trunk and several boulders which had been dragged across the road. Two 12 mm machine guns, manned by Partisans, opened fire; the riposte from the armoured car knocked out one of them. Anxious to press on quickly, Mussolini's armoured vehicle raised a white flag. The Partisans had limited fire power and plainly would be no match for the Germans if exchanges continued.

Negotiation was indicated; two Germans went forward to parley. Unaware of Mussolini's presence, the Partisans agreed to let the Germans go forward to the town of Dongo where the convoy would be searched. There was no time for an effective disguise of Mussolini who was persuaded to don the heavy overcoat of a corporal in an anti-aircraft unit and a steel helmet.

Inspection of the lorries at first revealed nothing. It was only when the search was nearly completed that a suspicious Partisan brought the deputy commissar of his brigade, Urbano Lazzaro, to inspect what appeared to be a drunken German soldier crouching between two cans of petrol.

Lazzaro confronted the man, demanding: 'Aren't you an Italian?' When Mussolini, his stubbled face ashen, admitted it, Lazzaro, momentarily taken aback, gasped the involuntary courtesy: 'Excellency! You *are* here.' Without attempting to use his weapon and mindful that he had told the German soldiers not to risk their own lives to save him, Mussolini allowed himself to be led from the lorry while the crowd which had gathered soon recognized him and cheered his capture loudly.

His last days were spent amid the squabbles of the Partisans. The moderates believed that he should be handed over to the Allies for trial as a war criminal. But powerful members of two groups, the Committee of National Liberation for North Italy and senior members of the Volunteer Freedom Corps, voted them down.

One of the latter was a tall, pale thirty-six-year-old book-keeper named Walter Audisio, otherwise known as 'Colonel Valerio', who later had the mission of bringing back Mussolini to Milan where his dead body would be put on show. Later, members of the National Liberation Committee were to complain that they had not been consulted over the decision to execute Mussolini and, indeed, did not even know it had been taken.

It made no difference. Mussolini and Claretta, reunited after she had been arrested, following a fruitless bid to deny her identity, were held at a farmhouse in Mezzegra, south of Dongo. Audisio, commandeering a black Fiat 100, raced to the house on the morning of 28 April. He hurtled up the stairs, brandishing a machine gun and making for the bedroom. The couple, not even allowed to finish dressing, were manhandled roughly into the waiting car. Their destination was the nearby Villa Belmonte, a large house standing back behind a stone wall.

For the final moments of Mussolini and Claretta historians have relied on accounts given by Walter Audisio, which were not fully corroborated and in some cases denied altogether. The generally accepted view was that the couple were taken out of the car by Audisio and made to stand outside the gates of the villa. So that there could be no possible escape, two Partisans, Guglielmo Cantoni and Guiseppe Frangi, who had followed on foot, were posted at the hairpin bend between the square and the villa. Another Partisan, Aldo Lampredi, stood between them and the car, while, Lampredi's companion, Michelle Moretti, was placed fifteen yards downhill in the direction of the lake.

Claretta threw her arms around her lover, screaming at Audisio: 'No! No! You mustn't do it. You mustn't!' Audisio ordered: 'Leave him alone or you'll get shot too!'

But Claretta in blind hysteria was beyond all reason now, clutching at Mussolini and attempting to grab the barrel of the gun while shouting: 'You cannot kill us like this.'

Then the gun jammed as did the pistol that Audisio tried next. With sweat pouring down his face, he yelled to Moretti: 'Bring me your gun.' The bullets from the French MAS 7.65 mm sub-machine-gun killed Claretta instantly. Mussolini did not lack courage in his last moments. He stood and faced his killer squarely, holding back the lapels of his jacket as he said: 'Shoot me in the chest.' Mussolini slumped back against the wall. He was still breathing at the moment that he took the second shot, this time from the pistol.

After noting the time as 4.10 pm, Audisio left Cantoni and Frangi in charge of the bodies. He returned to Dongo. There was a lot more killing to do. A clutch of ministers who had served in Mussolini's government were lined up outside Dongo town hall, facing the lake. At a signal they were mown down and their bodies thrown into a yellow removal van which was driven south, stopping to pick up the corpses of Mussolini and Claretta. Later the same night, the van parked in front of a garage where the corpses were tipped out and arranged in order.

A large crowd gathered in anger, recalling that on the same spot, nine months earlier, the Germans had ordered the execution of fifteen Italian hostages. Memories triggered an orgy of macabre vengeance. Repeated kicks were aimed at Mussolini's head and Claretta's body was trampled. Party Secretary Achille Starace, after being forced to witness what was happening, was marched to the square and executed. His body was flung onto the pile with the rest.

Then, under the cold gaze of movie cameras, ropes were tied around the ankles of Mussolini and Claretta. Their corpses, along with that of another executed Fascist, were hung from the garage's overhanging girders, where, still poked by the crowd, they swung obscenely. One woman yelled: 'I avenge the death of my five sons' as she emptied her pistol into Mussolini's body.

With the arrival of the Americans, the corpses were removed, labelled, numbered and interred. Benito Mussolini, the man who had once denounced democracy as 'a putrescent corpse', had become one himself.

Events moved fast from then on. The day following Mussolini's death, the German surrender was signed at Alexander's headquarters at Caserta, near Naples. At the last moment, German representatives had attempted to delay the proceedings by arguing that the approval of General Vietinghoff had not been received. The Americans went ahead and signed, anyway. For an exhausted Wolff, who had risked his own life and that of his family, the only reward was a rebuke from Kesselring for daring to act on his own.

With Mussolini's death, the Europe which he and Hitler had sought to create lay in ruins. The remaining jackal nations were also to pay the price of collaboration.

– 19 –

THE BITTER END

Heinrich Himmler had appeared almost wistful when addressing a meeting of his officers at Jagerhohe on 21 September, 1944, on the matter of loyalty, a commodity no longer to be depended upon from Germany's satellites:

> I would like to give another example of steadfastness, that of Marshal Tito. I must really say that he is a veteran Communist, this Herr Josif Broz, a consistent man. Unfortunately he is our enemy. He really has properly earned his title of Marshal. When we catch him we shall do him in at once. You can be sure of that; he is our enemy. But I wish we had a dozen Titos in Germany. . . . He is a Moscow man. He has never capitulated.

By then Tito had been fighting for three years against the Germans and was in sight of victory, following the entry of the Red Army to Belgrade the previous October. The Russians had been accompanied by the Free Yugoslav Legion, consisting of prisoners captured when fighting for the Germans and persuaded to change sides. They were not alone: a Bulgarian division also serving with the Red Army was poised to enter Belgrade.

At the end of October, the traditional Slavonic sympathy between Yugoslavia and Russia was cemented when the National Liberation Army had joined with Marshal Tolbukhin's 3rd Ukrainian Army to free Belgrade after several days of street fighting. Among the war damaged buildings, heavily armed Partisans patrolled the streets.

As the military situation deteriorated, panic gripped the hierarchy. They were divided between those who hoped to reach a deal with Russia and the Allies and those who were prepared to stick with Hitler until the end. With the latter group, Tito was prepared to do business.

In March, 1944, he had called on all Ustachi and others who had collaborated with the Germans to join the Partisans forthwith. Refusal would mean death as traitors. After the liberation, an undertaking was given that only those wanted for war crimes would be prosecuted. In Zagreb, the Ustachi had not much longer to run. With the Partisans in Belgrade, Pavelic had no arms, no hope and no future.

*　　*　　*

As for the Hungarians, the long nights seemed endless at the turn of 1944 and well into the New Year. In October, the Stavka, the Soviet high command, had ordered General Tolbukhin to prepare the forces of the Third Ukrainian Front for the coming battle for Budapest. Stalin's order had been stark: 'Take Budapest as quickly as possible.'

But twelve German divisions had blocked his progress. An eleven-day assault on the city reduced much of it to ruins. The Third Ukrainian Front battled its way to within seven miles of the city centre and emissaries were sent forward to discuss terms for a capitulation. But Hitler showed all the signs of being stuck in a pre-Stalingrad timewarp, envisaging a dramatic rescue of his forces. Budapest, would not be evacuated, but recaptured.

The Führer's illusions were fed by the Arrow Cross's Szalasi. After a meeting between the two dictators, a joint official communiqué proclaimed the 'firm determination of the German people and Hungarian people united under the revolutionary movement of Hungarists' to 'carry on the defensive struggle with all the means in their possession and in the spirit of the traditional and well-tried comradeship-in-arms and friendship of the two nations.'

In fact, by the time that the communiqué was published, the armies of Tolbukhin and those of Malinovsky's 2nd Ukrainian Front had virtually completed their encirclement of Budapest. At first Hitler had felt confident, commenting sarcastically: 'Unfortunately because of the treachery of our dear allies we are forced to retire gradually . . . Yet despite all this it has been possible on the whole to hold the Eastern Front.'

There had been some grounds for optimism. At first, Tiger tanks had crossed the Danube and knocked out Russians in the front of the advance. But by 27 December, the combined forces of Tolbukhin and Malinovsky had met to the west of the city; five German and four Hungarian divisions, together with 800,000 civilians, were encircled.

Then the Russian rocket assault began, blowing apart buildings evacuated by men with no desire to be cut down where they stood. Those unable to escape were butchered. Loudspeaker vehicles urged Hungarians to come out peacefully and join the Red Army. Those who complied pinned strips of red cloth to their uniforms; any feelings of humiliation were lessened in the sure knowledge that the alternative was internm ent and no prospect of return.

In pursuit of Hitler's bid to save the situation, dazed veterans of Army Group South found themselves taking part in Operation *Frühlingerwachen* (SPRING AWAKENING) which would not only destroy Tolbukhin's 3rd Ukrainian Front, and recapture Budapest but – again the old obsession – secure the Hungarian oilfields by establishing a barrier to the east of them.

It was an operation against all reason. It had long been known that the wells no longer supplied sufficient oil even to meet the requirements of Army Group South. Yet here was the Group being reinforced with train-loads of, among other forces, the formidably equipped manpower of Sepp Dietrich's 6th SS Panzer Army. In addition to his own two Panzer Corps, I and II SS, Dietrich now also had IV SS Panzer Corps (consisting of the *Wiking* and *Totenkopf* SS Panzer Divisions), two cavalry divisions and a Hungarian infantry division, under command.

There was widespread doubt about the whole enterprise. Heinz Guderian wrote in his memoirs: 'I was sceptical, since very little time had been allowed for preparation, and neither the troops nor the commanders possessed the same drive as in the old days.'

To the veteran tank commander the course of action had seemed obvious. The threat to the lower Oder, which the Red Army had reached, was surely what mattered; such forces as were available should be transferred to meet it. Hitler would have none of it, arguing that what was needed was the broader vision. He had argued: 'Hungary must be the objective. We'll throw the Russians back across the Danube and then we'll have the initiative for other victories.'

D-Day for *Frühlingerwachen* was 6 March, 1945. Army units breasted the Drau river in a rapid motor-boat assault and established a bridgehead. The main thrust was between Lake Balaton and the Velence Lake; the first objective of the Leibstandarte and Hitler Jugend Divisions of I SS Panzer Corps being to force bridgeheads across the Sio Canal.

But there was a serious flaw. The terrain, supposedly frozen hard, turned out to be wet and marshy – warnings from Hungarians who knew the ground had not been acted upon. Dietrich explained to Allied interrogators after the war:

For reasons of camouflage, I had been forbidden to make an earlier terrain reconnaissance. Now 132 tanks were sunk in the mud, and fifteen Royal Tigers were sunk up to their turrets, so that the attack could be continued only by infantry. Considerable losses of men followed.

The release of reserves and an attack south of Lake Balaton by Second Panzer Army made little impression. Then the Russians attacked and Dietrich was engaged in hard fighting against five tank corps, ten guards infantry divisions and four mechanized brigades, described by him as 'young, fresh troops, excellently trained and armed, among them some older veteran divisions.'

Without any preliminary artillery bombardment, the SS troops knifed through the fortifications held by 4th Guards and 26th Red Armies. For the prize of a two mile advance, the German losses were huge. The Leibstandarte managed a further four mile advance between Lake Balaton and the Saviz canal. But the Russians were soon in there to counter the blows.

Simontornya and Azora became of vital importance to both sides. The Russians held on tenaciously because they knew the SS needed to hold both these towns before there could be any further advance southwards. The Germans held Simontornya and established a bridgehead across the Sio canal. But the forward Panzer grenadiers were starved of petrol, ammunition and spares. Severe losses reduced 6 SS Panzer Army's total strength in tanks which became useless hulks as they eked out their fuel allowances by towing one another. The number of self-propelled guns dwindled, so that a mere 135 vehicles were operative.

Dietrich, with scant respect for the Führer's delusions, asked for the offensive to be called off. The Russians, with overwhelming superiority, threw in everything they had. An attempt at orderly withdrawal all too often became a rout. Six understrength divisions had the hopeless task of trying to hold 93 miles of front with low calibre manpower which, along with other sweepings, included barely trained Volkssturm and military academy pupils who had been hastily recruited.

General Otto von Wohler, the Commander of Army Group South, committed reserves to try and save the situation but failed. An attack south of Lake Balaton by Second Panzer Army fared no better. When the Hungarian oilfields were lost on 2 April, Hitler's reaction was wearily predictable: Wohler was dismissed.

For the cowering jackals of a fast disintegrating Reich now in the Soviet embrace, battlefield conditions in Hungary proved conspicuously grim. The encirclement of Budapest was completed on Christmas Eve. The extent of the devastation there could be gauged from a message put before the Berne Ministry for Foreign Affairs by the Swiss Legation, which left Budapest towards the end of March:

Half the city at a rough estimate is in ruins. Certain quarters have, according to the Russians, suffered more than Stalingrad. The quays along the Danube, and in particular the Elisabeth Bridge and the Chain Bridge, are utterly destroyed. On Palace Hill, there is practically nothing left standing. The Royal Palace has been burnt to the ground. The Coronation Church has collapsed. The Parliament buildings are badly damaged. . . .

In his memoirs, while recognizing the superiority in strength of the Red Army, Admiral Horthy commented bitterly: 'The Asiatic barbarians remained true to their past.'

Hungary, of course, did not have a monopoly of privation. Bulgaria, in particular, was made to suffer the consequences of its former loyalty. Tolbukhin's armies had driven across the frontier and Partisan groups had helped occupy Sofia, installing a Fatherland Front administration, a mishmash of Agrarians, Social Democrats and Communists. And now, under their new masters, 339,000 troops of the 1st, 2nd and 4th Bulgarian Armies, as part of Tolbukhin's Third Ukrainian Front, were mustered for Lake Balaton and came under withering fire. The 3rd Bulgarian Division, defending the Drau river line, was soundly trounced by Dietrich.

Romania's price for its collaboration had been humiliation. A major purge of the Romanian officer corps had been directed with particular venom at the 3rd and 4th Armies which had taken part in BAR-BAROSSA. Serious deficiencies had shown up during the struggle for Budapest. During the first two weeks of January, Romania's VII Corps had edged forward in street fighting unequalled in viciousness until the final apocalyptic days in Berlin.

Away from Budapest in the north-east lay a string of small mountain ranges affording the last natural defences before the Czech borders. Romanian units were ordered to secure them. A prize role went to the Tudor Vladimirescu Division, made up of Romanian prisoners of war, held in reserve by the Soviets until mid-December, when it broke through the Matra mountain range and so into Czechoslovakia. By then, the Red Army had entered Eger, less than 25 miles from the Slovak border.

The Germans had succeeded in clearing roads, rivers and valleys along which their armies in eastern Slovakia and Sub-Carpathian Ruthenia would need to escape. But Partisans were still holding out in mountainous areas. As for the Hlinka Guard, a secret intelligence report for Berlin of 30 November, 1944, referred in one breath to 3,579 Guardists on active service being in a mood of 'great' enthusiasm and in the next stating:

One can hear the men complain that they only receive their pay irregularly and many of them have to pay for their own food. This situation will have to be resolved quickly. In many areas, particularly where the Partisans used to live, the Guardists are too afraid to volunteer for active service and join, because they fear that secret Partisans who sit in their home villages in civilian clothes might take revenge on them.

During the same month, SS-Obersturmbannführer Dr Witiska of the *Sicherheitspolizei* in Bratislava received a gloomy assessment from a colleague:

> The political situation is very tense. . . . The population is unsure how it should react towards the Bolshevist danger. While there is a lot of fear of the Russians as well as [of] local Bolsheviks, the intelligentsia in particular is of the opinion that Bolshevism might not be quite as bad as propaganda has painted it. The mood among members of the Slovakian Army is more or less the same as in the days of the uprising. A large section of the troops has caught the Bolshevist virus and among almost all of them one can detect a feeling of hatred towards the Hlinka Guard.

But the truth was that Slovakia as a co-belligerent was a spent force. In Italy, for example, with the withdrawal to Rome went 4,700 Slovak troops, 3,000 of which managed to get back to Slovakia, after switching sides and throwing in their lot with the Italian Partisans.

A thrust through Hungary and Austria had been but one of Stalin's plans. The other provided for swift progress from Poland to Berlin. Between the two lay Czechoslovakia; in this secondary theatre, Stalin would stoke up continuous pressure with infantry armies.

Ahead of the 1st and 4th Romanian armies lay the Ore mountains, held tenaciously in vile weather by Hungarians and Germans. The bulk of the 4th Army was switched south to reinforce the front of the Soviet 4th Army. Six months were needed to clear the Ore mountains and draw up along the length of the Horn river.

The Russians made sure that the Romanians bore the brunt of suffering; about 66,000 men out of some 248,000 fell to the winter weather. The Russian message became only too easy to read over the coming months and weeks: the Romanians could say farewell to any dreams of political and social autonomy at the hands of their new masters. Co-belligerency, a status which had been afforded to Italy, was not to be theirs.

By March, 1945, a two-pronged effort to liberate Slovakia had the 2nd Ukrainian Front on course for teaming up with the 4th Ukrainian Front and aiming for Bratislava. Here was a gratifying role for the pro-Allied Czecho-Slovak Brigade of Colonel Svoboda, rolling towards Moravska Ostrava, with the Romanians seizing Banska Bystrica.

Bratislava was at last rid of the bullies of the fleeing Hlinka Guard. Defence of the capital was left to the Hungarian 3rd Army, and a sparse

German presence of bewildered teenagers under the tattered banner of 31st SS Division of Protectorate *Volksdeutsch*. Bratislava fell on 4 April, 1945. On that date also the Third Ukrainian Front had reached Vienna, sealed it off on three sides and joined hands with Malinovsky's Second Ukrainian Front, whose 46th Army had raced down from the north-east towards the Austrian capital.

One of Hitler's first acts after stripping Wohler of his command of Army Group South had been to give Sepp Dietrich and 6th Panzer Army the task of defending Vienna. By now the Führer was well installed in cloud-cuckoo land. With grim humour, Dietrich, stripped of all logistical support and with no prospect of securing any, commented with grim humour: 'We call ourself 6th Panzer Army because we have only six tanks left.' As it was he was able to hold out for two weeks, but it was only postponing the inevitable. On 9 May, one day after the end of hostilities in Europe, he surrendered to the US 36th Infantry Division.

Hungarian, Russian and French Partisans imprisoned in Stalag XVIIIB, south-east of Vienna, were treated to the operatic spectacle of mounted Russians galloping through the Stalag gates, holding aloft giant Red Flags.

Vienna aside, the catalogue of disasters that had faced the Reich had grown daily, Poznan had fallen early in February, Breslau shortly afterwards, followed by Königsberg after four days artillery barrage. From the west, the Allied supply columns ground inexorably towards the heart of the Reich, planning their foray from the Rhine to link up with the Red Army.

Meanwhile, in 'Fortress Berlin', in his concrete sarcophagus of the *Führerbunker* below the Reich Chancellery, Hitler sought succour from his sycophants and from a portrait of Frederick the Great, the Prussian monarch whom the Führer claimed as his military mentor.

Above ground, the German capital needed some 200,000 fully equipped and trained troops to defend it. The reality was that it was being crippled by relentless bombing and could not even summon a garrison. Instead there were assorted Volkssturm, Hitler Youth, engineer, police and anti-aircraft units. True, there were slit trenches, pillboxes and some tank barriers; the drawback was that there was no one to man them.

The streets were given over largely to Himmler's flying SS court-martial squads who shot those deemed to be deserters or dragged them away screaming to dangle from lamp posts. Placards pinned to their uniforms read: 'I hang here because I left my unit without permission.'

*   *   *

Those who were with Hitler in his subterranean cavern in the final weeks and days were faced with a dreadful physical spectre, awash with drugs, hunched and shaking, with faltering voice and staring eyes, his uniform hanging loose, the jacket blotched with fragments of food from hastily snatched meals. The appearance of premature senility was heightened by the slightly wobbling head, the left arm dangling slackly and the hand constantly trembling. A surgeon, Professor Schenck, who was one of those in the bunker in the very last days, concluded that here was a man in the grips of Parkinson's disease and likely, even if he lived, to become an incurable cripple.

Incredibly, even at this stage, Hitler could summon reserves of energy and the eyes would blaze with their old fire but only when talking of past triumphs. Certainly, there were none in the present. On 22 April, Berlin was cut off on three sides; Soviet tanks were reported to the west of the city. At his usual mid-day conference, Hitler launched a tirade of abuse. Wholly in character, he blamed everyone but himself for the course of the war. He was surrounded, he stormed, by cowardice, incompetence and treachery. Now, for the first time, he spoke the unmentionable. The war, he declared, was lost.

Four days later, the first Russian shells struck the Chancellery and soon the full force of the Red Army was less than a mile away.

Then, at about 10 pm, the Führer was handed a copy of a Reuters report that Himmler had contacted Count Folke Bernadotte, Deputy President of the Swedish Red Cross, in order to negotiate a surrender in the West. Hitler, according to the testimony of surviving witnesses, received the news at the same time as a hurricane of Russian shells blew in the roof of the Chancellery above.

In these grotesque circumstances, the Führer's eruption was terrible to behold. He was described as raging like a madman, thrusting the text of the message into the hands of everyone he met, as if seeking confirmation of the truth. He screamed out that his longest serving colleague – *der treue Heinrich* – had dealt him the cruellest blow of all.

Hard enough to stomach had been the earlier treachery, as he saw it, of Hermann Göring. The Reichsmarschall had remained mindful that by Führer decrees he was designated to replace Hitler should the latter become incapacitated or, in the event of Hitler's death, to replace him. Göring had dug out the decrees, satisfied himself that they were valid, and on 23 April, 1945, dashed off a telegram to Hitler, which contained the sentence: 'If no reply is received by 10 o'clock tonight, I shall take it for granted that you have lost your freedom of action, and shall consider the decree as fulfilled.' Göring had miscalculated disastrously. Hitler was persuaded that Göring's presumption amounted to a coup. The

Reichsmarschall was promptly stripped of all his offices and finally put under arrest on Hitler's orders by embarrassed SS men.

In the small hours of 29 April, Hitler married his long time mistress Eva Braun. A desperate air of jauntiness characterized the reception where champagne glasses were raised and past glories recalled. At about 2 am, Hitler retired with a secretary to prepare his political testament. It concluded with a final kick of venom:

> Above all, I charge the leaders of the nation and those under them to scrupu-lous observance of the laws of race and to merciless opposition to the universal poisoner of all peoples, international Jewry.

With gloomy masochism, Hitler ordered a final military conference in which General Karl Weidling, the Battle Commandant of Berlin, informed him that there was heavy fighting in the Tiergarten and the Potsdamer Platz, only a few blocks from the Chancellery. About 3.20 pm, Hitler and his bride withdrew. Outside the door the inhabitants of the Bunker waited as Hitler shot himself with his Walther 7.65 calibre pistol, probably simultaneously biting into a poison capsule. Eva Braun also took poison.

There was one last macabre ceremony: the Viking funeral. The bodies were carried to the Chancellery garden, soaked in petrol and set alight. In the Bunker, from the moment it was known that Hitler had intended to kill himself, there had been scant suggestion of mourning.

The historian Hugh Trevor-Roper (later Lord Dacre), who later inter-viewed many of the Bunker's survivors with the aid of British Intelligence, sardonically captured the mood: 'A great and heavy cloud seemed to roll away from the spirits of the Bunker-dwellers. The terrible sorcerer, the tyrant who had charged their days with intolerable melodramatic tension, would soon be gone and for a brief twilight moment they could play. In the canteen of the Chancellery, where the soldiers and orderlies took their meals, there was a dance. The news was brought; but no one allowed that to interfere with the business of pleasure. A message from the Führerbunker told them to be quieter; but the dance went on . . .'

Two secretaries were later told that Hitler was dead. But they already knew because they noticed that everyone in the Bunker was smoking which had been strictly forbidden in the Führer's lifetime. In the words of Trevor-Roper, 'Now the headmaster had gone and the boys could break the rules.'

The prevailing mood was one of relief, not just for those who remained in the Bunker but to the world outside when it learnt of Hitler's death. On 14 May, 150,000 Germans surrendered to the Red Army in East Prussia, six days after Germany's formal surrender to the Allies. A further

150,000, the remnants of the German force in Yugoslavia, laid down their arms to the Russians and the Yugoslavs. Over four years, Yugoslavia had lost in terms of the military, Jews and Serbs and Partisans a total of 1,700,000 men.

Relief tinged with sadness was not the emotion of every country. Among Nazi Germany's collaborator nations lurked something like fear.

– 20 –

AFTERMATH

Revenge was not a dish that the newly constituted governments of Hitler's former collaborators were prepared to eat cold. Bulgaria provided a grim example. The Communists, following the September, 1944, coup, took indiscriminate vengeance; hatred was reserved especially for the monarchy and its associates. Even King Boris was not allowed to rest in peace. Initially buried amid much solemnity at the Rila Monastery, the Communists insisted that his body should be dug up and removed to the privacy of the family's country estate at Vrana. With the abolition of the monarchy, it was removed yet again to an unknown location.

The mystery which had surrounded the King's death persisted with a macabre touch. A heart was found in the grounds of the former royal palace and tests demonstrated that, if it did belong to the King, his cause of death would have been heart failure. But for the mystery-mongers the legend could not be left there. Rumours abounded that the *real* heart of Boris had been buried elsewhere.

Boris's successor, Simeon, had been six years old in 1943; a regency had been formed, consisting of Bogdan Filov, Prince Cyrill, Boris's brother, and General Mikov, a professional soldier. On trial before the people's court, set up by a decree of October, 1944, to try 'collaborators' and 'war criminals', Filov could have had few doubts as to his fate. The previous March, Hitler had warned him that a Soviet victory would mean implementation of Stalin's avowed aim to incorporate Bulgaria into the Soviet system and all that implied. Among the charges read to Filov was the passing of the so-called Law for the Peace of the Nation for which he was held responsible and which 'transformed the Jews into despised beings at the instigation of Germany.'

But the general feeling was that Filov and the others were to be eliminated because of their past associations with the old order, rather than their involvement in wartime atrocities. The verdict was never in doubt. On 2 February, 1945, the three Regents were executed, along with another ex-Premier, Ivan Bagrianov, sixty-eight Narodno *Sobranije* deputies, two dozen former cabinet ministers and several royal advisers. The fact that former premier Dobri Bozhilov had tried to steer the country away from its pro-German policy, did not save him, either.

The bloodbath was barely in its stride. Soon Radio Sofia was announcing that nine Bulgarian generals, five colonels and nine other senior officers had been shot for ordering brutal treatment for British and American prisoners of war and of personally directing reprisals and atrocities in Yugoslavia and Greece. Retribution was not confined to Sofia; humble functionaries of the old regime were hunted down in the countryside and eliminated.

The Hungarians proved equally impatient for revenge. In Hungary, in October, 1945, scores were brought before courts in Budapest's music academy. Hundreds turned out to witness the hanging of Ferenc Szalasi. With his hands tied behind his back, the Arrow Cross leader was lifted up to the gallows by two men in black coats and black hats while a priest held a crucifix which the condemned man leant forward to kiss before he was hanged. The gallows also claimed General Szibard Bakay, a military confident of Admiral Horthy, and Dr Laszo Andre, a former judge, who had effected an interview with Adolf Eichmann which led to his appointment as Secretary of State for Political Affairs, a deliberately vague office which in fact was concerned with the 'Jewish question' and all its implications.

The administration of justice inevitably brought anomalies and puzzling verdicts. Dr Edmund Veesenmayer, the Commandant for Hungary and the pet of Himmler, was thought lucky to escape with a sentence of a mere twenty years.

Sympathy was a rare commodity when it came to war crimes; Marshal Antonescu had his share when his trial opened in Bucharest on 6 May, 1946. For nearly two years, the former Conductator and some of his closest colleagues had been kept in the Lubianka prison in Moscow. Deaf to the widely held view that an accused was responsible not only for the crime for which he was charged but for all consequences flowing from it, Antonescu argued that the only reason for his *rapprochement* with Hitler had been to prevent Romania becoming a vassal state as a Nazi protectorate. Such a disingenuous defence would, in any circumstances, have stood no chance. The major charges, carrying the death sentence, were formidable. They included waging an aggressive war against the Soviet Union and the Allies, breaking the international rules of conduct in war, mistreating prisoners of war and hostages, ordering massacres of civilians and mass racial and political repression through deportation and forced labour.

Knowledge that the Marshal had endured a lengthy ordeal in the Lubianka and that his wife, Maria, had been driven half insane by solitary confinement, drew some added sympathy, not least from King Michael who argued that the war was over and that the Romanian constitution did not allow the death penalty during peace. Since the crimes had been committed in time of war, the argument was doomed. Besides, the rule of the Soviet-appointed Prime Minister Petru Groza and the Romanian Communist Party leader Lucretiu Patrascanu was tightening as fast as the King's influence was declining.

Michael was powerless to save the lives of the Marshal, former Foreign Minister Mikai Antonescu, Professor Gheorghe Alexianu, who had been Governor of Transnistra and General Piki Vasiliu, Under Secretary at the Interior Ministry. Michael was allowed only to reprieve three of the lesser fry.

Antonescu's execution, which survives on film, could only be described as a bloody shambles. Some indication of the depth of feeling in favour of a reprieve was shown by the difficulty the authorities found in selecting a firing squad. Those eventually assembled at Jilava military prison were a scratch lot of ill-trained home guard and security wardens from public buildings who were stuffed into police uniforms and later described as being 'more used to clubs and sub-machine guns than rifles.' Antonescu, who had refused to have his eyes covered, delivered his formal last words: 'Gentlemen, we are ready. Aim true. Long live Romania!' The *coup de grace* in the back of the neck was delivered by the sergeant in charge of the firing squad.

Josef Tiso and what remained of his Slovak government in early April, 1945, scurried into Austria on the coat tails of German forces. In a broadcast over Austrian radio in Kremunster, he continued the call for Slovak separatism. But time ran out. Early in the following month, the American occupation authorities handed Tiso and Alexander Mach, his former minister, over to the Czechoslovak government.

The Communists, who were not to gain total rule until 1948, seized the opportunity afforded by Tiso's trial. The organs of State Security were under the orders of a Communist Minister of the Interior who shunted the accused back to Bratislava in chains. Popular demonstrations involving Partisans, former political prisoners, troops who had taken part in the uprising were organized to oppose any clemency being shown to Tiso. Anti-Communist leaders within the Slovak Council and the Czechoslovak government leaders were bombarded with intimidation and threats. Even so, pleas for mercy came from both Catholic and Protestant churchmen in Slovakia. An approach to Pope Pius XII, however, was met with a rebuff. The former Minister of the Slovak State to the Vatican, Karol Sidor, was reminded that Tiso had been warned in vain that, since he was a priest, he should not have accepted the office of President of the Slovak state.

At the trial, presided over by a Communist Dr Igo Daxner, Tiso's defence council argued that his client, as a former President, was entitled to Parliamentary immunity and should be tried by an international court. The plea was overruled; the reading of a 213-page indictment went ahead. It stated that the accused had sought contact with Göring, Ribbentrop and other leading Nazis to enlist their help in severing Slovakia from the Czechoslovak state via direct negotiations with Hitler. Furthermore he had encouraged 'German terrorists' to be sent to Bratislava for a programme of intimidation against politicians.

Apart from the declaration of war on Britain and the United States and the aid given to Germany, there had been the brutal reprisals against Partisans. Countless examples were cited proving that the former professor of theology was Hitler's creature. It was cited that on 30 October, 1944, in celebration of the occupation of Banska Bystrica by German troops, Tiso had proclaimed: 'Honour to the Protector Adolf Hitler! Glory to his Army and the SS, glory to General Hoffle and other divisional commanders! . . . We have a protector in the German Reich, a magnanimous guardian, Adolf Hitler.'

A total of 111 capital charges, involving deportation of Jews, were stacked against the obese cleric. A character witness, Archbishop Karol Kmetko of Neutra, a prominent churchman in Slovakia and former mentor of Tiso, claimed that Tiso was primarily an ardent Slovak nationalist and not a pro-Nazi. On the question of the accused's attitude to the Jews, Kmetko was asked: 'Would the deportation of Jews have been possible if the accused had spoken out?' He replied: 'It could have meant that he would have been relieved of his office. Perhaps he thought that he could serve the nation and the Jews better by staying.'

The argument did not impress the court; Tiso was sentenced to death and hanged on 18 April, 1947. Alexander Mach drew a sentence of thirty years. Pressure on Bratislava from the Czech and Slovak Communists grew apace. The Slovak separatist movement was doomed and, by 1948, the Communist Party of Czechoslovakia was in power.

By no means all retribution by gallows or firing squad won the approval of the Western powers, certainly not the execution of Draza Mihailovic in March, 1946. The rivalry between Chetnik forces and Communist Partisans, thorns in the side of the Allied governments, had resulted in Churchill's decision to support the more ruthless Tito as representing the most effective fighting force. Mihailovic's Chetniks had little alternative but to find supporters where they could, initially with the occupying Italians. Support for his royalist champion was withdrawn by the exiled King Peter.

Mihailovic's trial, concentrated on his alleged collaboration with the Germans. From the dock, the Chetnik leader, fortified with brandy, impressed the court with his dignity, but it was impervious to his claim that he had been the victim of events. A guilty verdict brought the death sentence, which was widely considered too harsh. Those in favour pointed out that any other verdict would have dismayed Tito's Partisans and the victims of the Chetniks. Mihailovic and eight others were shot early on the morning of 17 July. At Voerde, a small German town occupied by dissident Yugoslavs, hundreds of officers and men wearing Royal Yugoslav army uniform with mourning bands attended a local church service.

Luck, accompanied by an element of farce, had aided the escape in early May of the Croatian leader Ante Pavelic. A final appearance in the streets of Zagreb had been accompanied by a bombastic declaration: 'If we must die let us fall as true heroes, not as cowards crying for mercy.' But there was no one to listen; the architect of the Ustachi accompanied by a knot of his followers, fled to the comparative safety of the Austrian border and eventually to Argentina. He remained true to type, surviving an assassination attempt to surface in the company of Paraguayan secret police in the interrogation of the country's alleged insurgents.

After ten years in Buenos Aires, his extradition was requested by Yugoslavia. He escaped again. The trail ran cold until 30 December, 1959, with newspapers reporting a terse notice in a Spanish newspaper which read: 'Don Ante Pavelic aged 70 years, died in Madrid.'

For those who had been powerless to stop the alliance of their countries with the Axis powers there was no relief and no justice, certainly no consolation for crowned heads striving to survive in Communist states. With ninety per cent of Romania handed over to Stalin at the Yalta Conference, Andrei Vyshinsky, who had forced the appointment of Petru Groza on King Michael, was able to sneer at the monarch: 'I am Yalta.'

When the final coup came, the young King was newly engaged. He told the journalist Simon Sebag-Montefiore what happened:

They said they wished to see me about 'a family matter'. So I thought it was about my fiancée. . . . They produced a bit of paper. It was the abdication. . . . The grammar was not good. They could hardly even write; so I would not sign. But they said: 'Your guards have been arrested; the telephone is cut; and there is artillery pointing at this very office.' I looked out of the window. Everything they said was true; there was a howitzer pointing at me. I tried to delay, suggesting that we ask the people. 'No time to ask the people', they said. 'There'll be disturbances and we'll shoot the whole lot and it would be *your* fault.' I was disgusted at how low these people were. And I signed.

Outside, Communist troops had disarmed the royal guard; tanks rolled the surrounding streets. Had he not done so, it was made clear that he would have been arrested for allegedly plotting with Great Britain and the United States of America, sworn enemies of Communism, against his own government.

King Michael's father, King Carol, who died in the 1950s, had escaped with riches. Michael went into exile with a threadbare suit and, later, the American Legion of Honour for, in the words of President Harry Truman, 'an outstanding contribution to the cause of freedom and democracy.'

Inevitably, one man's tragedy, however poignant, was dwarfed by that of millions of others struggling to rebuild their shattered lives amid the ruins of their towns and cities. Those on the roads of Europe in the week following VE-Day were put at nine-and-a-half million, tens of thousands of them deportees from Bulgaria, Romania, Hungary and Yugoslavia, while into Germany poured the *Volksdeutsche*, driven from what had been the homes of their forebears for generations.

Nationals of the jackal countries, whether active collaborators or those (in the poignant words of Draza Mihailovic) caught up 'in the whirlwind of the world', suffered appalling privations and atrocities at the hands of the recently installed Communist governments. In Hungary, rapes were in the tens of thousands. The Soviet NKVD arrested an estimated 600,000 citizens who served long sentences or perished in the labour camps.

Three prominent players were lucky enough to survive. Conspicuous among them was Miklos Horthy, the Regent of Hungary, who was captured and interrogated by American officers following his deportation to Austria by the Germans but not charged with war crimes. He died in exile in Portugal in 1957. Until 1989, Horthy was portrayed as a Fascist leader by Hungary's Communists but four years later, more than 80,000 people attended his reburial at his home village of Kenderes in central Hungary.

It was an occasion for tribute to, in the words of Hungarian Prime Minister Josef Antall, a 'committed patriot.' Defenders of Horthy pointed out that towards the end of the war, he had refused to allow the deportation of Budapest's Jewish community, even though Eichmann himself had been sent to oversee their removal. But, Jewish groups added the rider that this had not been before an estimated 400,000 Hungarian Jews, mainly from rural areas, had perished in concentration camps.

Luck proved to be on the side of Hitler's more hesitant partners. As

President, Marshal Mannerheim, in tough negotiation with the emissaries of Stalin had engineered a ceasefire early in September, 1944. The terms obliged the Russians not to press further territorial claims and for the Finns to expel the Germans from their soil. General Siilasvuo's 3rd Corps became the hunter, forcing scattered Nazi forces to jettison their equipment and flee; by October, 1944, the tail of the German column was at Kemi, making for Norway. A clash near the border town of Tornio on the Swedish frontier was the last hurrah; Finland's war role was at an end and the task of rebuilding began.

The era of the old-style dictators was over. The one exception was provided by Spain's General Francisco Franco. Although overtly neutral, the Spaniards fed the German war effort until the end. In April, 1945, SS Standartenführer Miguel Ezquerra, a former Blue Division Captain, was in command of three companies of Spaniards plus some survivors from Belgian and French SS Divisions, under the name of Unit Esquerra. They were among the last troops fighting the Russians in Berlin. It took another nine years for the last soldiers of the Blue Division to be repatriated from the Soviet camps.

But neither Axis collaborators nor their Allied opponents were able to escape the inevitable consequence of war in terms of mental and physical scars. The inheritance is with their descendants still. The poignant words of the historian Sir Martin Gilbert which conclude his *Second World War* remain particularly applicable: 'The greatest unfinished business of the Second World War is human pain.'

SELECT BIBLIOGRAPHY

Abbot, Peter; Thomas, Nigel; Chappell, Mike: *Germany's Eastern Front Allies 1941–45*. (Osprey, 1982.)

Axworthy, Mark; Scafes, Cornel; Craciunoiu, Cristian: *Third Axis Fourth Ally: Romanian Armed Forces in the European War, 1941–1945*. (Arms & Armour Press, 1995.)

Butnaru, I C: *The Silent Holocaust: Romania and its Jews*. (Greenwood Press, US, 1992.)

Butnaru, I C: *Waiting for Jerusalem: Surviving the Holocaust in Romania*. (Greenwood Press, US, 1993.)

Calvocoressi, Peter and Witt, Guy: *Total War: Causes and Courses of the Second World War*. (Allen Lane, The Penguin Press, 1972.)

Cameron Watt, D: *How War Came*. (Heineman, 1989.)

Carell, Paul: *Hitler's War on Russia*. (Harrap & Co, 1964.)

Carell, Paul: *Scorched Earth: The Russian-German War 1943-1944*. (Schiffer Military History, 1994.)

Chary, Frederick B: *The Bulgarian Jews and the Final Solution*. (University of Pittsburgh Press, 1972.)

Churchill, Winston: *The Second World War, Volume III: The Grand Alliance*. (Cassell, 1950.)

Clark, Alan: *Barbarossa. The Russian-German Conflict, 1941–1945*. (Hutchinson, 1965.)

Clogg, Richard: *A Concise History of Greece*. (Cambridge University Press, 1992.)

Collier, Richard: *The World in Flames*. (Hamish Hamilton, 1979.)

Crampton, R J: *A Short History of Modern Bulgaria*. (Cambridge University Press, 1987.)

Cross, Robin: *Fallen Eagle: The Last Days of the Third Reich*. (Michael O'Mara Books, 1995.)

Dawidowicz, Lucy S: *The War Against the Jews 1933–1945*. (Bantam Books, 1978.)

Deighton, Len: *Blood, Tears & Folly*. (Jonathan Cape, 1993.)

De Vere Summers, Anthony: *War and the Royal Houses of Europe in the 20th Century*. (Arms & Armour Press, 1996.)

Keegan, John (Ed.): *Documents on German Foreign Policy 1918–1945.* (HMSO. Series D. Vol 4. The Second World War, 1989.)

Erickson, John: *The Road to Stalingrad: Stalin's War With Germany, Vol 1.* (Weidenfeld & Nicholson, 1975.)

Everett, Susan; Young, Brigadier Peter: *Wars of the 20th Century.* (Bison Books, 1985.)

Fenyo, Mario D: *Hitler, Horthy and Hungary.* (Yale University Press, 1972.)

Gervase, Frank: *The Violent Decade.* (W W Norton, 1989.)

Gibson, Hugh (Ed): *The Ciano Diaries 1939–1945.* (Doubleday, 1946.)

Gilbert, Martin: *The Holocaust: The Jewish Tragedy.* (Collins, 1986.)

Gilbert, Martin: *Second World War.* (Weidenfeld & Nicholson, 1989.)

Hibbert, Christopher: *Benito Mussolini.* (Longmans, 1962.)

Hillberg, Paul: *Destruction of European Jews.* (Holmes & Meier, NY, 1985.)

History of the Second World War, various volumes. (Purnell & Sons, 1966.)

Hohne, Heinz: *Canaris: Patriot im Zwielicht.* (C Bertelsmann Verlag GMBH, Munchen, 1976.)

Horthy, Admiral: *Memoirs.* (Hutchinson, 1956.)

Infield, Glenn H: *Skorzeny, Hitler's Commando.* (Military Heritage Press, 1981.)

Irving, David: *Hitler's War and The War Path.* (Special Edition), (Focal Point Publications, 1991.)

Irving, David: *Göring.* (Macmillan, 1989.)

Jelinek, Yeshayahu: *The Parish Republic: Hlinka's Slovak People's Party (1939–1945). East European Quarterly.* (Boulder Press, NY and London, 1976.)

Kee, Robert: *The World We Fought For.* (Guild Publishing, 1985.)

Keegan, John: *The Second World War.* (Hutchinson, 1989.)

Kessler, Leo: *Kommando.* (Leo Cooper, 1995.)

Kesselring, Albrecht, Feldmarschall: *Memoirs.* (Greenhill Books, 1953.)

Lee Gould, Arthur: *Crown Against Sickle: The Story of King Michael of Romania.* (Hutchinson, 1950.)

Lettrich, Josef: *History of Modern Slovakia.* (Atlantic Press, London, 1956.)

Levekaun, Paul: *German Military Intelligence.* (Weidenfeld & Nicholson, 1954.)

Littlejohn, David: *Foreign Legions of the Third Reich.* (R James Bender Publishing, 1994.)

Littlejohn, David; Dodkins, Col C M, assisted by Roger James Bender: *Orders, Decorations, Medals and Badges of the Third Reich (Vol 2).* (R James Bender Publishing, 1973.)

Lucas, James: *Germany's Elite Panzer Force: Grossdeutschland.* (Macdonald & Jane's, 1978.)

Lucas, James; Cooper, Matthew: *Hitler's Elite: Leibstandarte SS.* (Macdonald & Jane's, 1975.)

Lucas, James: *Storming Eagles: German Airborne Forces in World War Two.* (Arms & Armour Press, 1988.)

Mack Smith, Denis: *Mussolini's Roman Empire.* (Longman, 1976.)

Messenger, Charles: *Hitler's Gladiator: The Life and Times of Oberstgruppenführer and Panzergeneral-Oberst der Waffen SS Sepp Dietrich.* (Brassey's Defence Publishers, 1988.)

Messenger, Charles: *The Last Prussian: A Biography of Feldmarschall Gerd von Rundstedt 1875–1953.* (Brassey's UK, 1991.)

Noel-Baker, Francis, MP: *Greece: The Whole Story.* (Hodder & Co, 1946.)

Padfield, Peter: *Himmler Reichsführer SS.* (Macmillan, 1990.)

Pierik, Perry: *Hungary, 1944–1945.* (Aspekt, 1966.)

Ready, J Lee: *World War Two Nation by Nation.* (Arms & Armour Press, 1995.)

Shirer, William J: *The Rise and Fall of the Third Reich.* (Secker & Warburg, 1959.)

Scurr, John: *Germany's Spanish Volunteers 1941–45.* (Osprey, 1980.)

Tanner, M: *Croatia: A Nation Forged in War.* (Yale University Press, 1997.)

Thomas, N; Mikulan, K: *Axis Forces in Yugoslavia.* (Osprey, 1995.)

Tarrant, V E: *Stalingrad.* (Leo Cooper, 1992.)

Toland, John: *The Last 100 Days.* (Arthur Baker, 1965.)

Trevor-Roper, H R (Ed): *Hitler's War Directives.* (Sidgwick & Jackson, 1954.)

Trevor-Roper, H R: *The Last Days of Hitler.* (Macmillan, 1947.)

Wagner, Bernd: *Hitler's Politsche Soldaten die Waffen-SS.* (Ferdinand Schoningh, Paderborn, 1982.)

West, Richard: *Tito and the Rise and Fall of Yugoslavia.* (Sinclair-Stevenson, 1994.)

Wilmott, Chester: *The Struggle for Europe.* (William Collins, 1954.)

Wiskemann, E: *Rome-Berlin Axis.* (OUP, 1949.)

World At Arms: The Reader's Digest Illustrated History of World War II. (Reader's Digest Association Ltd, 1989.)

INDEX